LOLA

A GHOST STORY

AN ONI PRESS PUBLICATION

LETTERED BY
JILL BEATON

ART ASSIST BY
ROBO MONKEY
PIXEL FIGHTERS

◆

BOOK DESIGN BY
KEITH WOOD
&
SONJA SYNAK

EDITED BY
JAMES LUCAS JONES
&
JILL BEATON

PAPERBACK EDITED BY
ROBIN HERRERA

LOLA

A GHOST STORY

WRITTEN BY
J. TORRES

ILLUSTRATED BY
ELBERT OR

PUBLISHED BY ONI-LION FORGE PUBLISHING GROUP, LLC

JAMES LUCAS JONES
PRESIDENT & PUBLISHER

SARAH GAYDOS
EDITOR IN CHIEF

CHARLIE CHU
E.V.P. OF CREATIVE & BUSINESS DEVELOPMENT

BRAD ROOKS
DIRECTOR OF OPERATIONS

AMBER O'NEILL
SPECIAL PROJECTS MANAGER

HARRIS FISH
EVENTS MANAGER

MARGOT WOOD
DIRECTOR OF MARKETING & SALES

JEREMY ATKINS
DIRECTOR OF BRAND COMMUNICATIONS

DEVIN FUNCHES
SALES & MARKETING MANAGER

TARA LEHMANN
MARKETING & PUBLICITY ASSOCIATE

TROY LOOK
DIRECTOR OF DESIGN & PRODUCTION

KATE Z. STONE
SENIOR GRAPHIC DESIGNER

SONJA SYNAK
GRAPHIC DESIGNER

HILARY THOMPSON
GRAPHIC DESIGNER

ANGIE KNOWLES
DIGITAL PREPRESS LEAD

SHAWNA GORE
SENIOR EDITOR

ROBIN HERRERA
SENIOR EDITOR

AMANDA MEADOWS
SENIOR EDITOR

JASMINE AMIRI
EDITOR

GRACE BORNHOFT
EDITOR

ZACK SOTO
EDITOR

STEVE ELLIS
VICE PRESIDENT OF GAMES

BEN EISNER
GAME DEVELOPER

MICHELLE NGUYEN
EXECUTIVE ASSISTANT

JUNG LEE
LOGISTICS COORDINATOR

JOE NOZEMACK
PUBLISHER EMERITUS

FIRST EDITION: MARCH 2020
ISBN 978-1-62010-691-4
eISBN 978-1-62010-703-4

1 3 5 7 9 10 8 6 4 2

LIBRARY OF CONGRESS CONTROL NUMBER:
2019940895

PRINTED IN CHINA

ONI PRESS, INC.
1319 SE MARTIN LUTHER KING JR. BLVD.
SUITE 240
PORTLAND, OR 97214
ONIPRESS.COM | LIONFORGE.COM
FACEBOOK.COM/ONIPRESS | FACEBOOK.COM/LIONFORGE
TWITTER.COM/ONIPRESS | TWITTER.COM/LIONFORGE
INSTAGRAM.COM/ONIPRESS | INSTAGRAM.COM/LIONFORGE

FOREWORD

By Jennifer de Guzman

MY MOTHER HATED SCARY STORIES. As a child, she listened with horror to the stories that her father's friends, the manongs, told about ghosts, spirits, and supernatural creatures. No matter that these specters and monsters didn't seem to make the same journey across the sea as her father, existing only in the Philippines, and she lived in her family's cozy house on Foothill Boulevard in Oakland—they filled her with a dread that kept her up at night. Fifty years later, she still closed her eyes and cringed just thinking about these stories, which she refused to repeat to me, much to my disappointment. She was so frightened by them, so traumatized, that she came to believe that any story that caused a frisson of terror was the work of Satan. And as the work of Satan, those stories should not just be avoided, they—whether they be urban legends, books, or movies— should also be condemned. And forbidden from our home.

This was a problem for me as I grew into a black-clad teen who loved horror stories. I read Stephen King's *Carrie* secretly at school; at the movie theater, I sneaked into *Dracula* with a friend after we told our parents we were going to see *The Last of the Mohicans*. Even Tim Burton's *Edward Scissorhands* and the comic book *Sandman* inspired my mother's suspicion. There was just something creepy about them, she said.

All of this just made horror more intriguing to me, of course. Once my mother no longer got to say what I could and couldn't watch or read, I started researching folklore about ghosts and monsters from the Philippines to find out what might have scared her so much as a child.

And that is how I found aswang—a multitude of types of supernatural creatures who might shape-shift, cast spells, stalk human prey, or eat corpses. They might have blood-curdling howls or they might be so silent that you wouldn't know they're near until too late. The manananggal especially intrigued me. The speaker in the poem "Aswang" by Vince Gotera describes one:

> That night, I was strolling by Carding's house,
> and I saw his mother, a pretty mestiza widow,
> her face hidden by her hair hanging down
> as she bent far forward from the waist.
> A manananggal, the worst kind of aswang:
> women who can detach themselves at the hips,
> shucking their legs at night like a wrinkled slip.
> They fly, just a face and breasts, to prey on infants.

The poem also describes the manangganal's

> ...pretty cousin who could
> pierce your jugular with her hollow tongue
> like sharpened bamboo, then delicately sip your blood,
> her eyes darting crimson.

These pretty women become dangerous monsters who are the opposite of what a virtuous Filipina is—instead of protecting and loving children, she eats them; instead of stuffing people full of nourishing food, she drains them of their life's blood. My mother was a virtuous Filipina. Perhaps these stories of aswang revolted everything that was good in her. As a mother myself now, I understand that. She was also separated by a generation and an ocean from the land of her ancestry. I like to think that if we were living in the Ilocos Sur village where her father was born instead of the California Bay Area, her way of protecting me from the terror of aswang would not have been to forbid me from even knowing about them. She might have been more like Jesse's Lola in this lovely graphic novel that tells a uniquely Filipino story of family love and devotion, using her faith to keep us safe.

JENNIFER DE GUZMAN IS A WRITER FROM THE SAN FRANCISCO BAY AREA, WHERE HER GRANDFATHER SETTLED AFTER ARRIVING FROM THE PHILIPPINES IN THE LATE 1920S. SHE SPENDS HER TIME WRITING FICTION, REVIEWING GRAPHIC NOVELS, DRINKING TEA, AND NURTURING HER LATEST POP CULTURE OBSESSIONS. HER SHORT COMICS STORY "THE VESTA," WITH ARTIST LEIGH DRAGOON, WAS PUBLISHED IN *WOMANTHOLOGY: SPACE* AND HER NOVEL *HALF A PERSON* IS AVAILABLE DIGITALLY. SHE HAS AN MFA IN LITERATURE AND CREATIVE WRITING FROM SAN JOSE STATE UNIVERSITY.

For my beloved Lola Gloria, whose
stories inspired this story.
—JT
∞

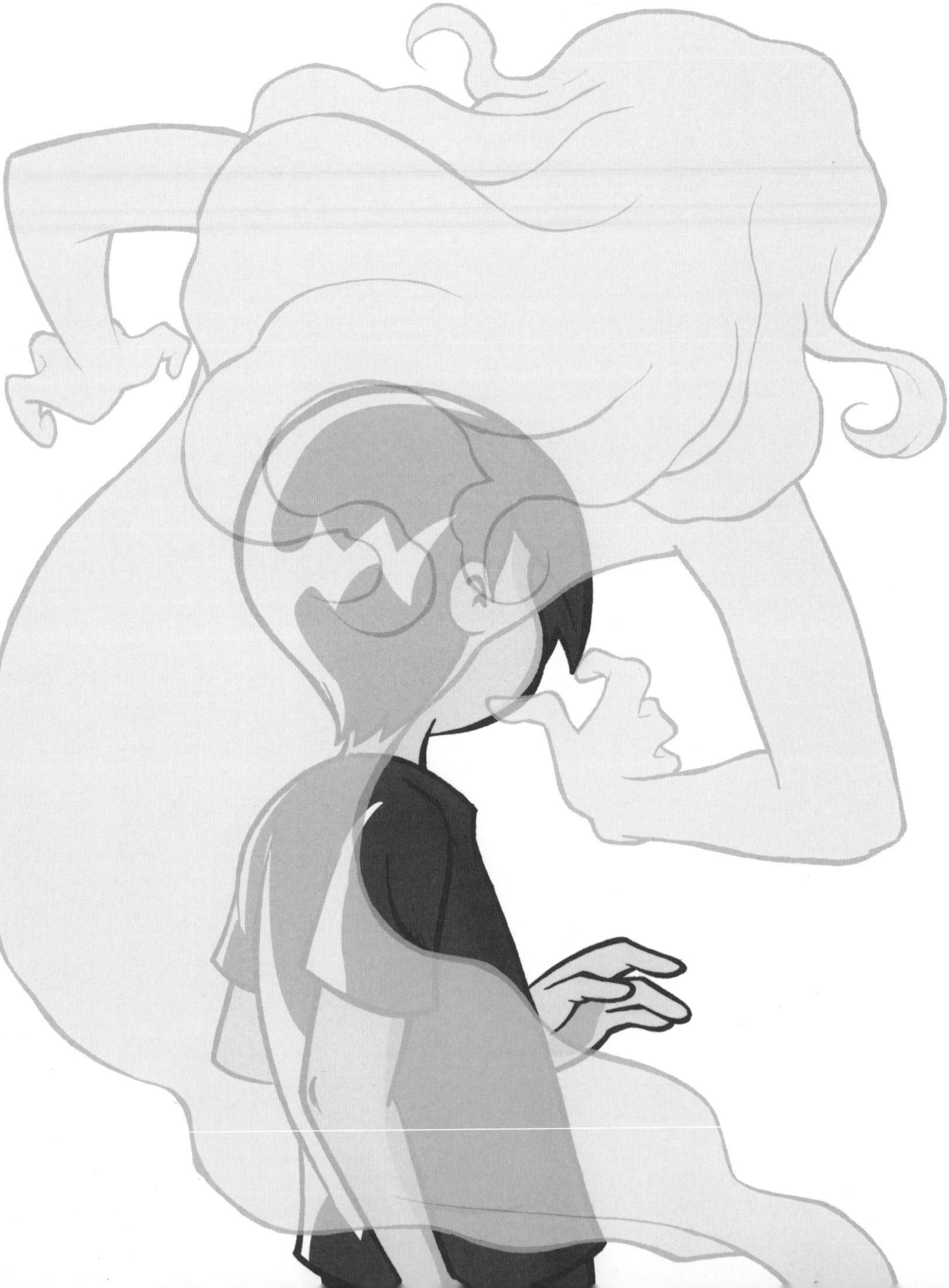

ACT

I

LOLA

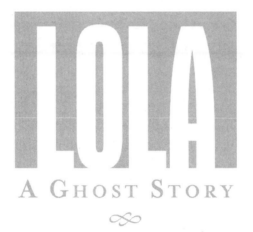

A Ghost Story

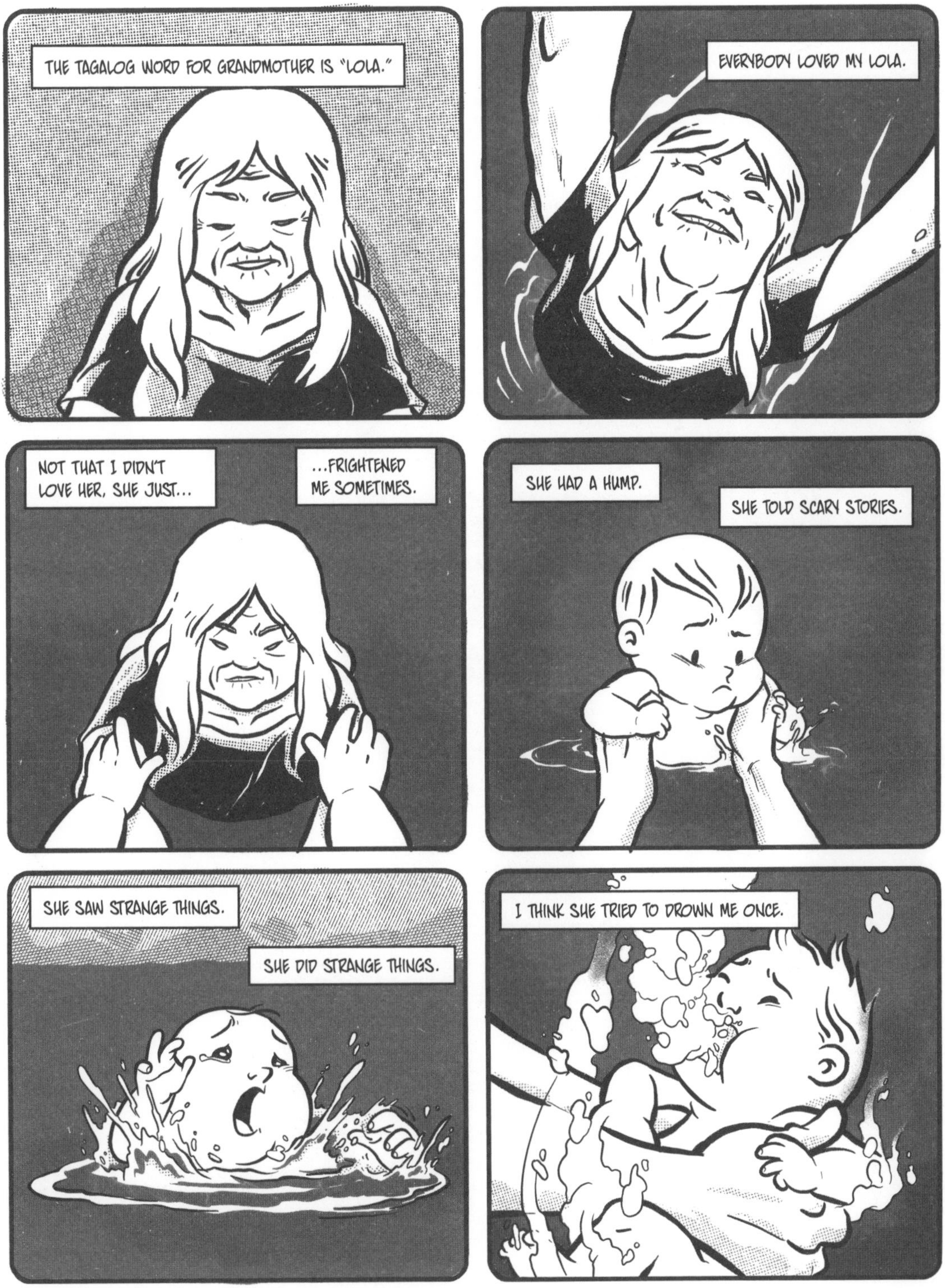
THE TAGALOG WORD FOR GRANDMOTHER IS "LOLA."
EVERYBODY LOVED MY LOLA.
NOT THAT I DIDN'T LOVE HER, SHE JUST...
...FRIGHTENED ME SOMETIMES.
SHE HAD A HUMP.
SHE TOLD SCARY STORIES.
SHE SAW STRANGE THINGS.
SHE DID STRANGE THINGS.
I THINK SHE TRIED TO DROWN ME ONCE.

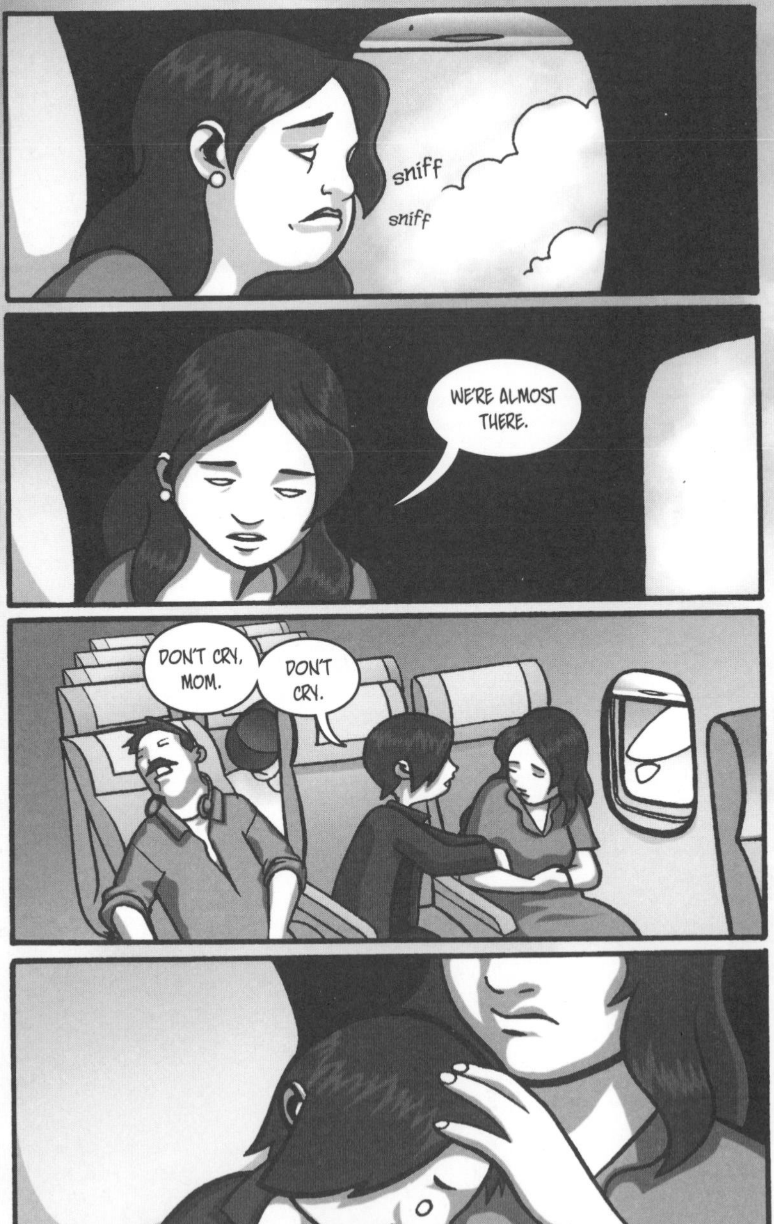
sniff
sniff
WE'RE ALMOST THERE.
DON'T CRY, MOM.
DON'T CRY.

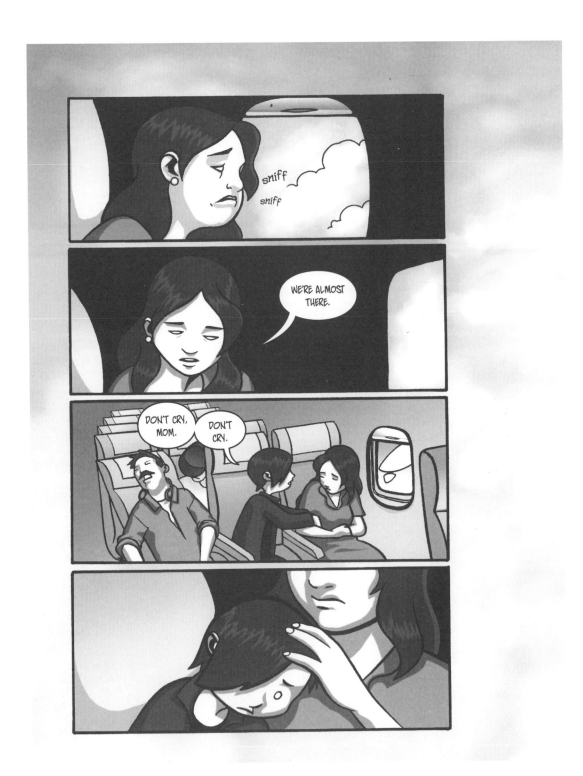

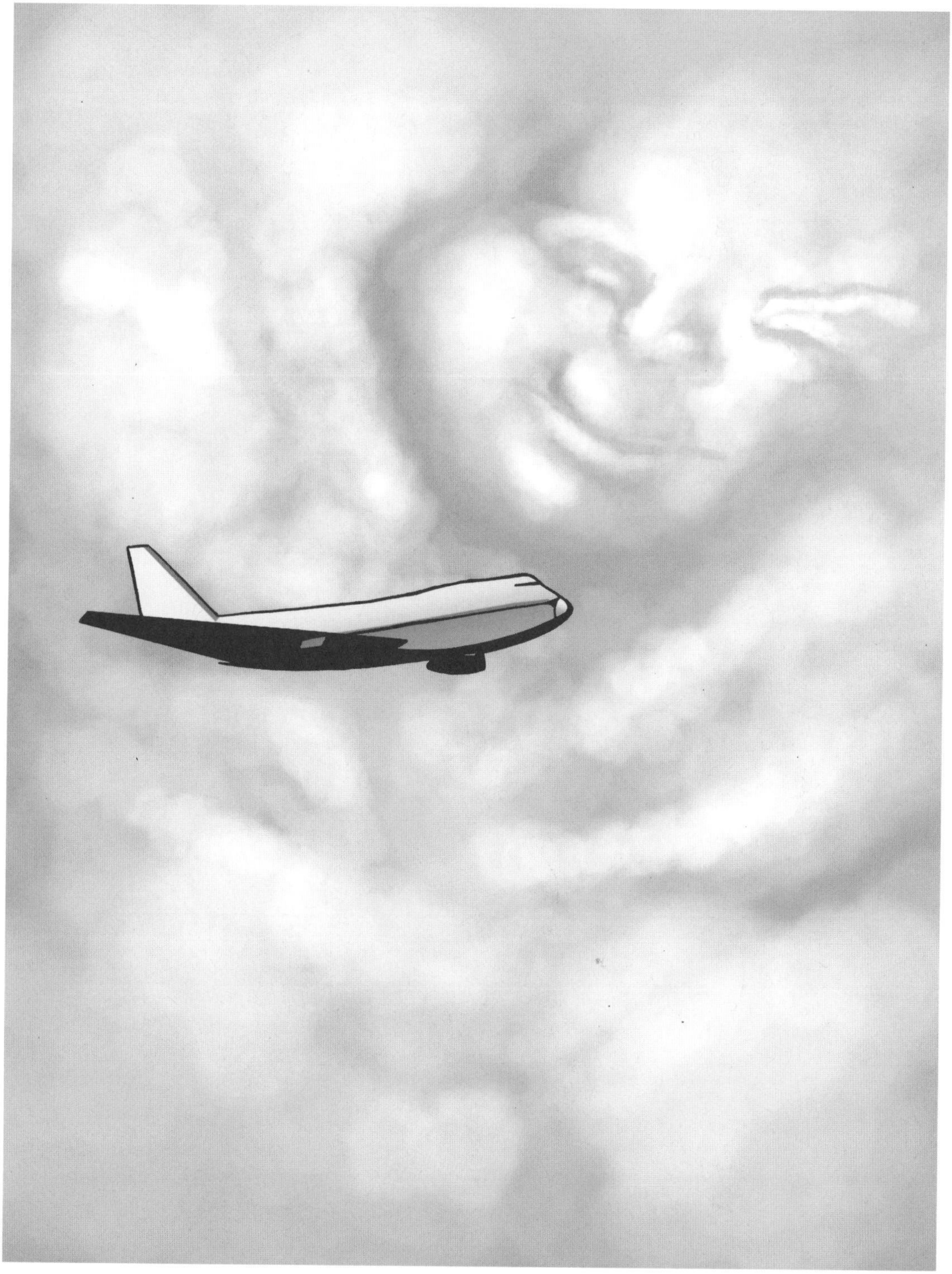

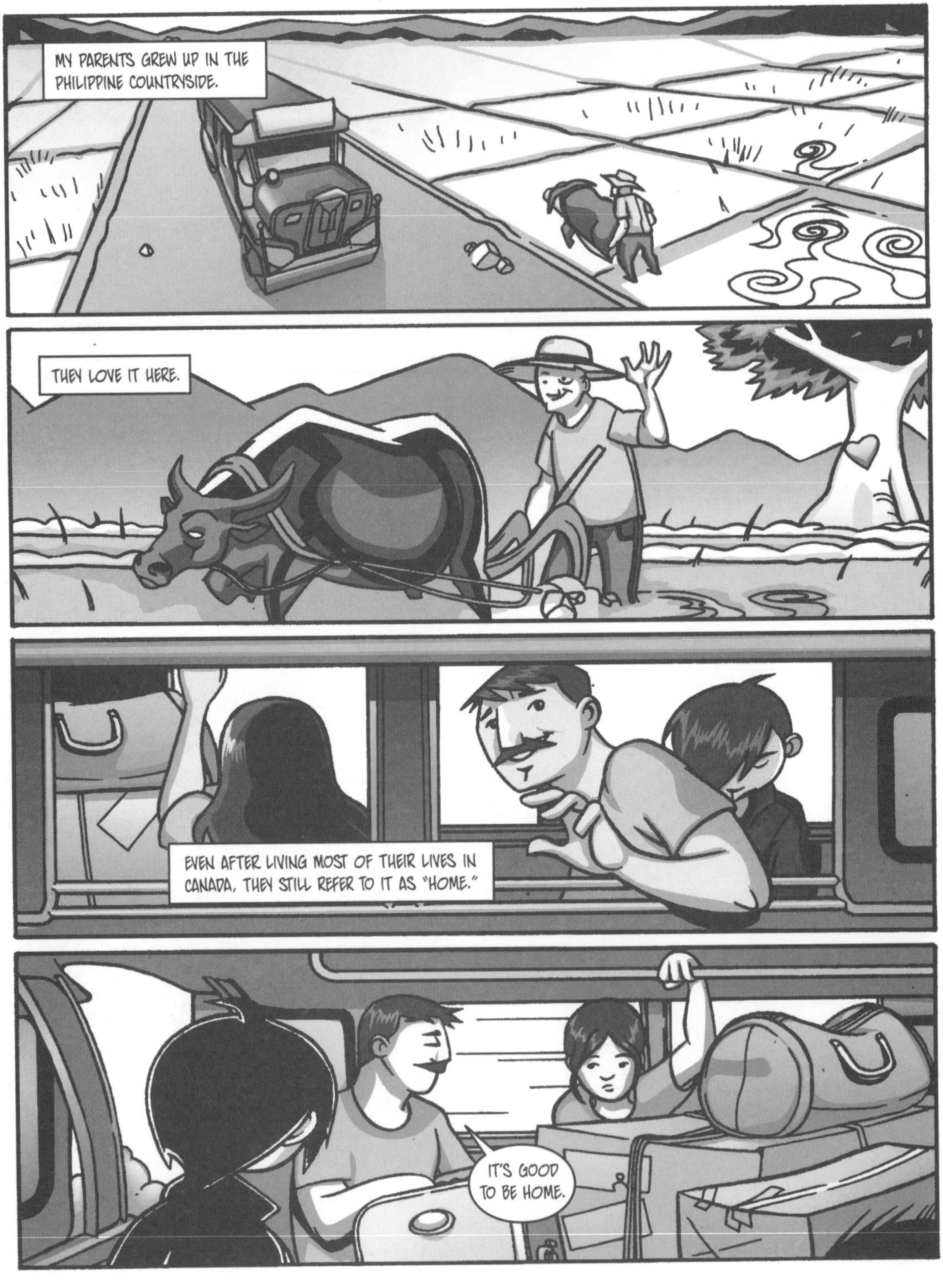
MY PARENTS GREW UP IN THE PHILIPPINE COUNTRYSIDE.
THEY LOVE IT HERE.
EVEN AFTER LIVING MOST OF THEIR LIVES IN CANADA, THEY STILL REFER TO IT AS "HOME."
IT'S GOOD TO BE HOME.

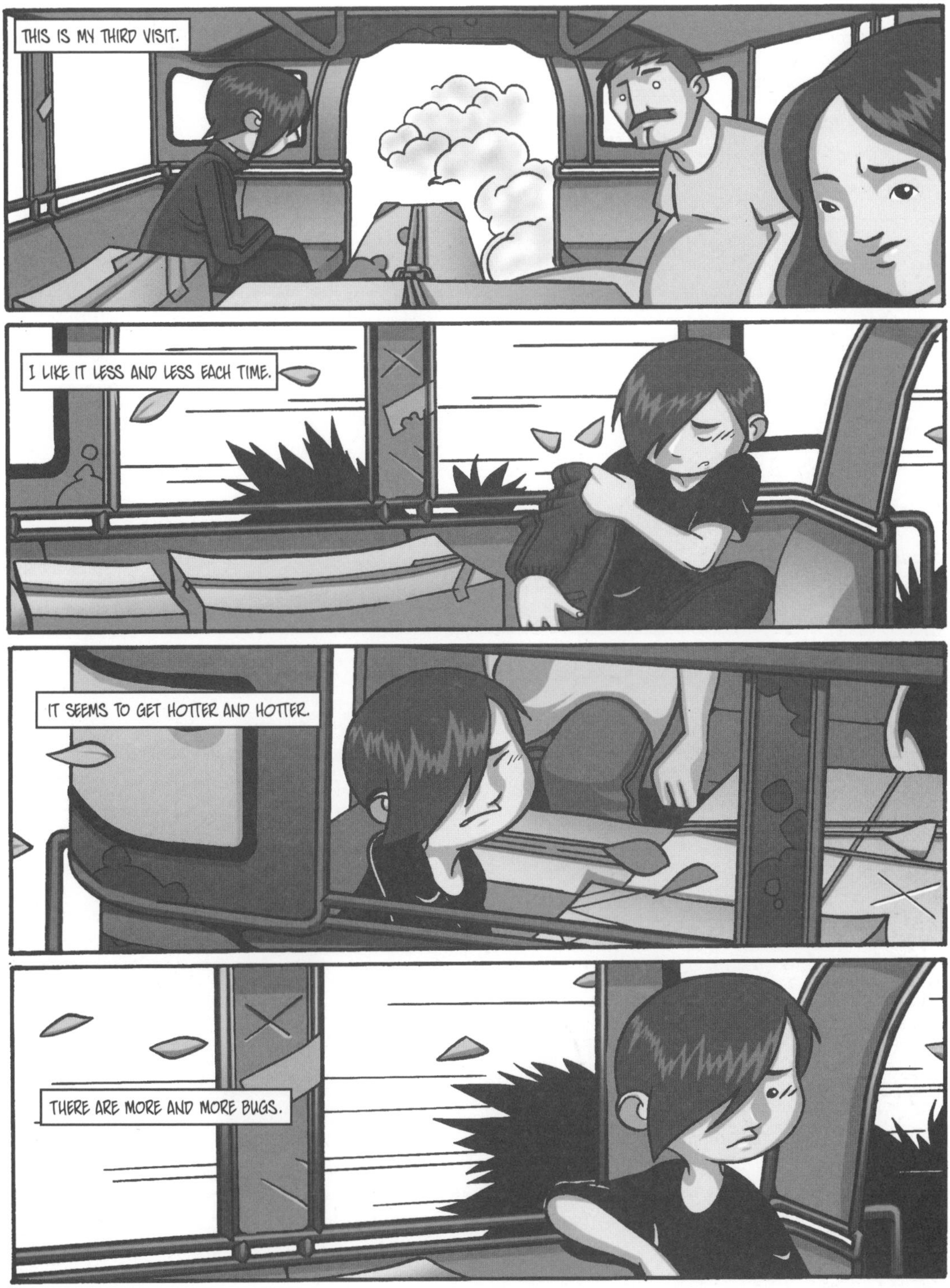
THIS IS MY THIRD VISIT.
I LIKE IT LESS AND LESS EACH TIME.
IT SEEMS TO GET HOTTER AND HOTTER.
THERE ARE MORE AND MORE BUGS.

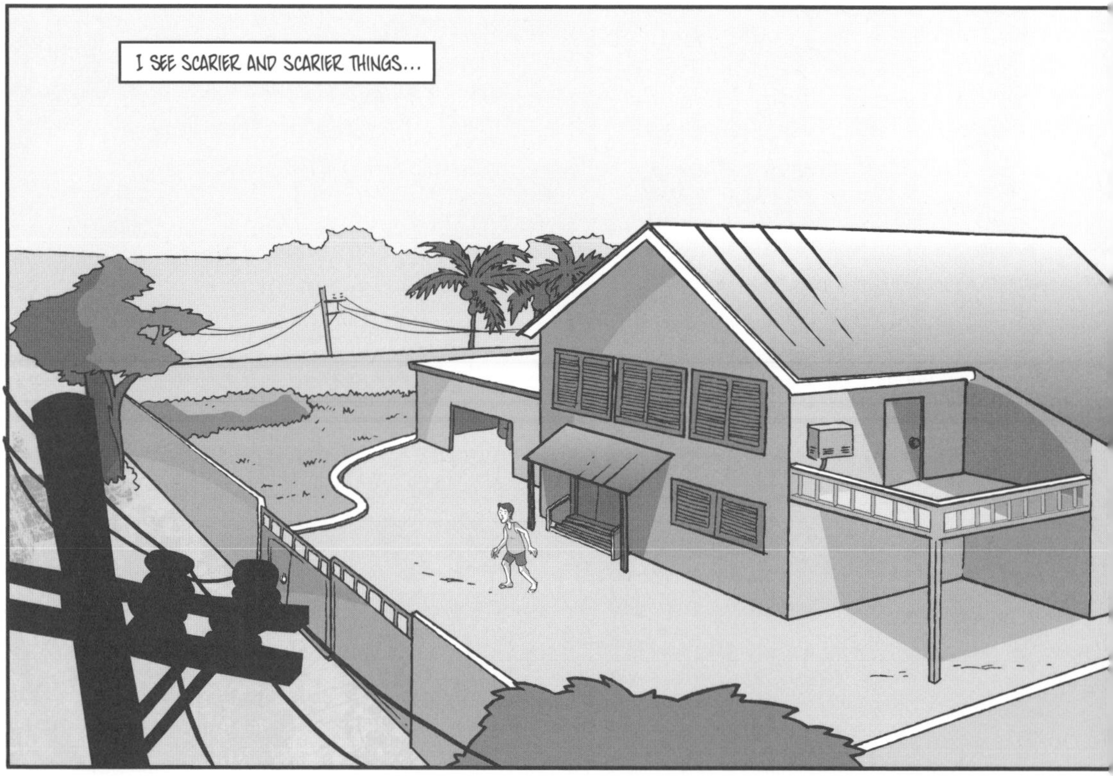
I SEE SCARIER AND SCARIER THINGS...

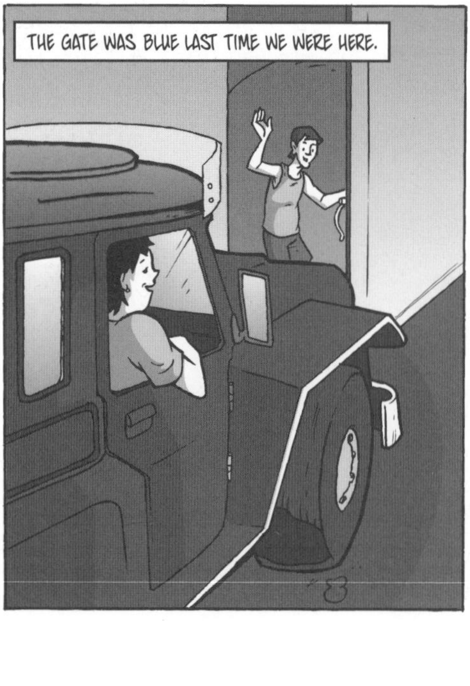
THE GATE WAS BLUE LAST TIME WE WERE HERE.

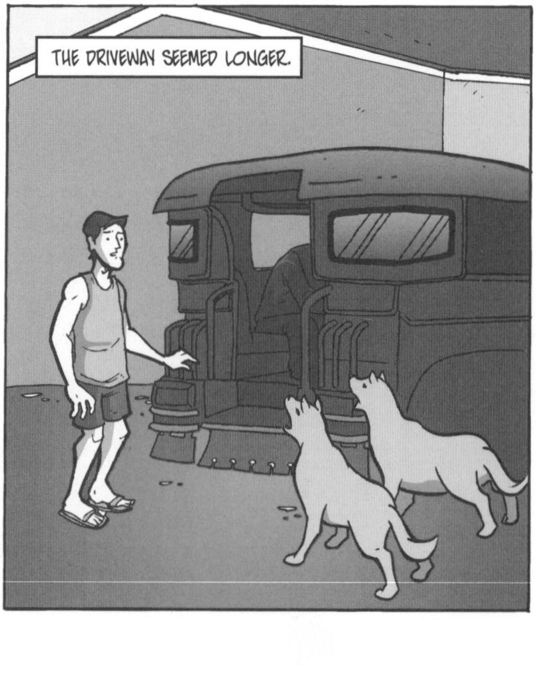
THE DRIVEWAY SEEMED LONGER.

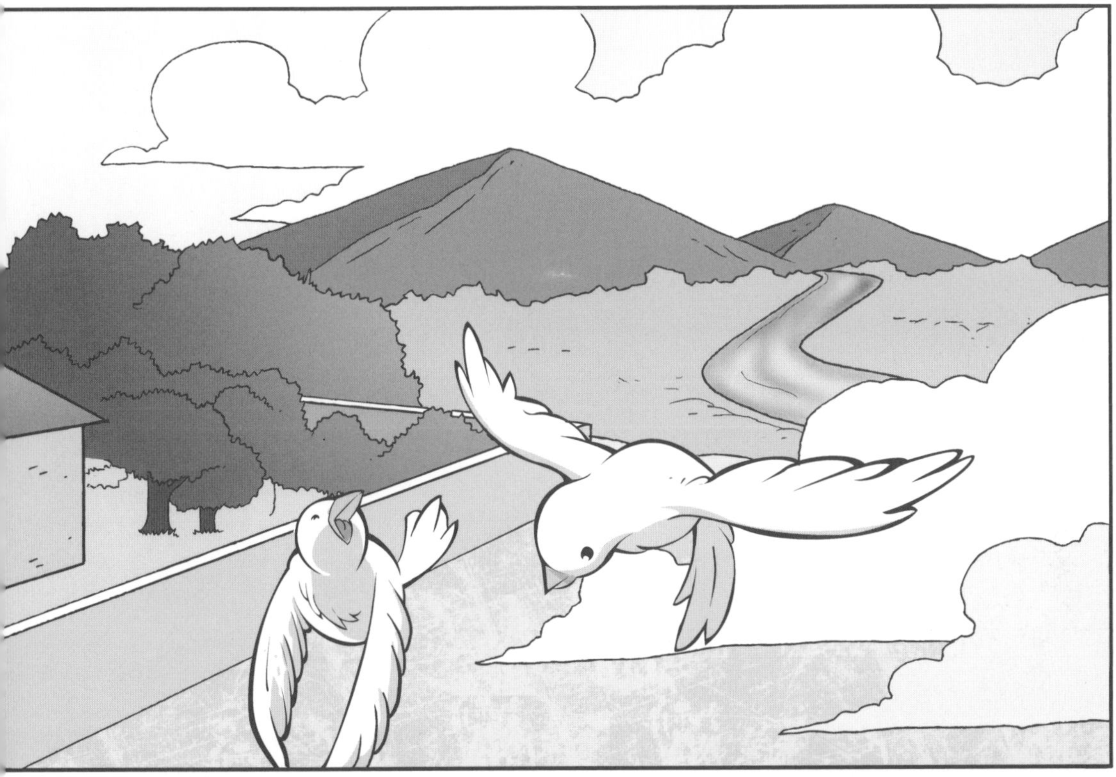

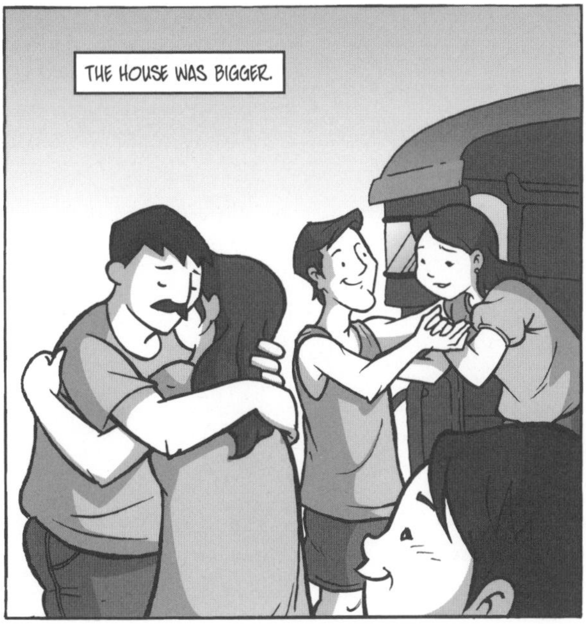
THE HOUSE WAS BIGGER.

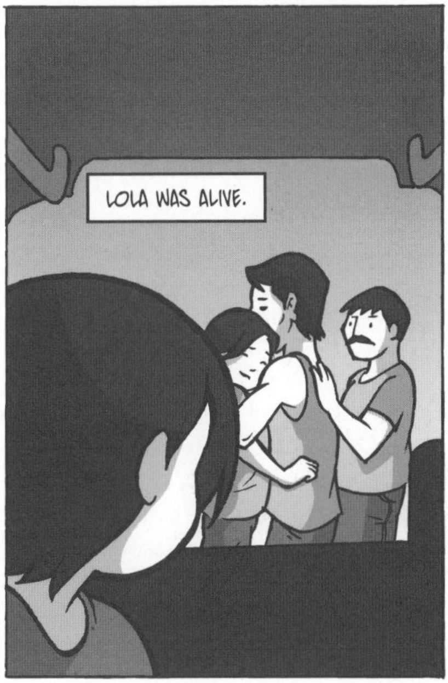
LOLA WAS ALIVE.

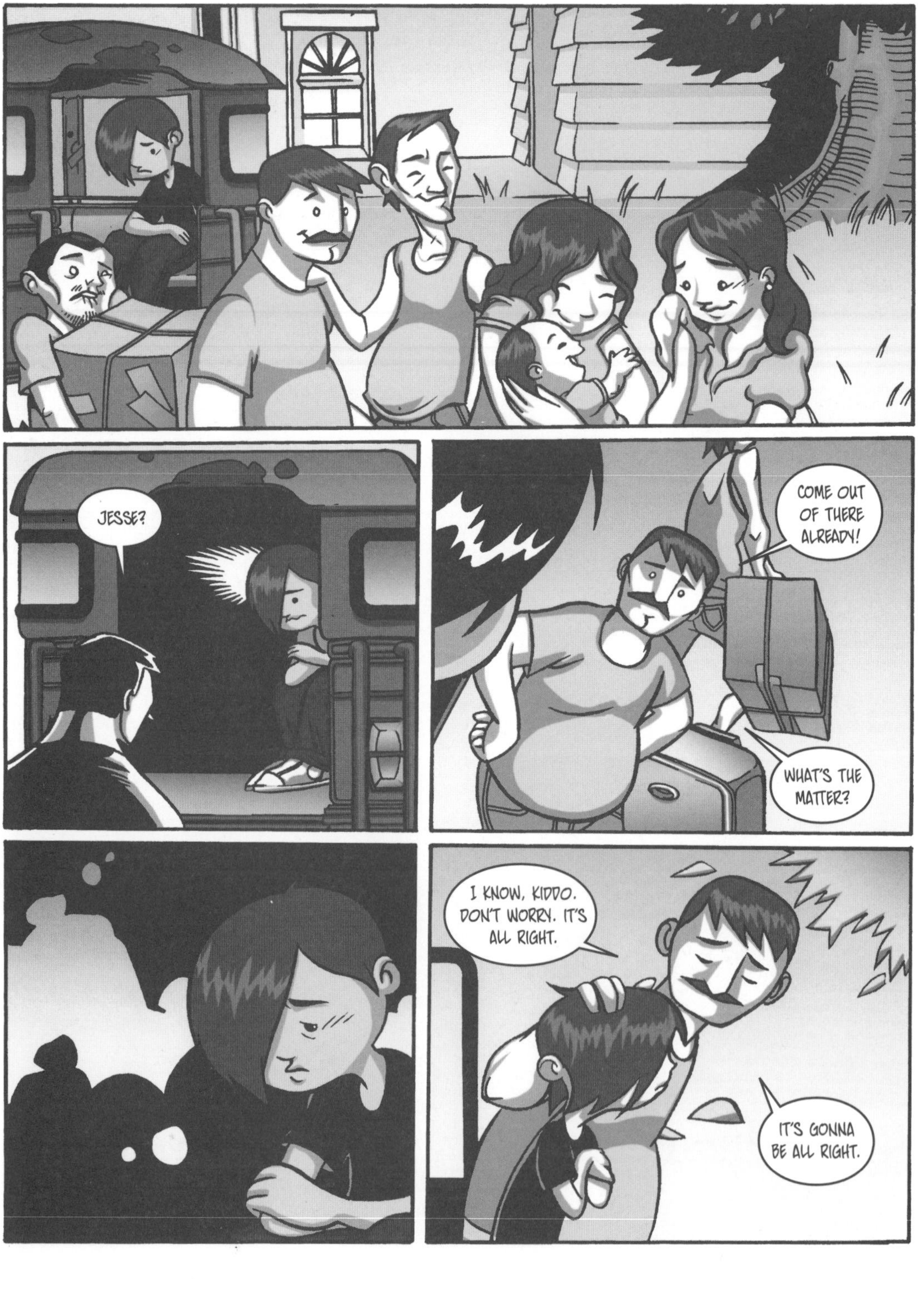
JESSE?
COME OUT OF THERE ALREADY!
WHAT'S THE MATTER?
I KNOW, KIDDO. DON'T WORRY. IT'S ALL RIGHT.
IT'S GONNA BE ALL RIGHT.

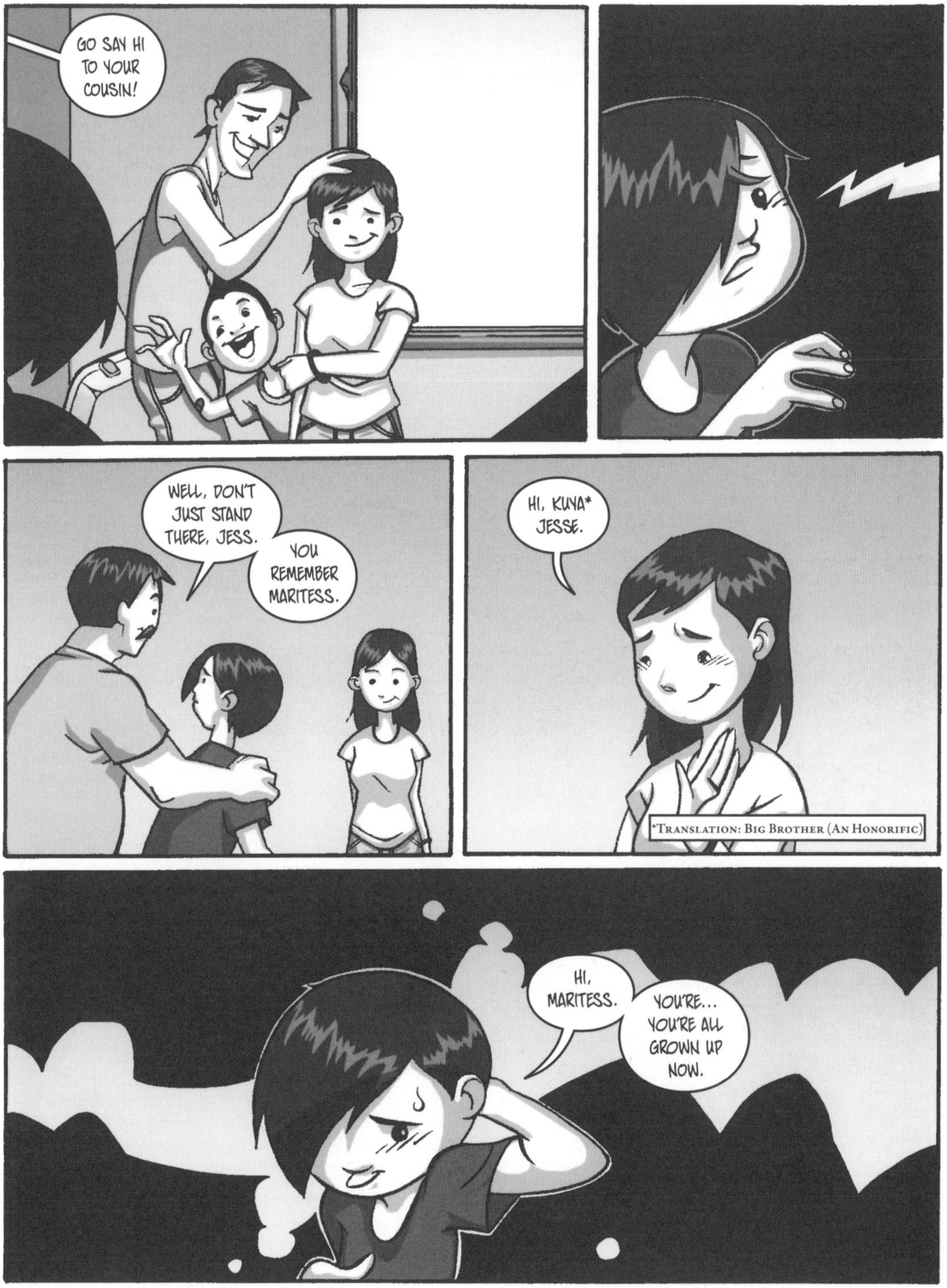
GO SAY HI TO YOUR COUSIN!
WELL, DON'T JUST STAND THERE, JESS.
YOU REMEMBER MARITESS.
HI, KUYA* JESSE.
*Translation: Big Brother (An Honorific)
HI, MARITESS.
YOU'RE... YOU'RE ALL GROWN UP NOW.

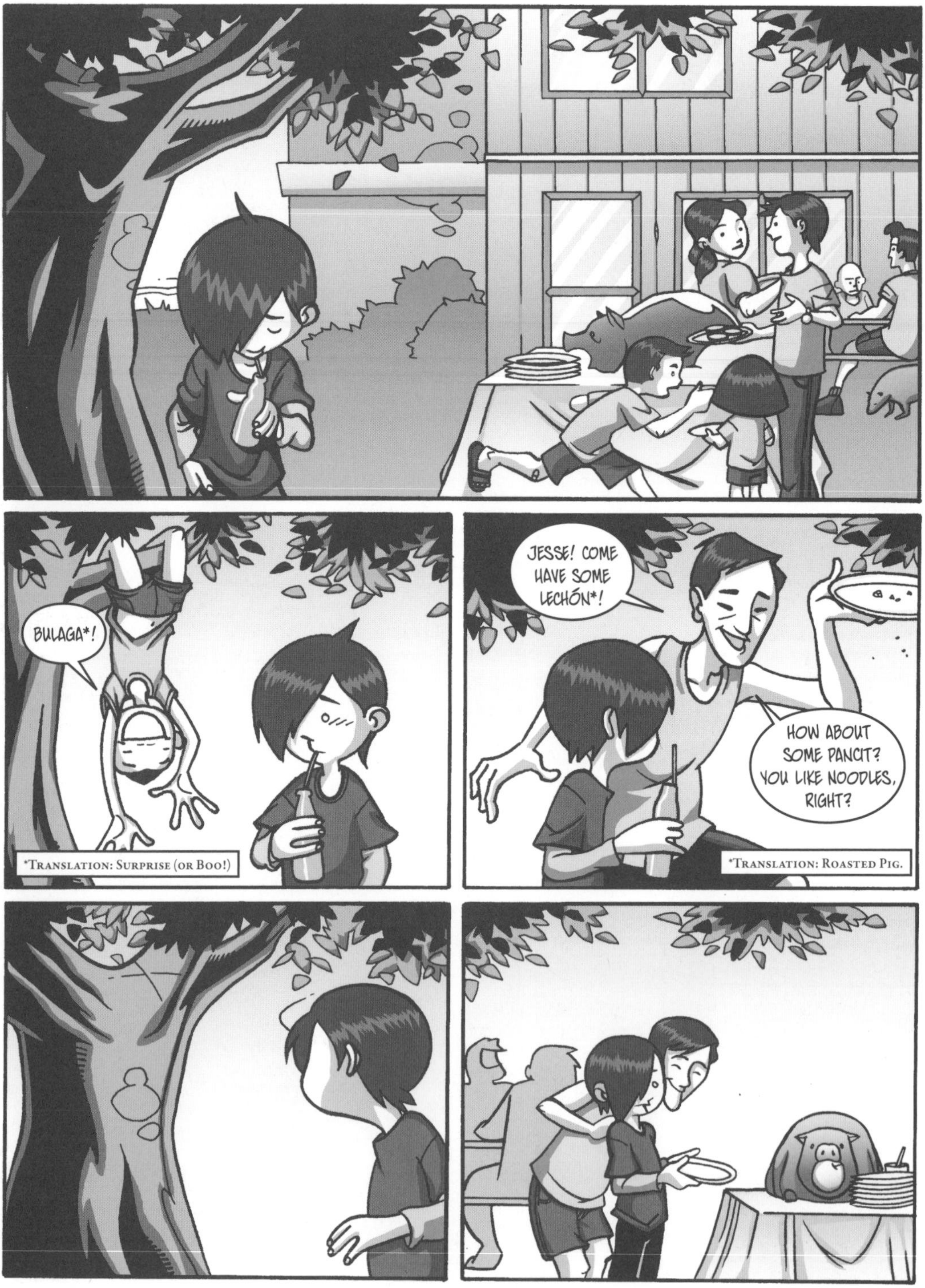
BULAGA*!
*Translation: Surprise (or Boo!)
JESSE! COME HAVE SOME LECHÓN*!
HOW ABOUT SOME PANCIT? YOU LIKE NOODLES, RIGHT?
*Translation: Roasted Pig.

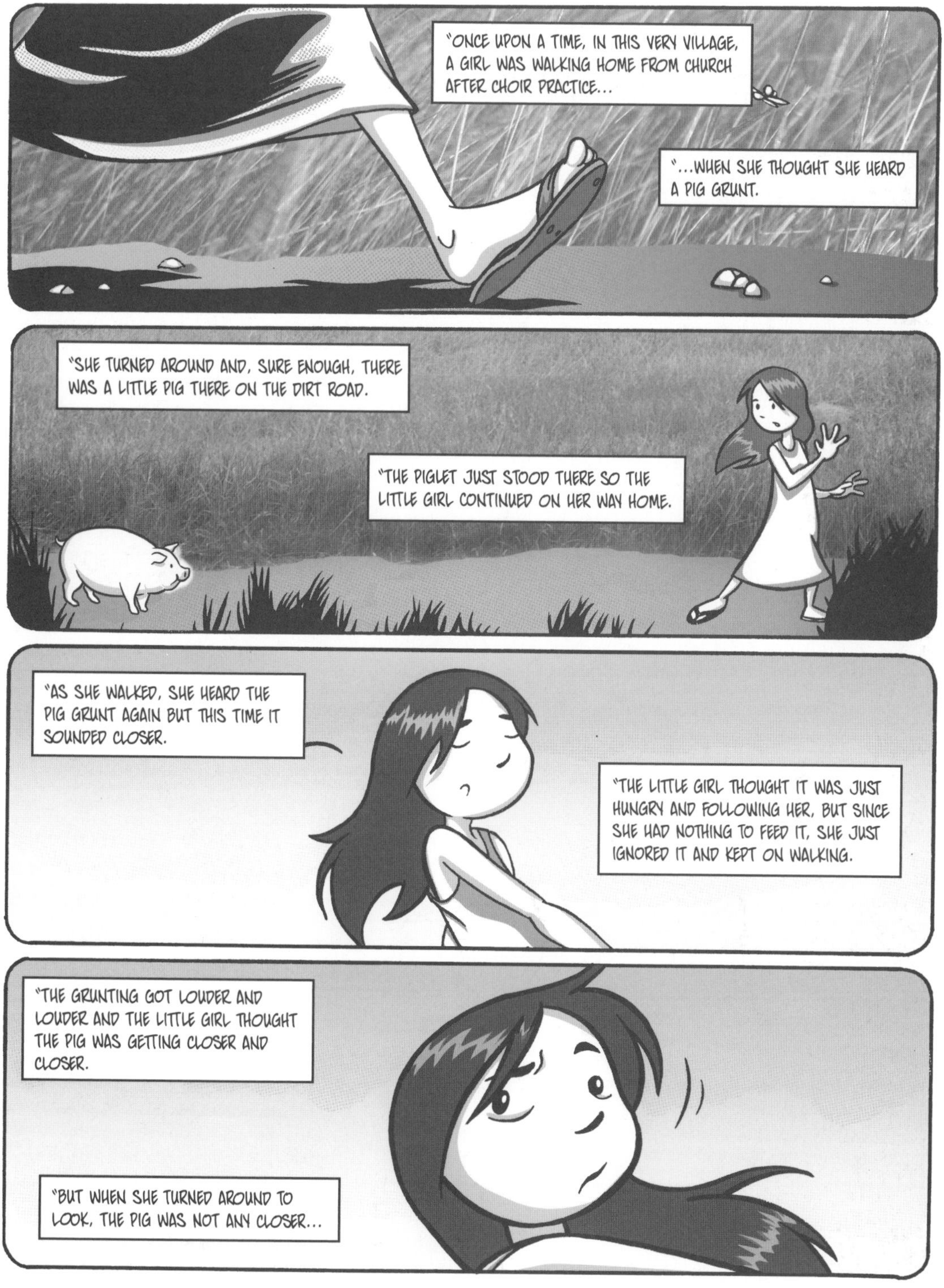
"ONCE UPON A TIME, IN THIS VERY VILLAGE, A GIRL WAS WALKING HOME FROM CHURCH AFTER CHOIR PRACTICE...
"...WHEN SHE THOUGHT SHE HEARD A PIG GRUNT.
"SHE TURNED AROUND AND, SURE ENOUGH, THERE WAS A LITTLE PIG THERE ON THE DIRT ROAD.
"THE PIGLET JUST STOOD THERE SO THE LITTLE GIRL CONTINUED ON HER WAY HOME.
"AS SHE WALKED, SHE HEARD THE PIG GRUNT AGAIN BUT THIS TIME IT SOUNDED CLOSER.
"THE LITTLE GIRL THOUGHT IT WAS JUST HUNGRY AND FOLLOWING HER, BUT SINCE SHE HAD NOTHING TO FEED IT, SHE JUST IGNORED IT AND KEPT ON WALKING.
"THE GRUNTING GOT LOUDER AND LOUDER AND THE LITTLE GIRL THOUGHT THE PIG WAS GETTING CLOSER AND CLOSER.
"BUT WHEN SHE TURNED AROUND TO LOOK, THE PIG WAS NOT ANY CLOSER...

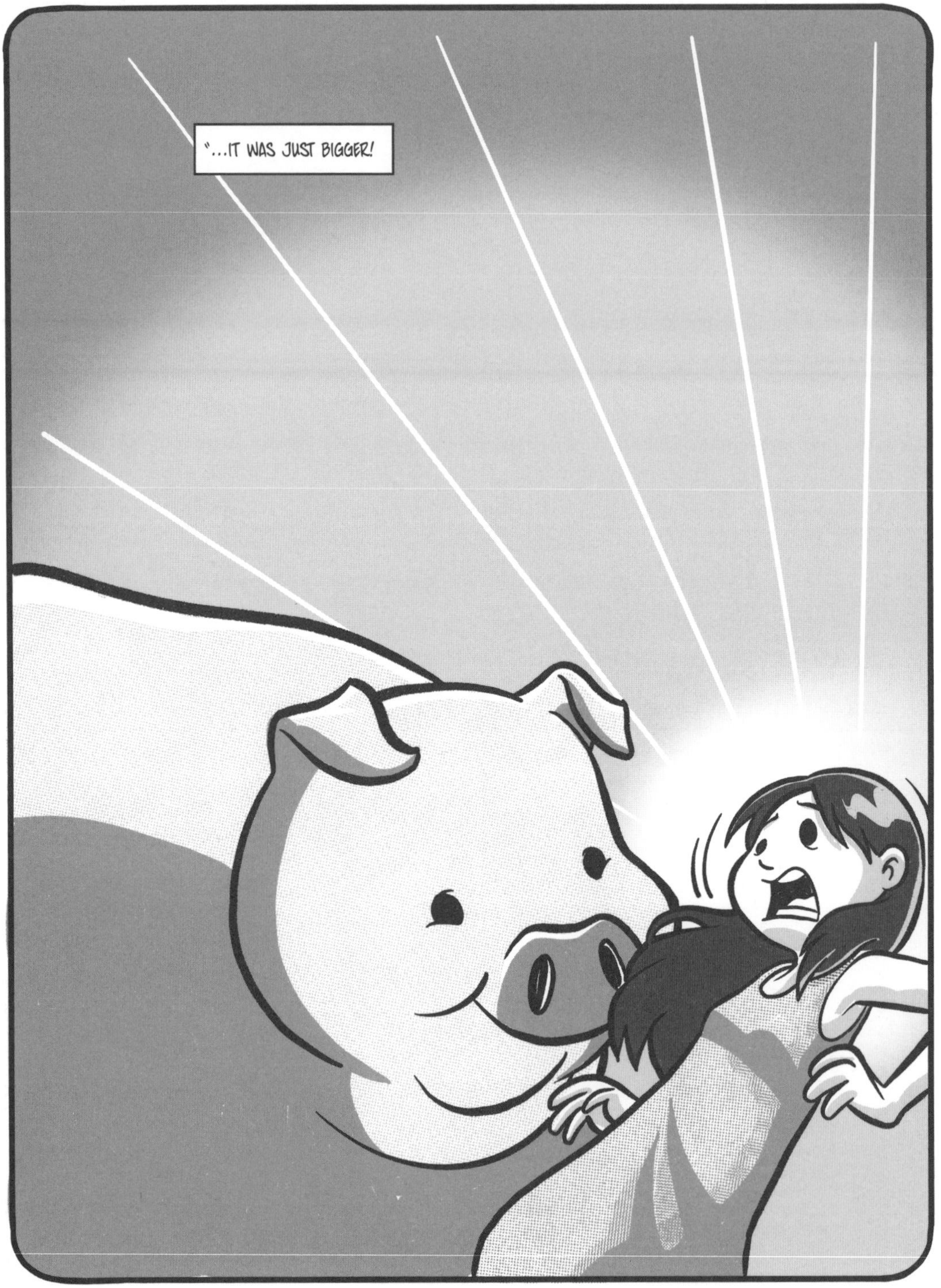
"...IT WAS JUST BIGGER!

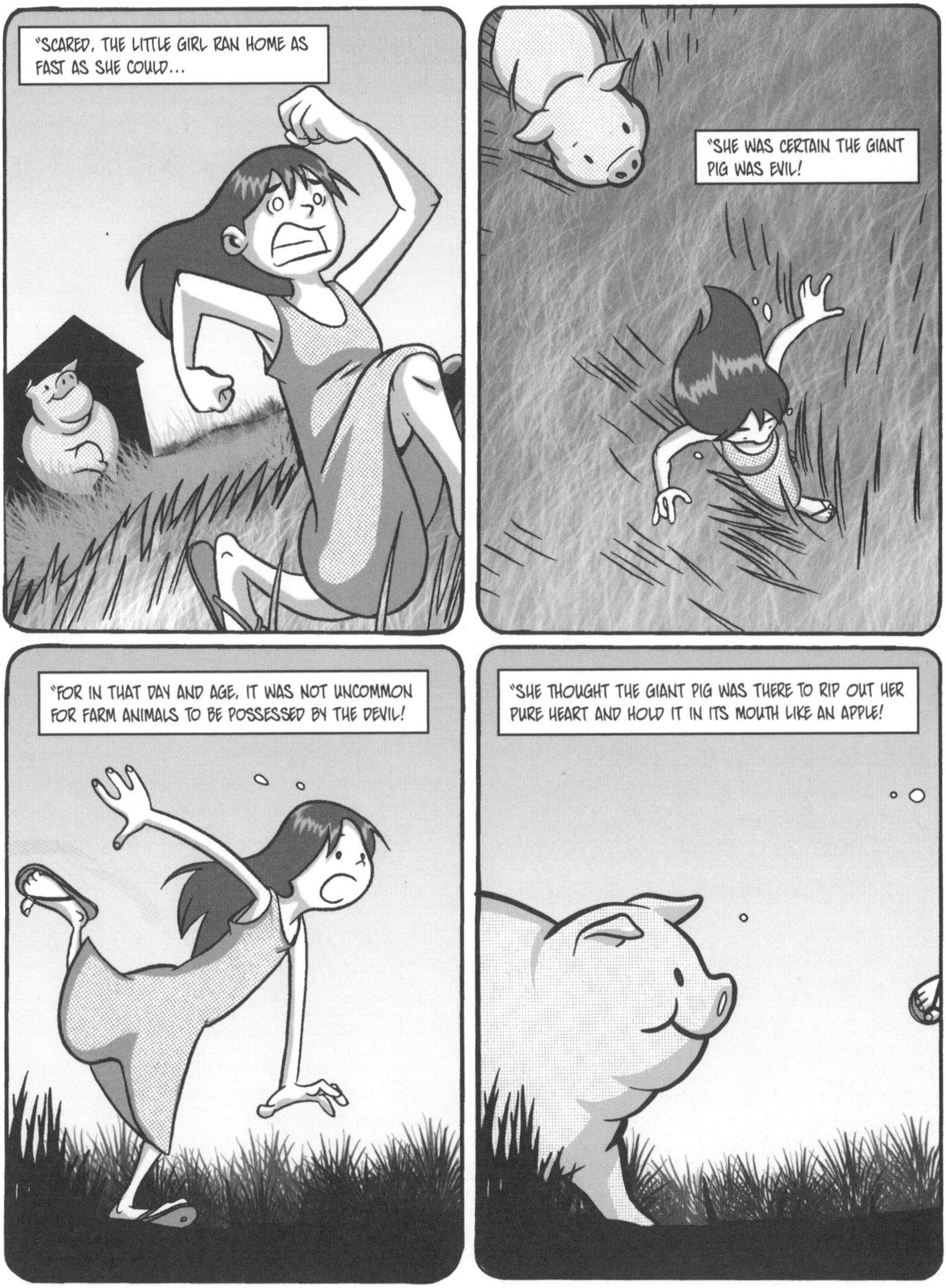
"SCARED, THE LITTLE GIRL RAN HOME AS FAST AS SHE COULD...
"SHE WAS CERTAIN THE GIANT PIG WAS EVIL!
"FOR IN THAT DAY AND AGE, IT WAS NOT UNCOMMON FOR FARM ANIMALS TO BE POSSESSED BY THE DEVIL!
"SHE THOUGHT THE GIANT PIG WAS THERE TO RIP OUT HER PURE HEART AND HOLD IT IN ITS MOUTH LIKE AN APPLE!

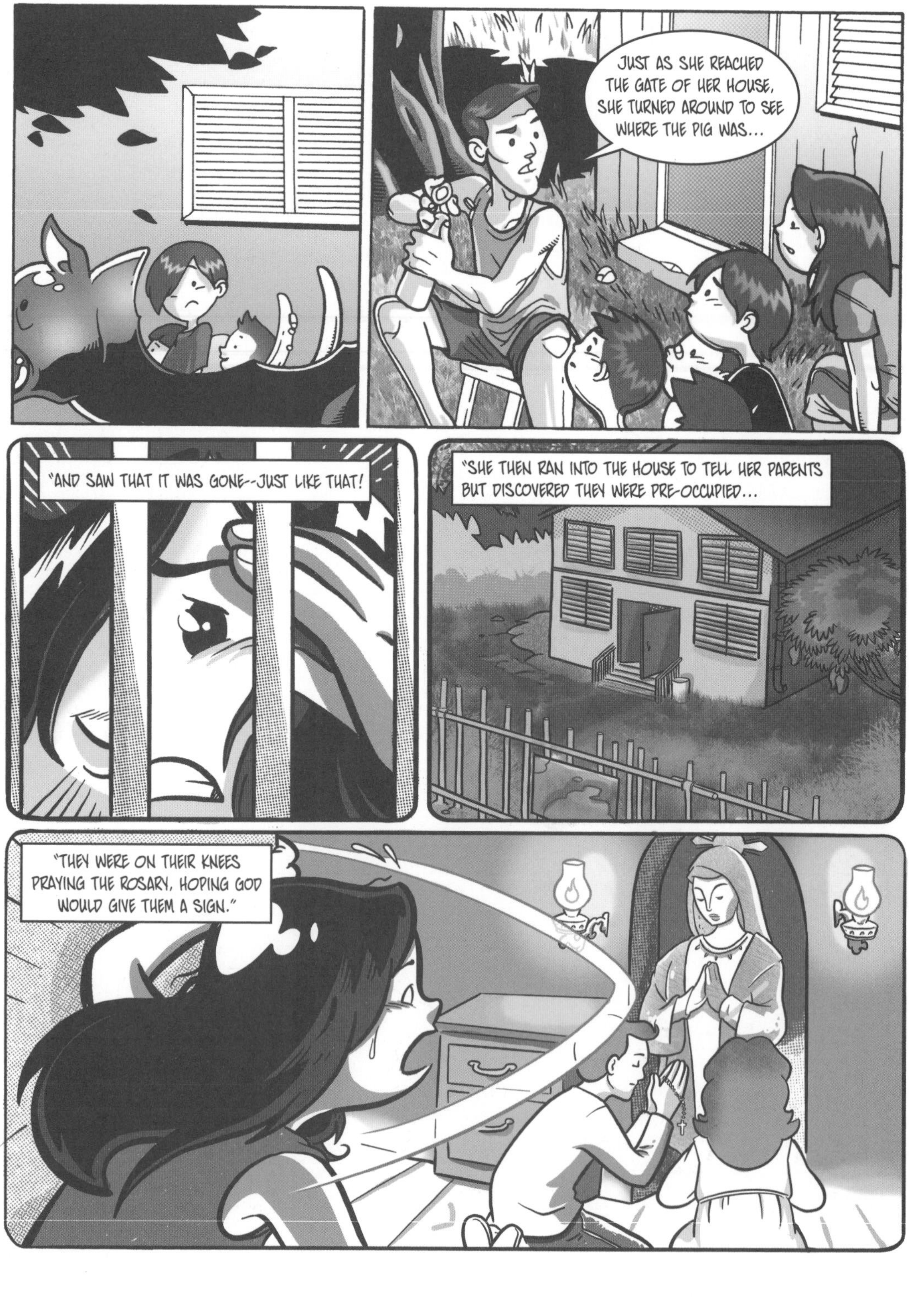
JUST AS SHE REACHED THE GATE OF HER HOUSE, SHE TURNED AROUND TO SEE WHERE THE PIG WAS...
"AND SAW THAT IT WAS GONE--JUST LIKE THAT!
"SHE THEN RAN INTO THE HOUSE TO TELL HER PARENTS BUT DISCOVERED THEY WERE PRE-OCCUPIED...
"THEY WERE ON THEIR KNEES PRAYING THE ROSARY, HOPING GOD WOULD GIVE THEM A SIGN."

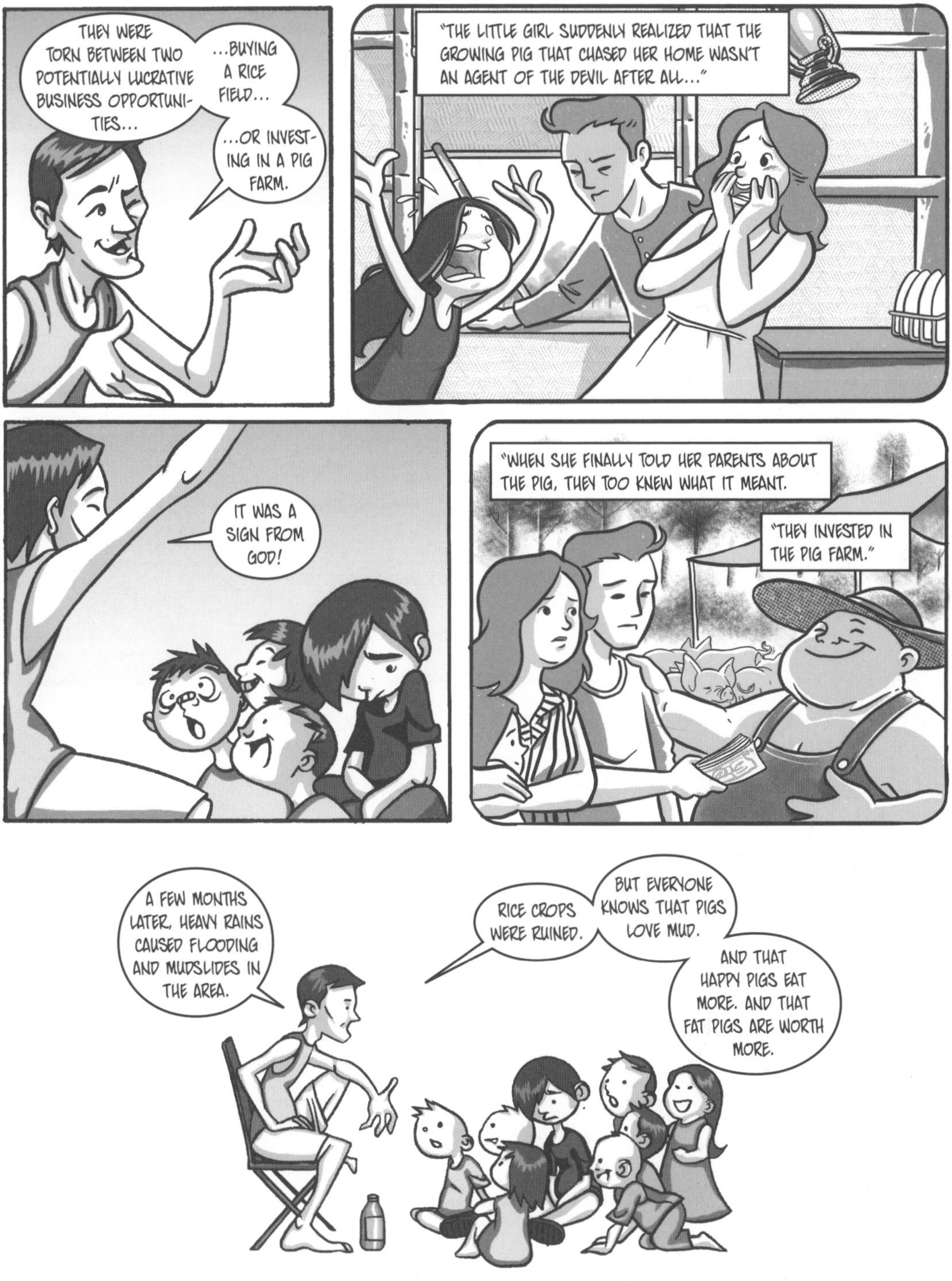
THEY WERE TORN BETWEEN TWO POTENTIALLY LUCRATIVE BUSINESS OPPORTUNITIES...
...BUYING A RICE FIELD...
...OR INVESTING IN A PIG FARM.
"THE LITTLE GIRL SUDDENLY REALIZED THAT THE GROWING PIG THAT CHASED HER HOME WASN'T AN AGENT OF THE DEVIL AFTER ALL..."
IT WAS A SIGN FROM GOD!
"WHEN SHE FINALLY TOLD HER PARENTS ABOUT THE PIG, THEY TOO KNEW WHAT IT MEANT.
"THEY INVESTED IN THE PIG FARM."
A FEW MONTHS LATER, HEAVY RAINS CAUSED FLOODING AND MUDSLIDES IN THE AREA.
RICE CROPS WERE RUINED.
BUT EVERYONE KNOWS THAT PIGS LOVE MUD.
AND THAT HAPPY PIGS EAT MORE. AND THAT FAT PIGS ARE WORTH MORE.

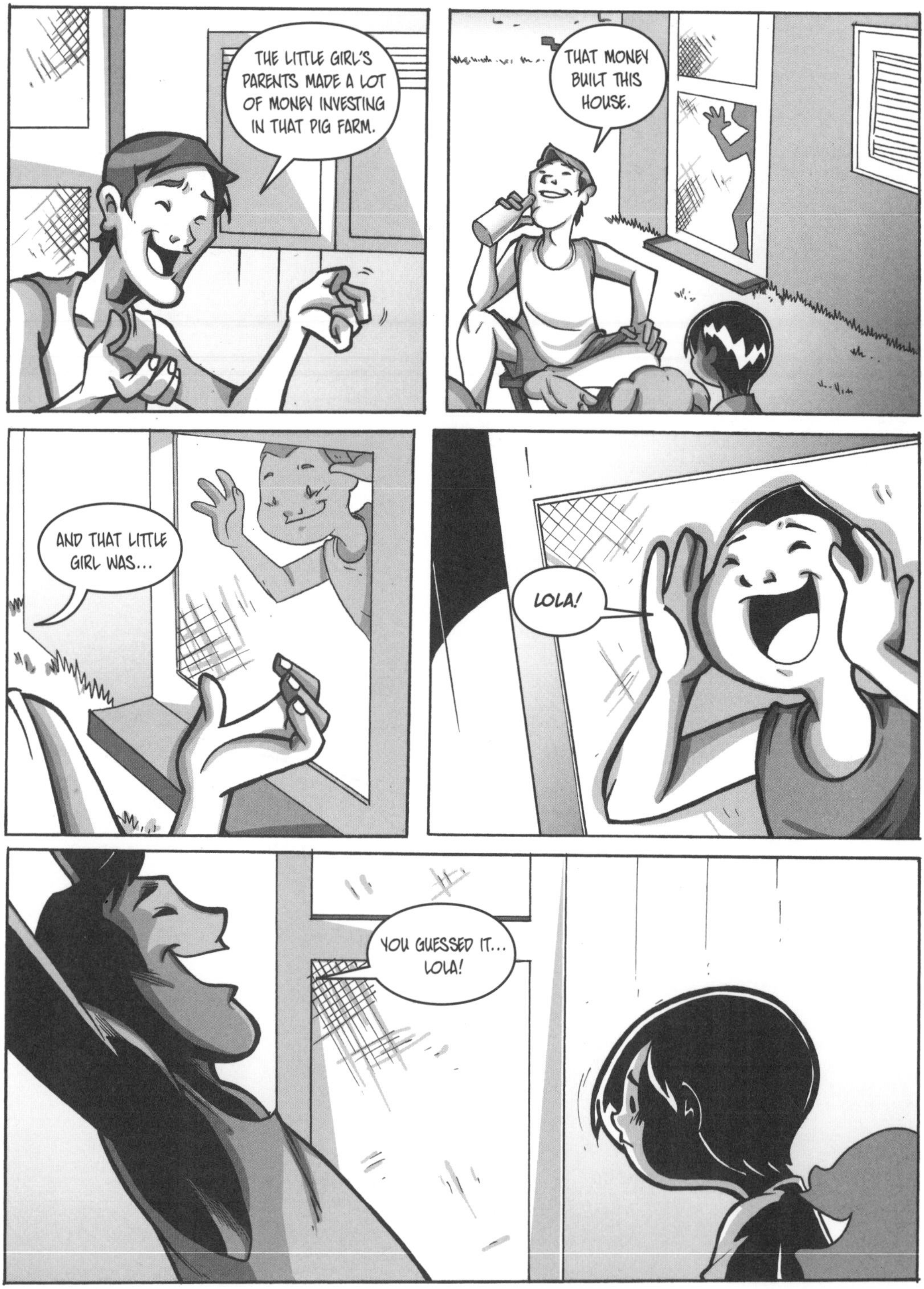
THE LITTLE GIRL'S PARENTS MADE A LOT OF MONEY INVESTING IN THAT PIG FARM.
THAT MONEY BUILT THIS HOUSE.
AND THAT LITTLE GIRL WAS...
LOLA!
YOU GUESSED IT... LOLA!

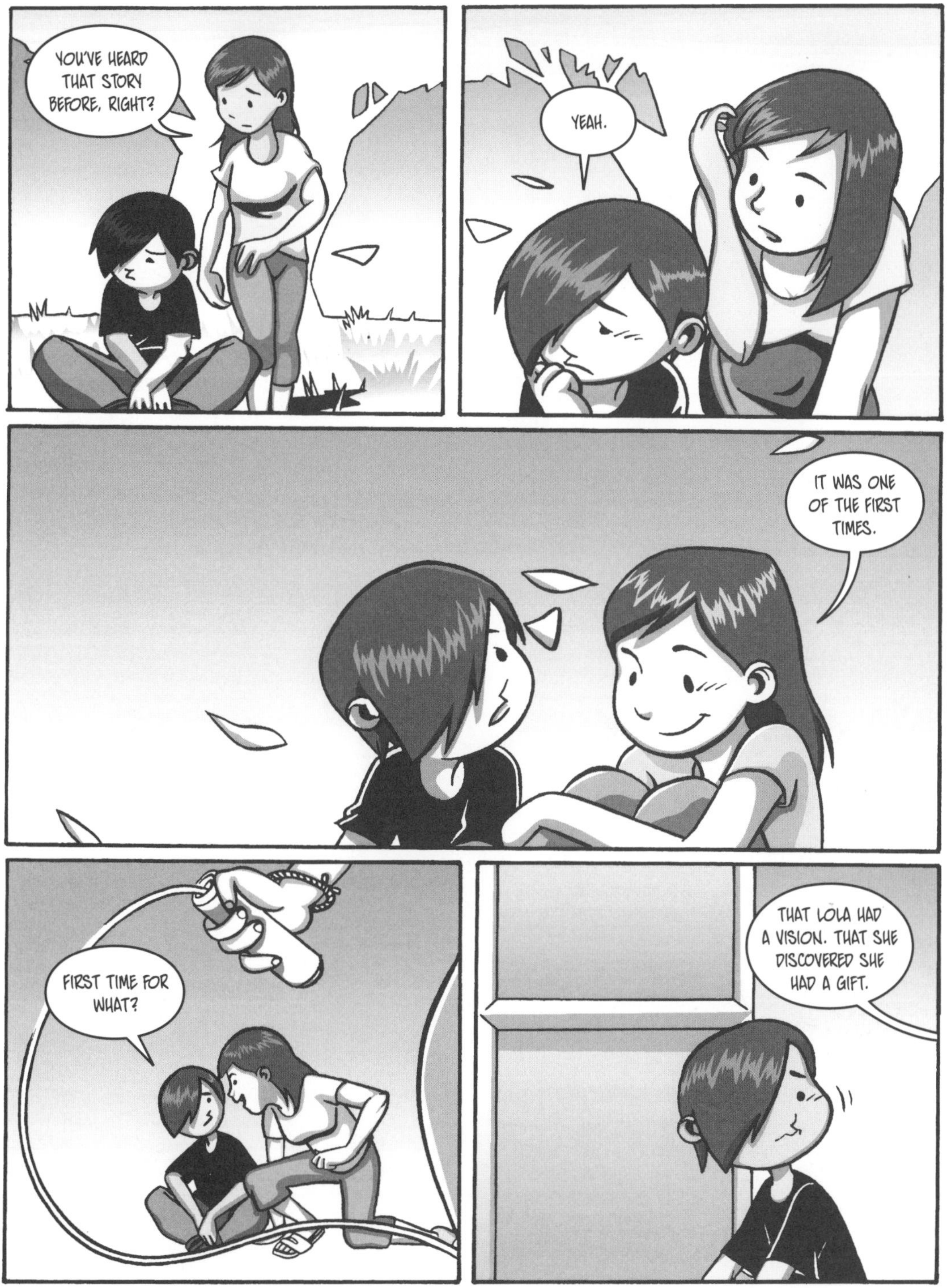
YOU'VE HEARD THAT STORY BEFORE, RIGHT?
YEAH.
IT WAS ONE OF THE FIRST TIMES.
FIRST TIME FOR WHAT?
THAT LOLA HAD A VISION. THAT SHE DISCOVERED SHE HAD A GIFT.

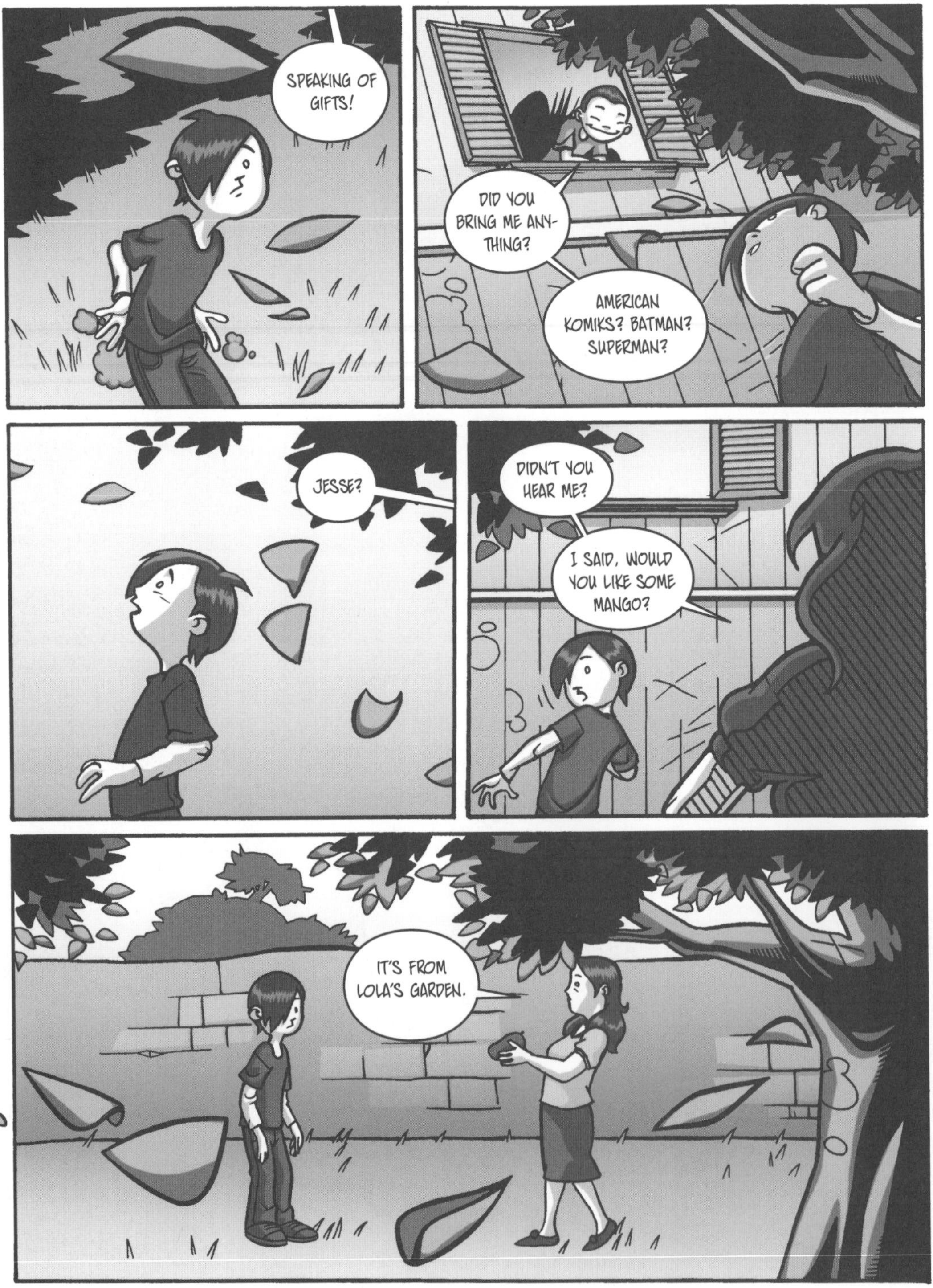
SPEAKING OF GIFTS!
DID YOU BRING ME ANY-THING?
AMERICAN KOMIKS? BATMAN? SUPERMAN?
JESSE?
DIDN'T YOU HEAR ME?
I SAID, WOULD YOU LIKE SOME MANGO?
IT'S FROM LOLA'S GARDEN.

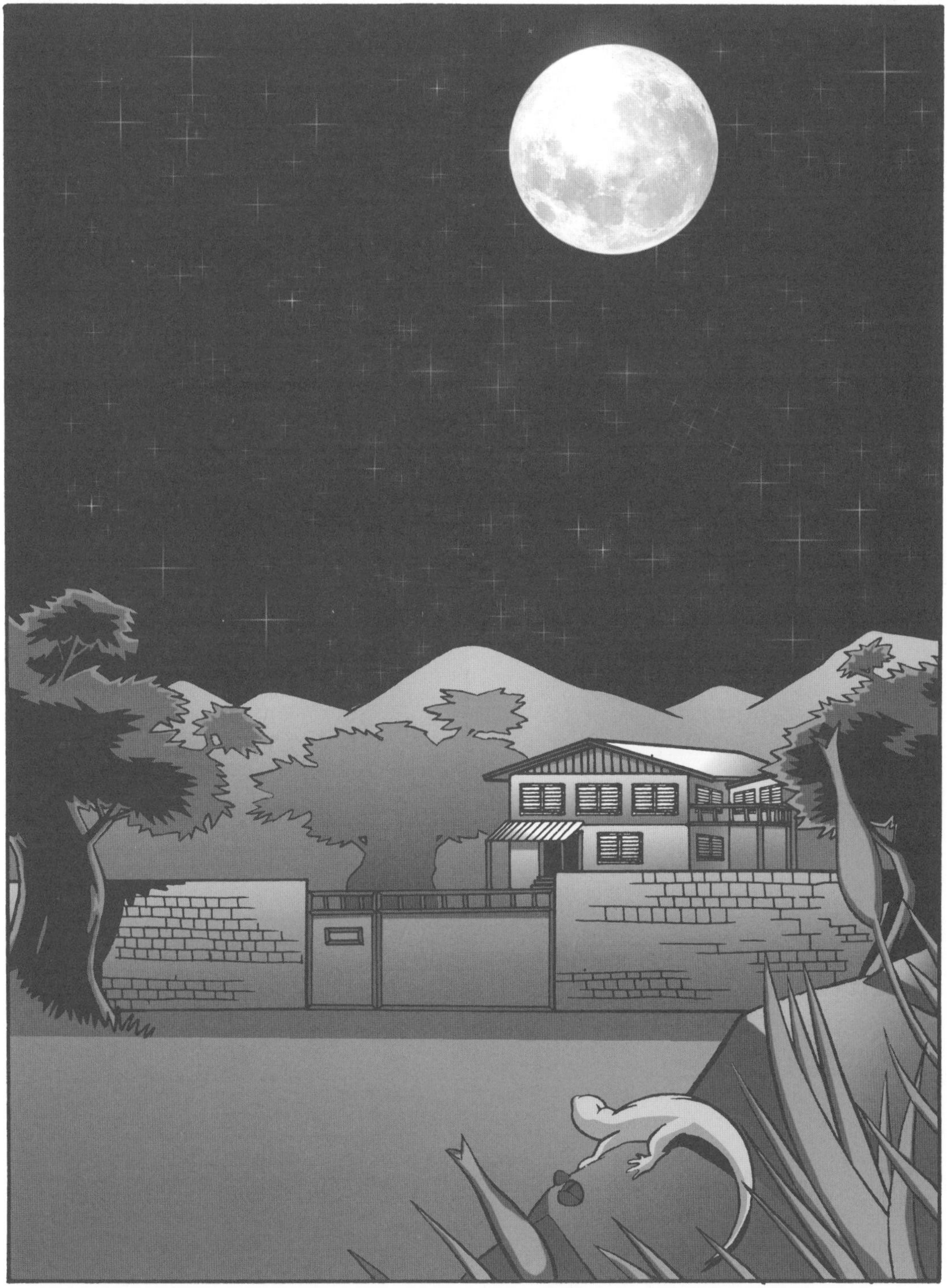

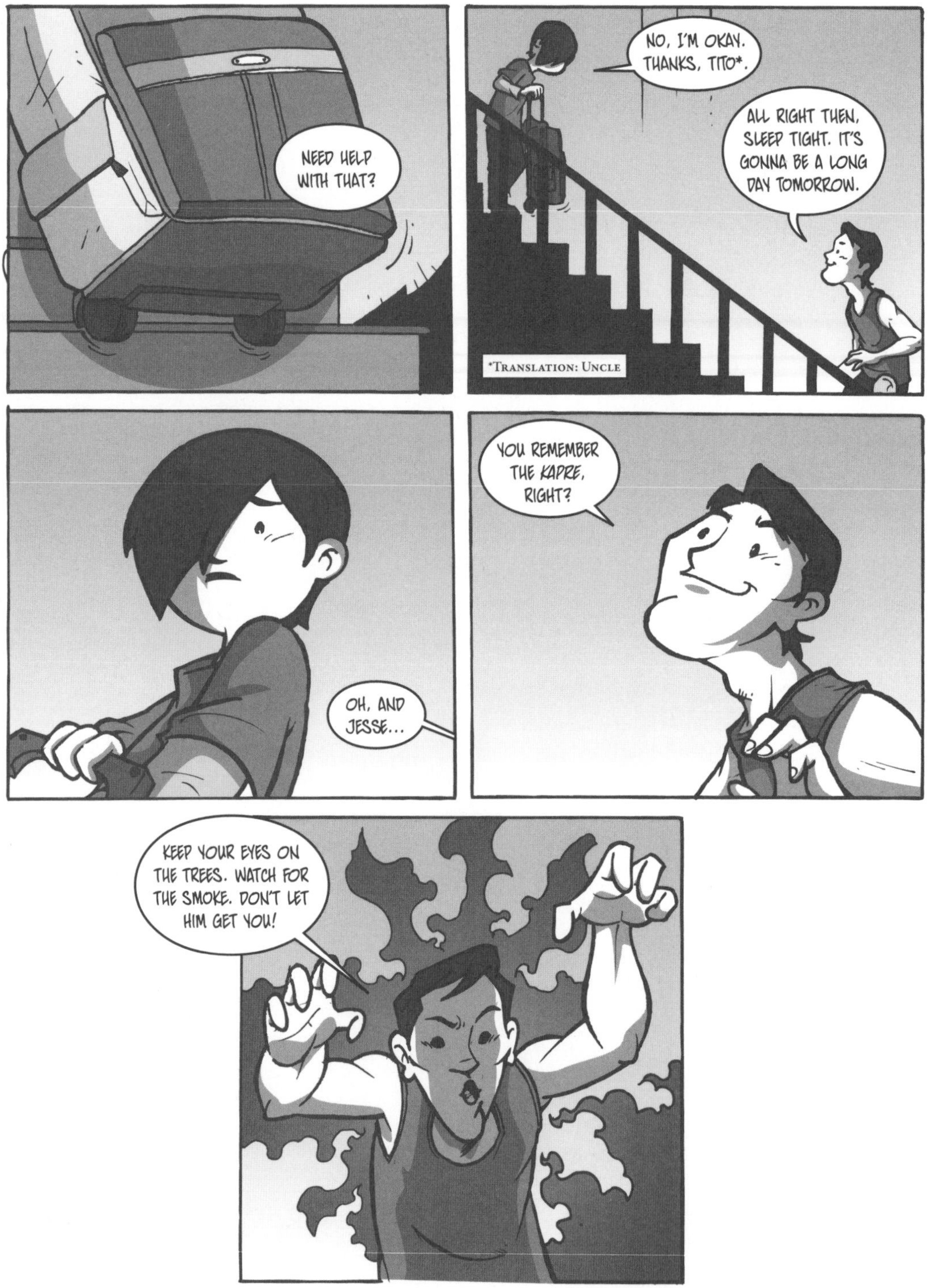
NEED HELP WITH THAT?
NO, I'M OKAY. THANKS, TITO*.
ALL RIGHT THEN, SLEEP TIGHT. IT'S GONNA BE A LONG DAY TOMORROW.
*Translation: Uncle
OH, AND JESSE...
YOU REMEMBER THE KAPRE, RIGHT?
KEEP YOUR EYES ON THE TREES. WATCH FOR THE SMOKE. DON'T LET HIM GET YOU!

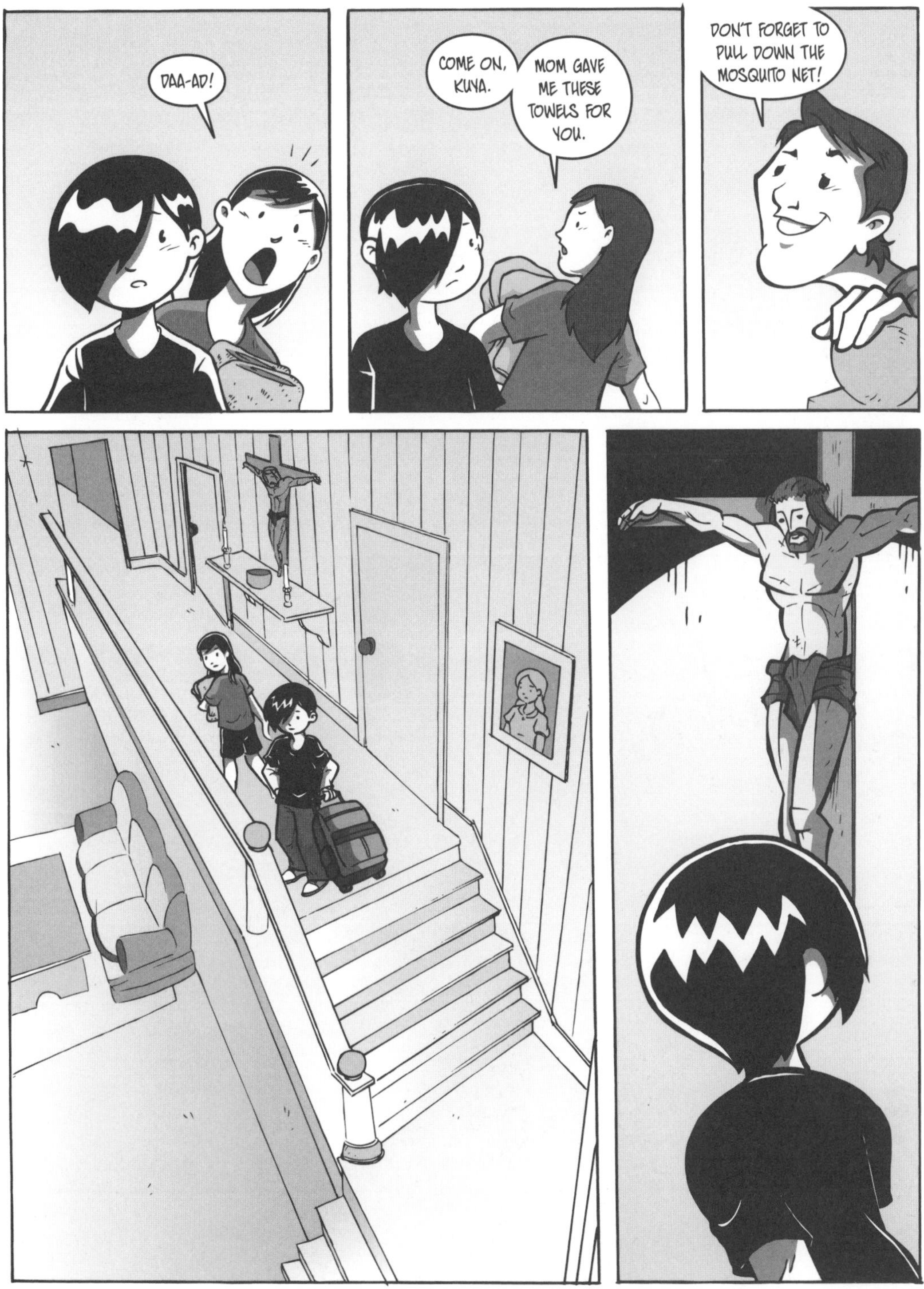
DAA-AD!
COME ON, KUYA.
MOM GAVE ME THESE TOWELS FOR YOU.
DON'T FORGET TO PULL DOWN THE MOSQUITO NET!

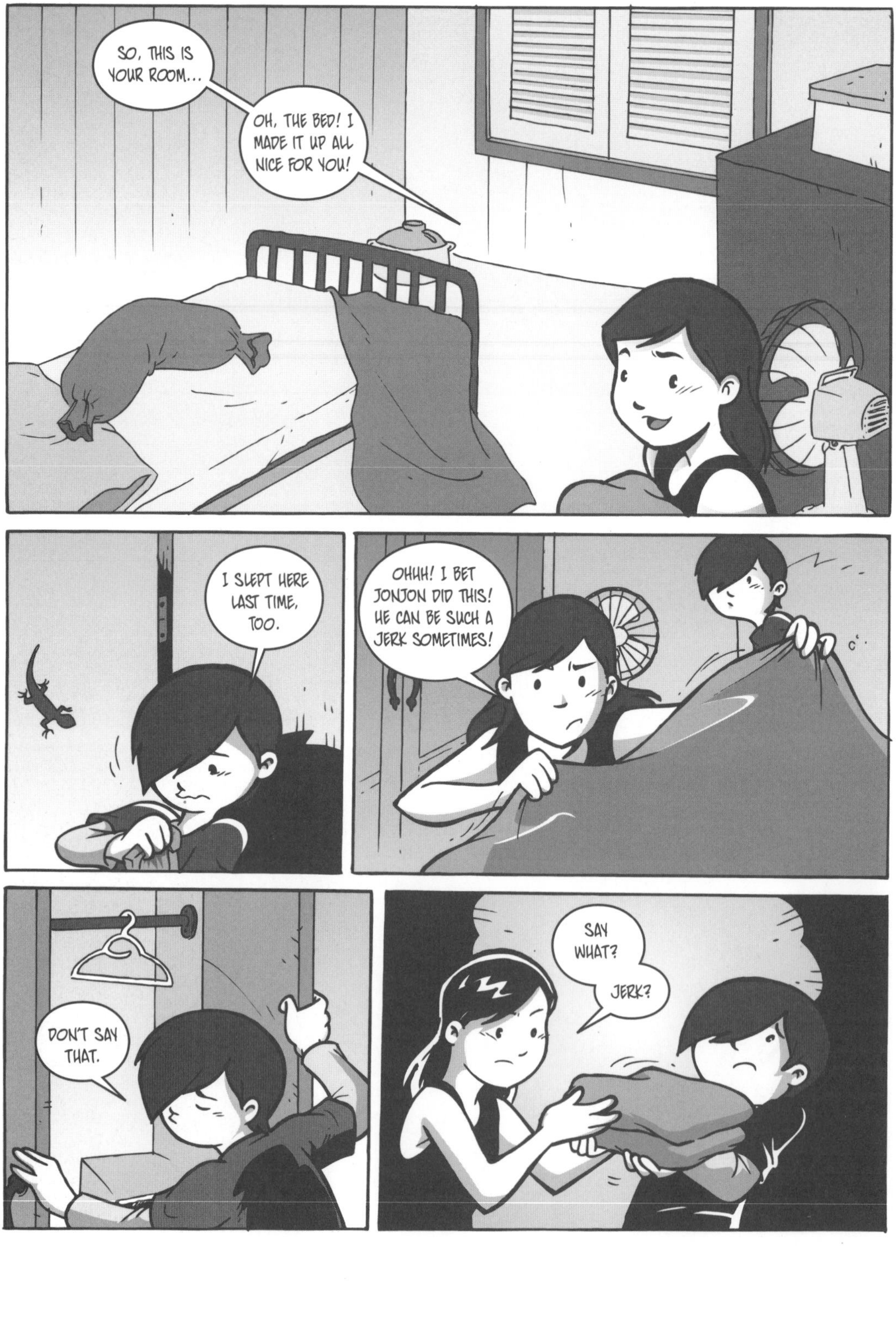
SO, THIS IS YOUR ROOM...
OH, THE BED! I MADE IT UP ALL NICE FOR YOU!
I SLEPT HERE LAST TIME, TOO.
OHHH! I BET JONJON DID THIS! HE CAN BE SUCH A JERK SOMETIMES!
DON'T SAY THAT.
SAY WHAT?
JERK?

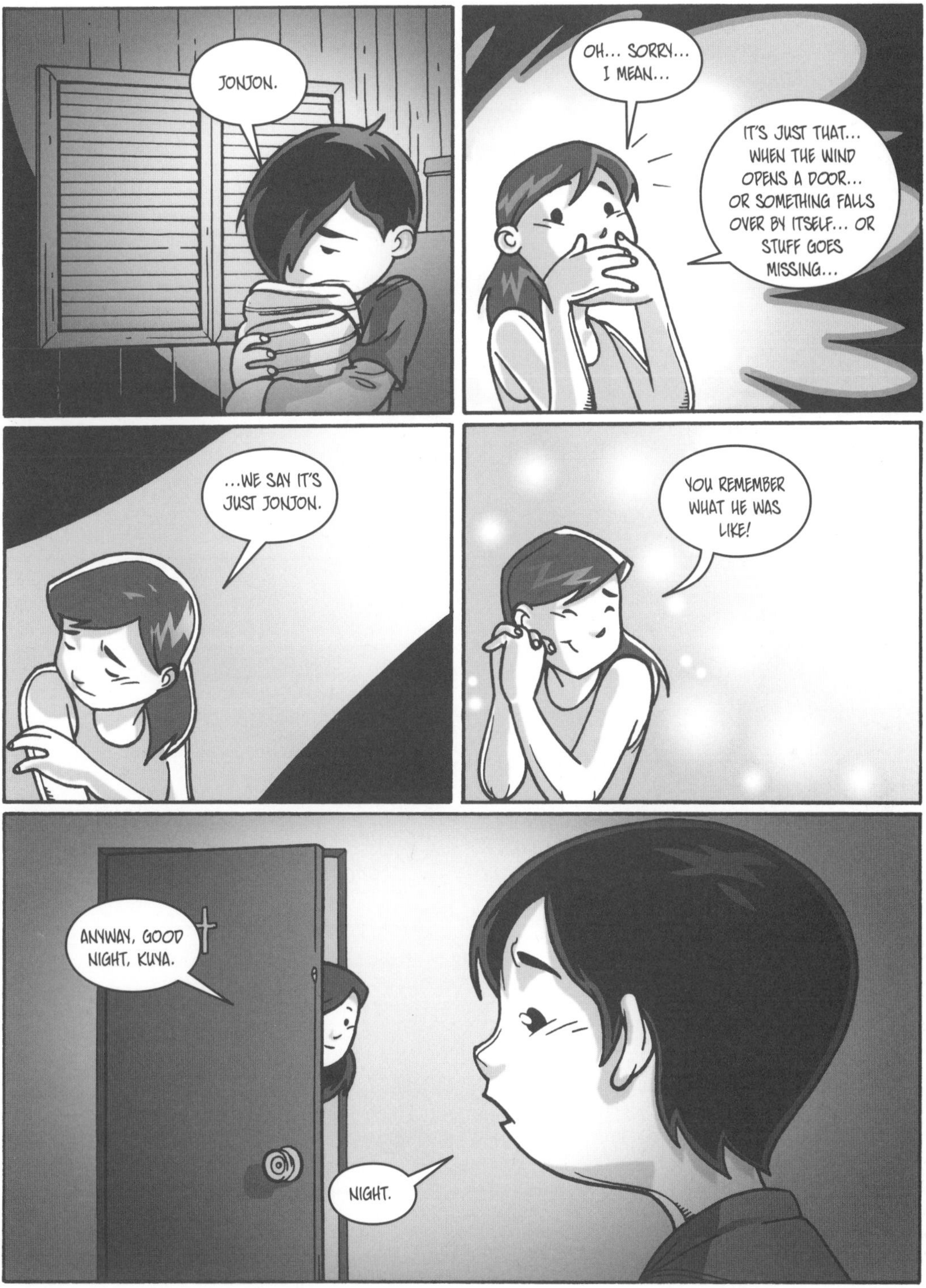
JONJON.
OH... SORRY... I MEAN...
IT'S JUST THAT... WHEN THE WIND OPENS A DOOR... OR SOMETHING FALLS OVER BY ITSELF... OR STUFF GOES MISSING...
...WE SAY IT'S JUST JONJON.
YOU REMEMBER WHAT HE WAS LIKE!
ANYWAY, GOOD NIGHT, KUYA.
NIGHT.

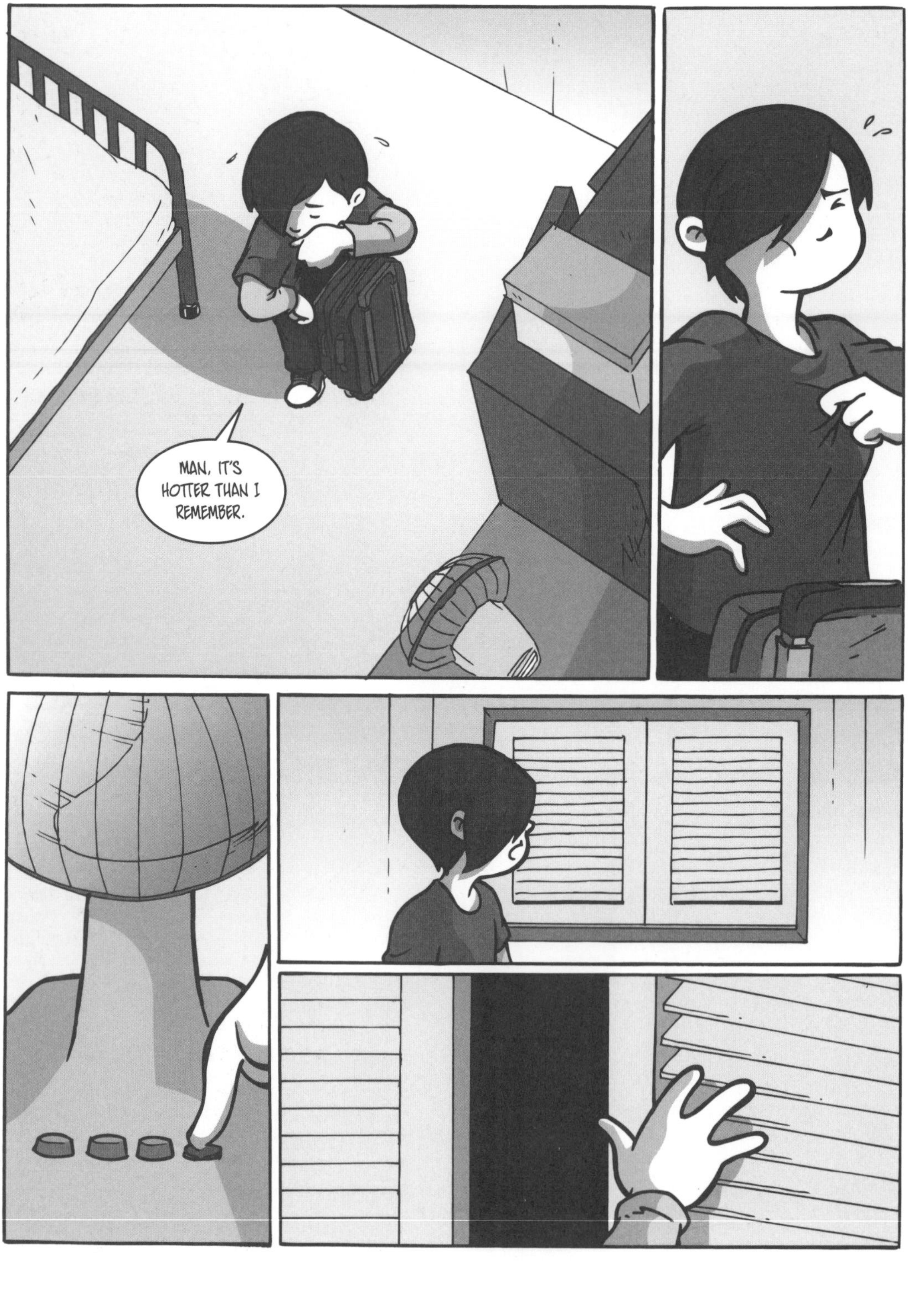
MAN, IT'S HOTTER THAN I REMEMBER.

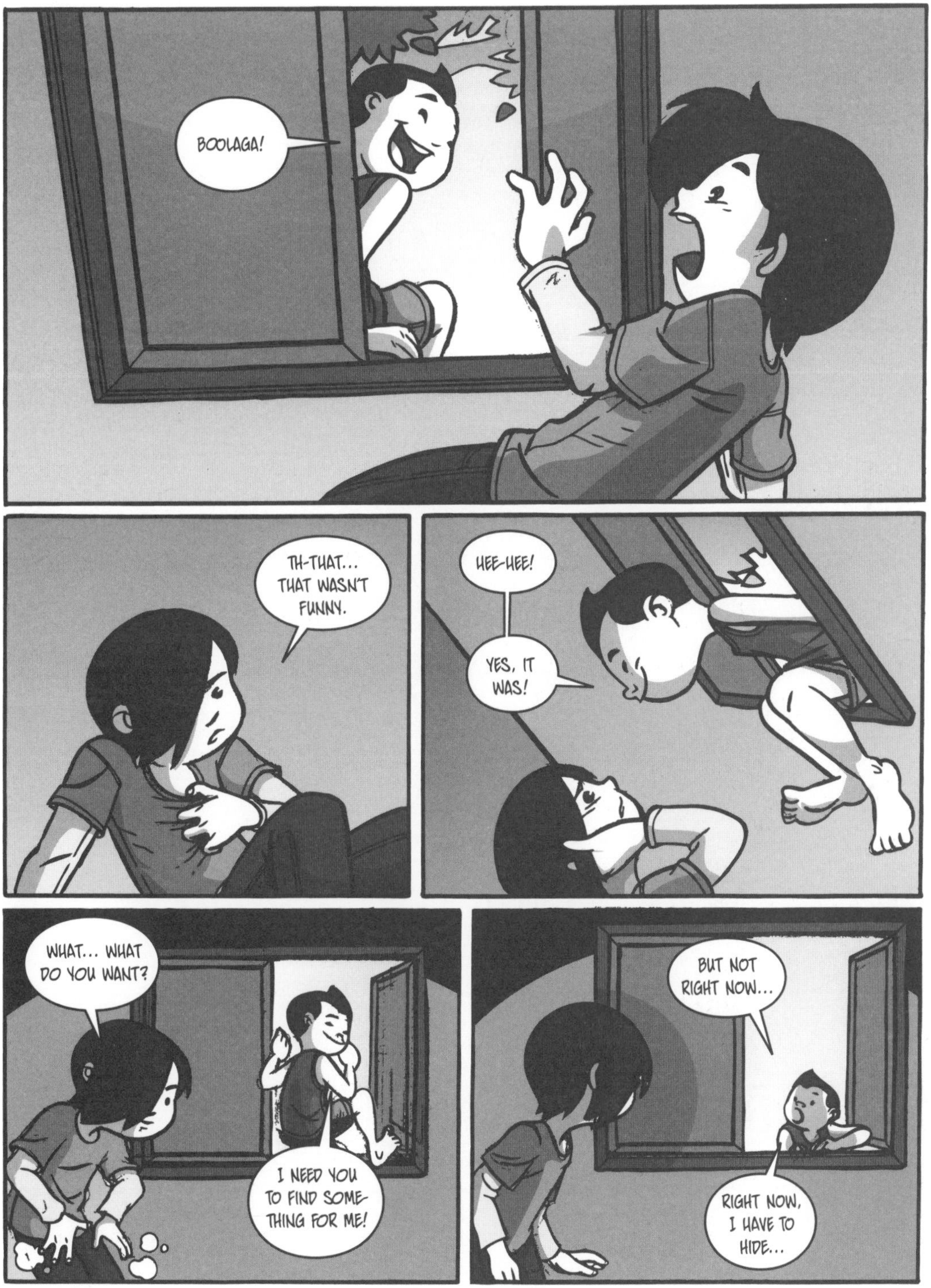
BOOLAGA!
TH-THAT... THAT WASN'T FUNNY.
HEE-HEE!
YES, IT WAS!
WHAT... WHAT DO YOU WANT?
I NEED YOU TO FIND SOME-THING FOR ME!
BUT NOT RIGHT NOW...
RIGHT NOW, I HAVE TO HIDE...

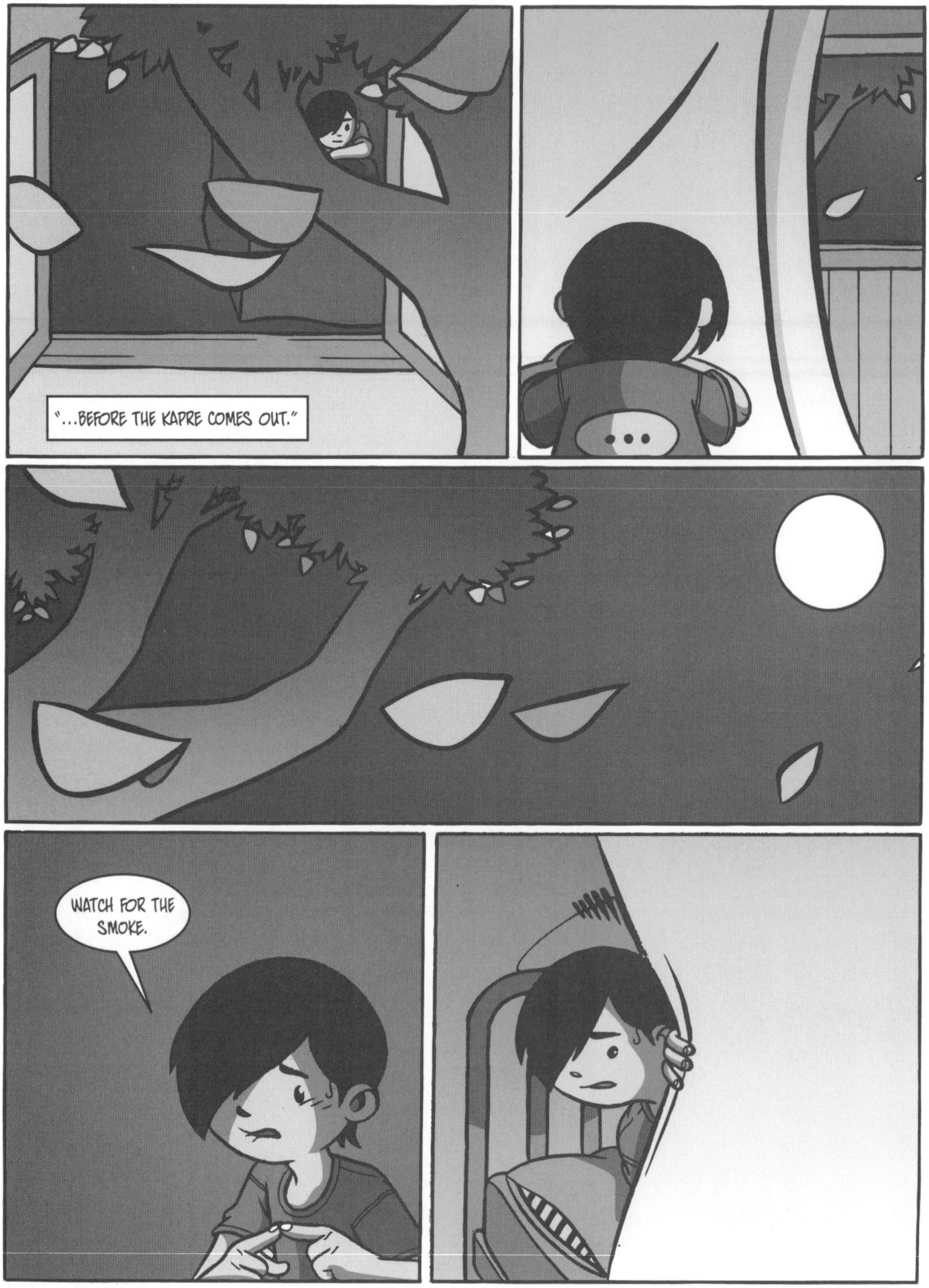
"...BEFORE THE KAPRE COMES OUT."
...
WATCH FOR THE SMOKE.

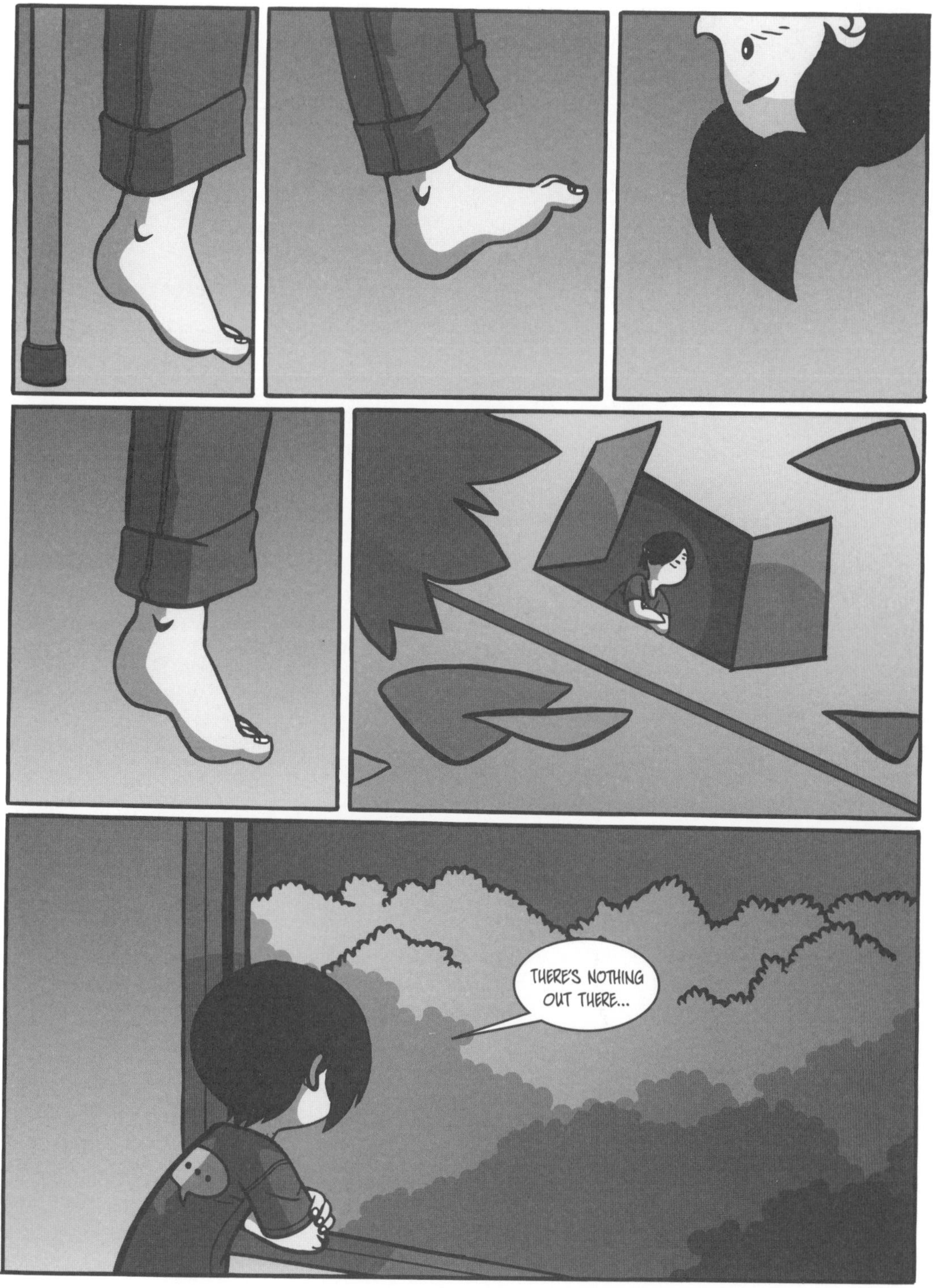
THERE'S NOTHING OUT THERE...

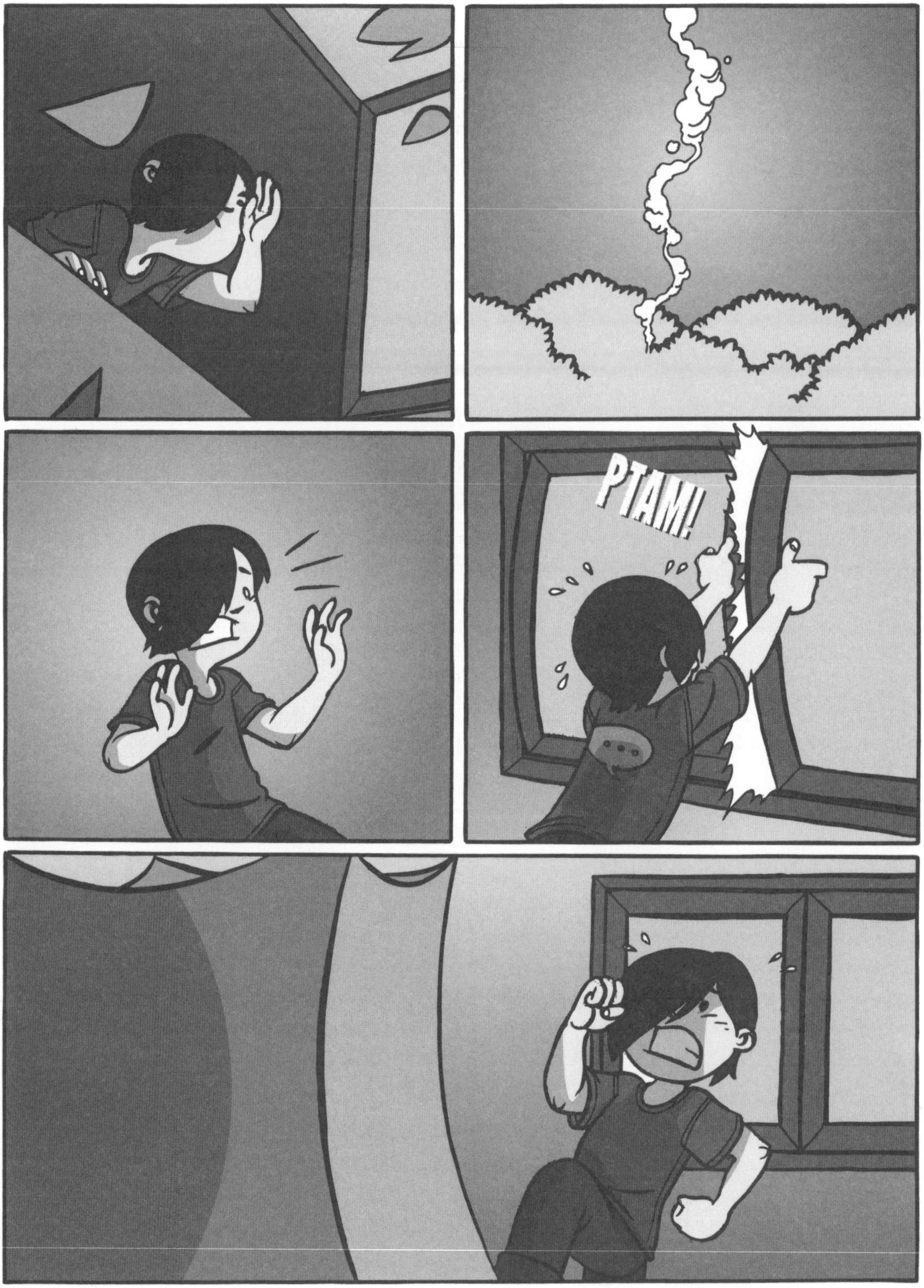
PTAM!

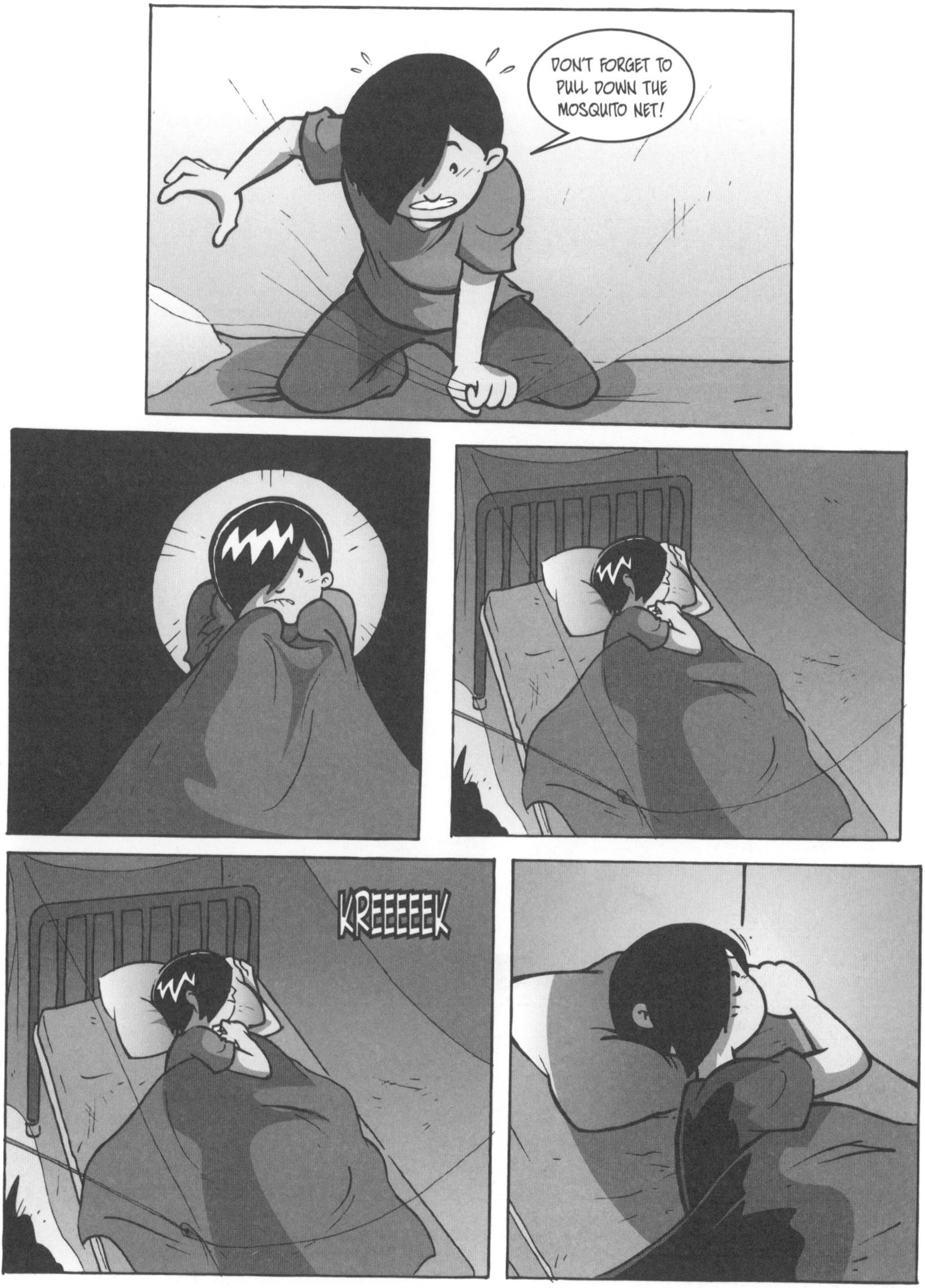
DON'T FORGET TO PULL DOWN THE MOSQUITO NET!
KREEEEEK

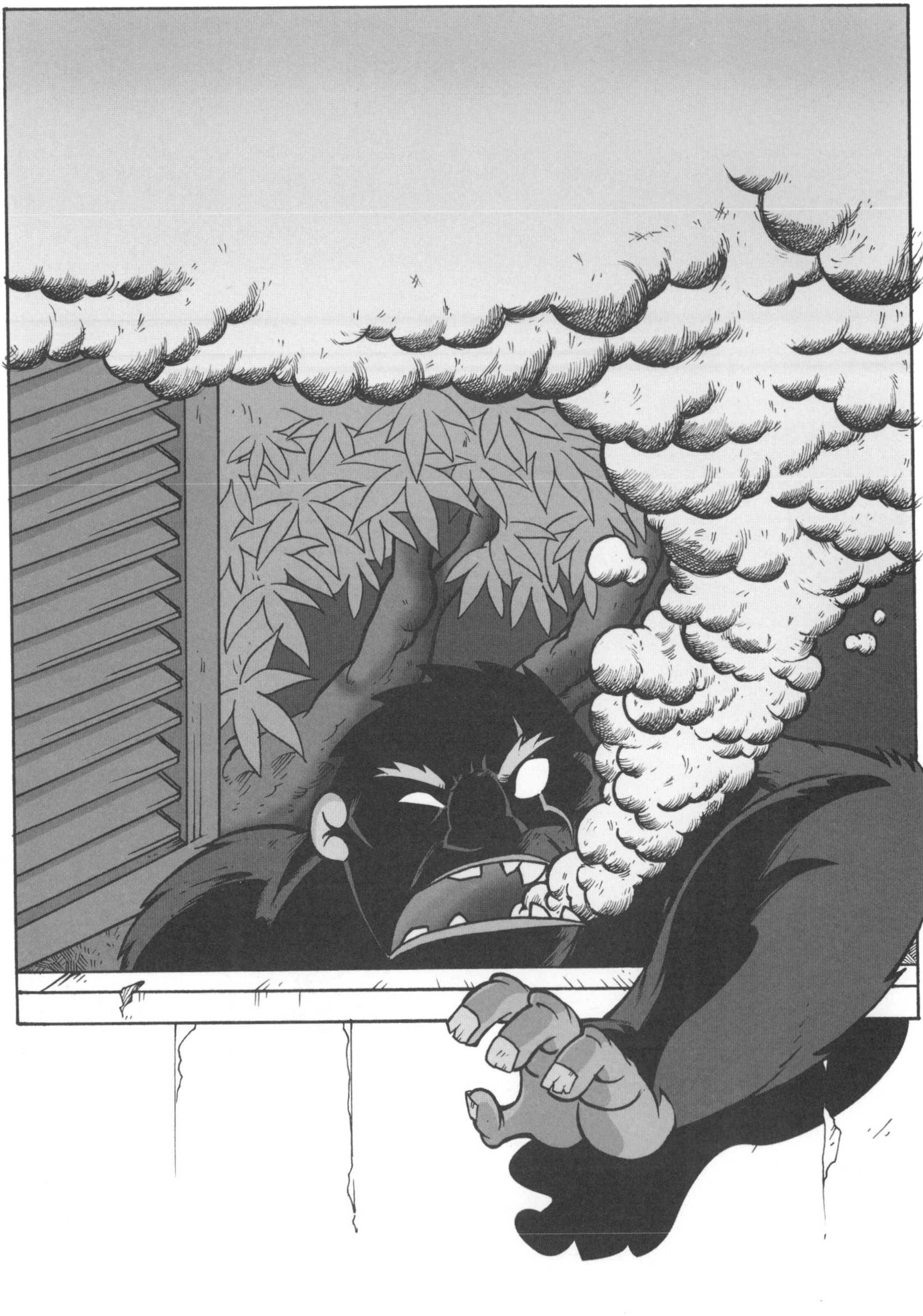

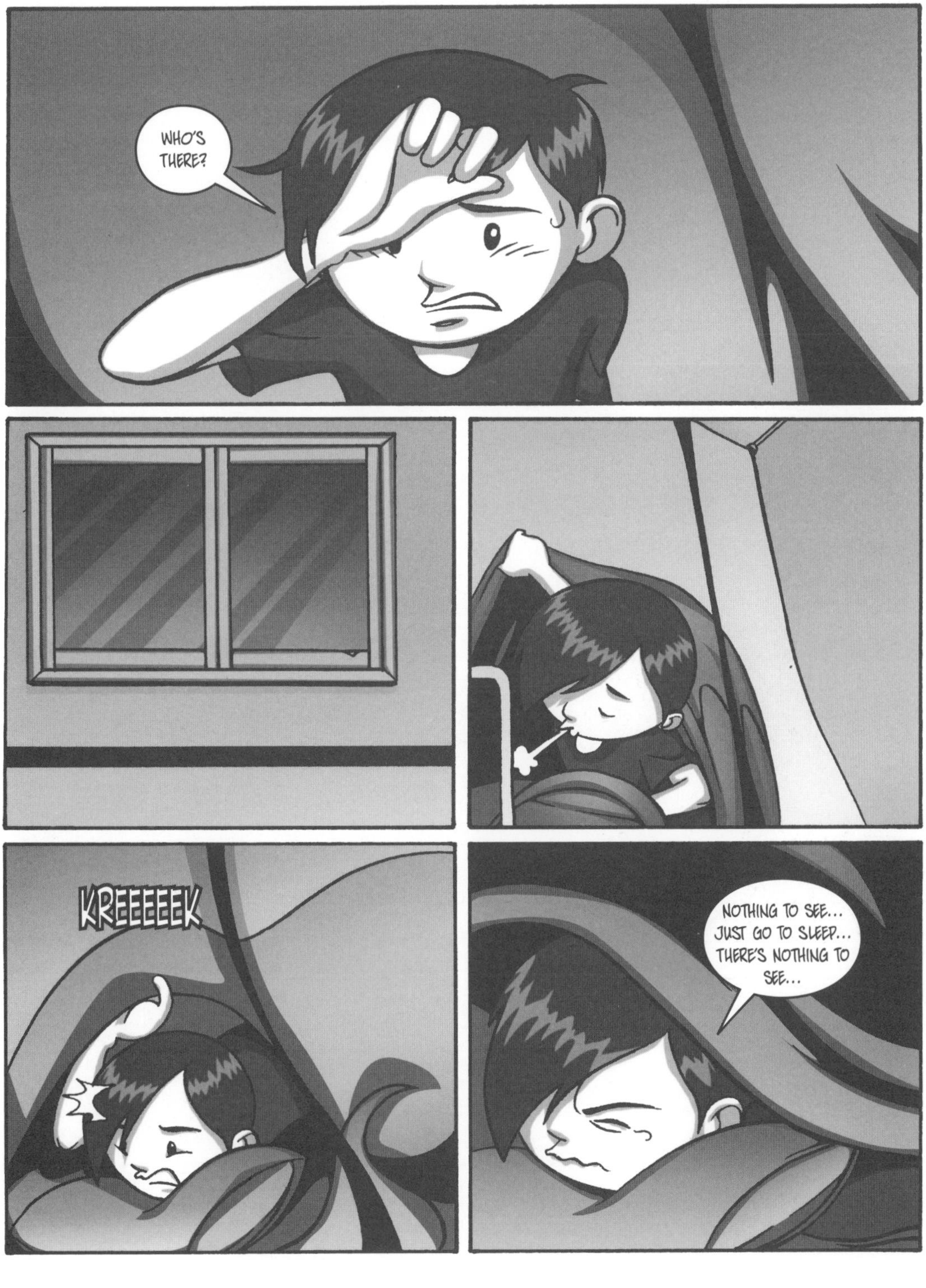
WHO'S THERE?
KREEEEEK
NOTHING TO SEE... JUST GO TO SLEEP... THERE'S NOTHING TO SEE...

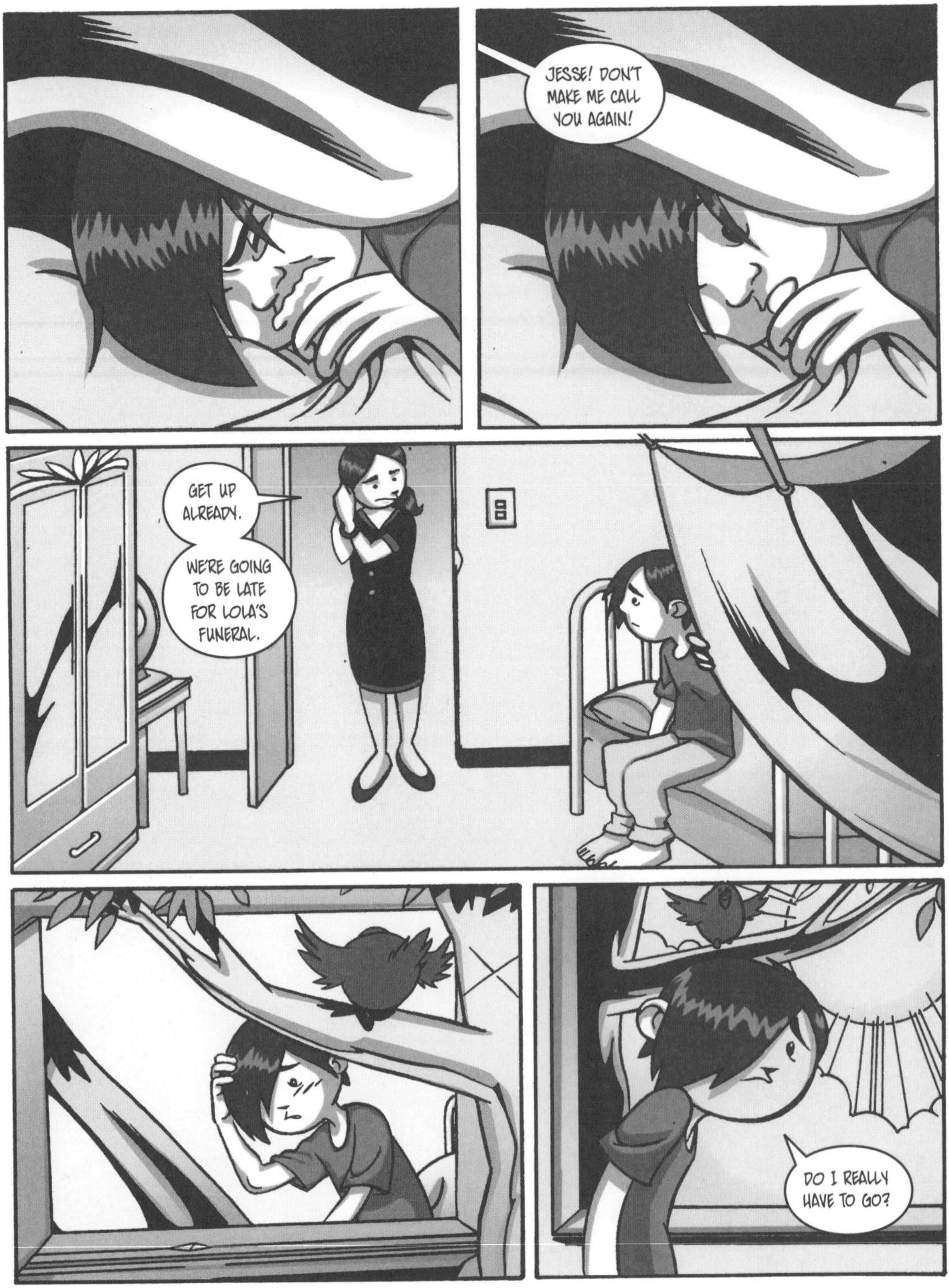
JESSE! DON'T MAKE ME CALL YOU AGAIN!
GET UP ALREADY.
WE'RE GOING TO BE LATE FOR LOLA'S FUNERAL.
DO I REALLY HAVE TO GO?

ACT

II

LOLA

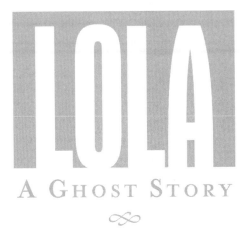

A Ghost Story

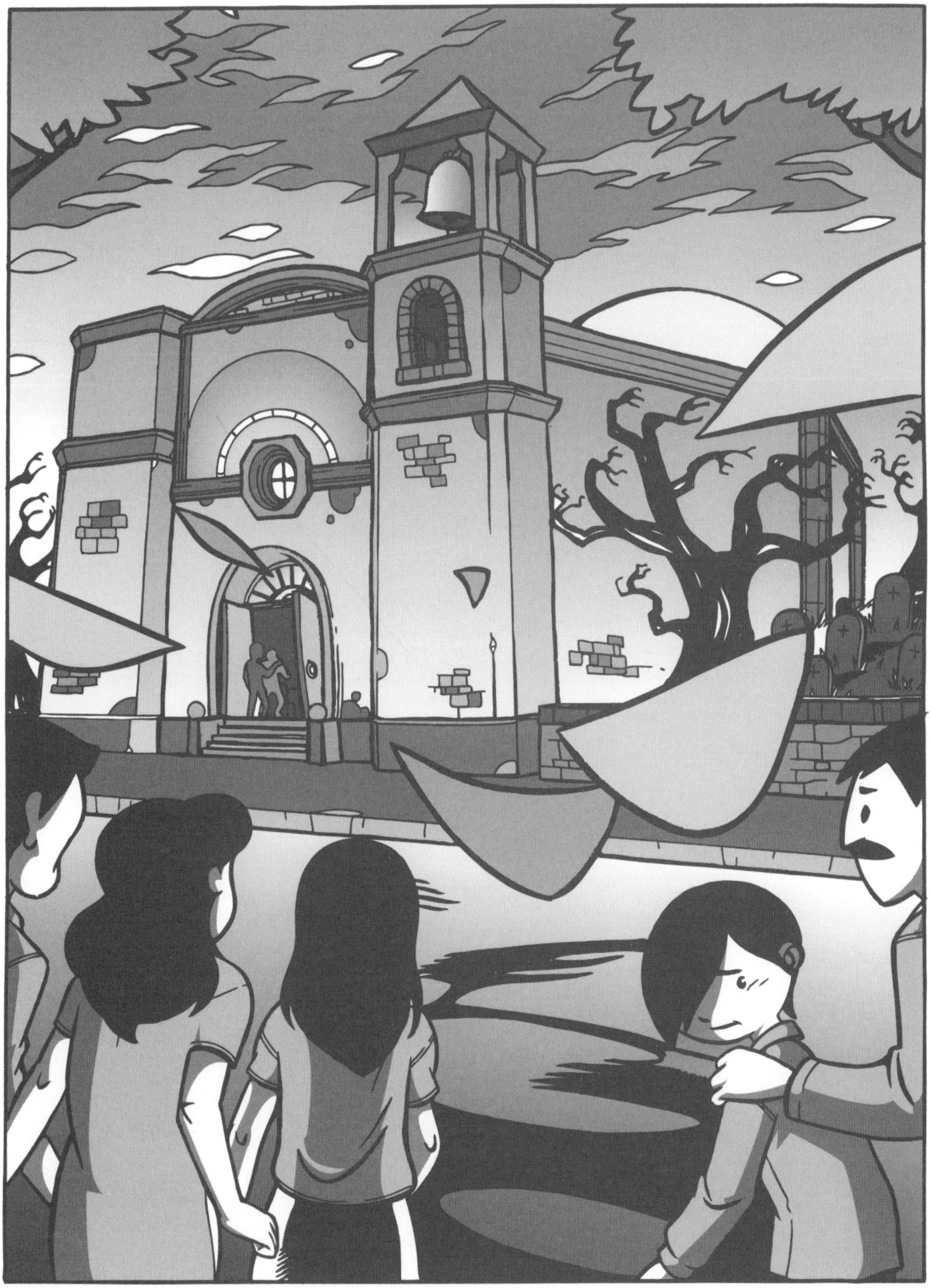

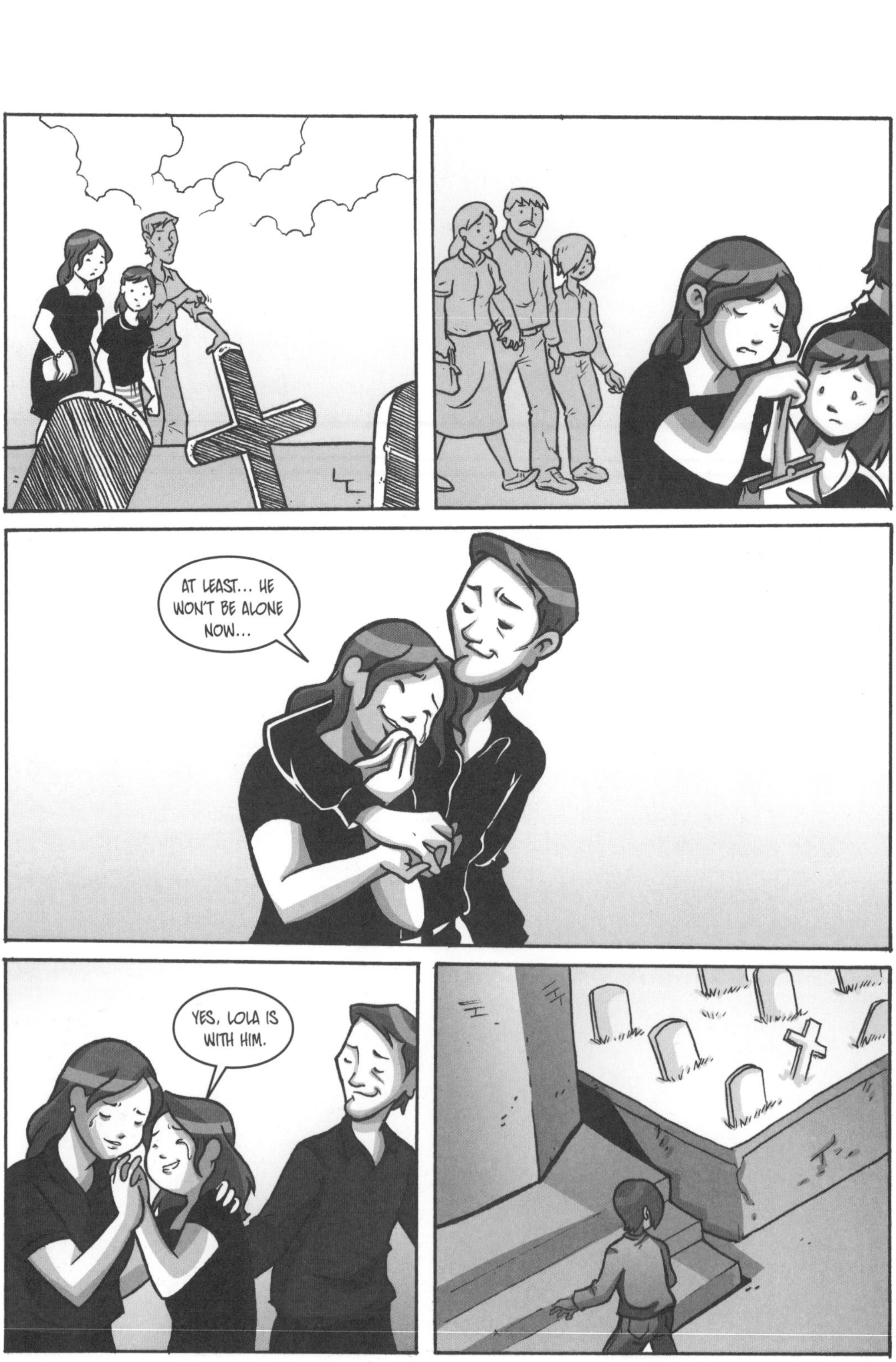
AT LEAST... HE WON'T BE ALONE NOW...
YES, LOLA IS WITH HIM.

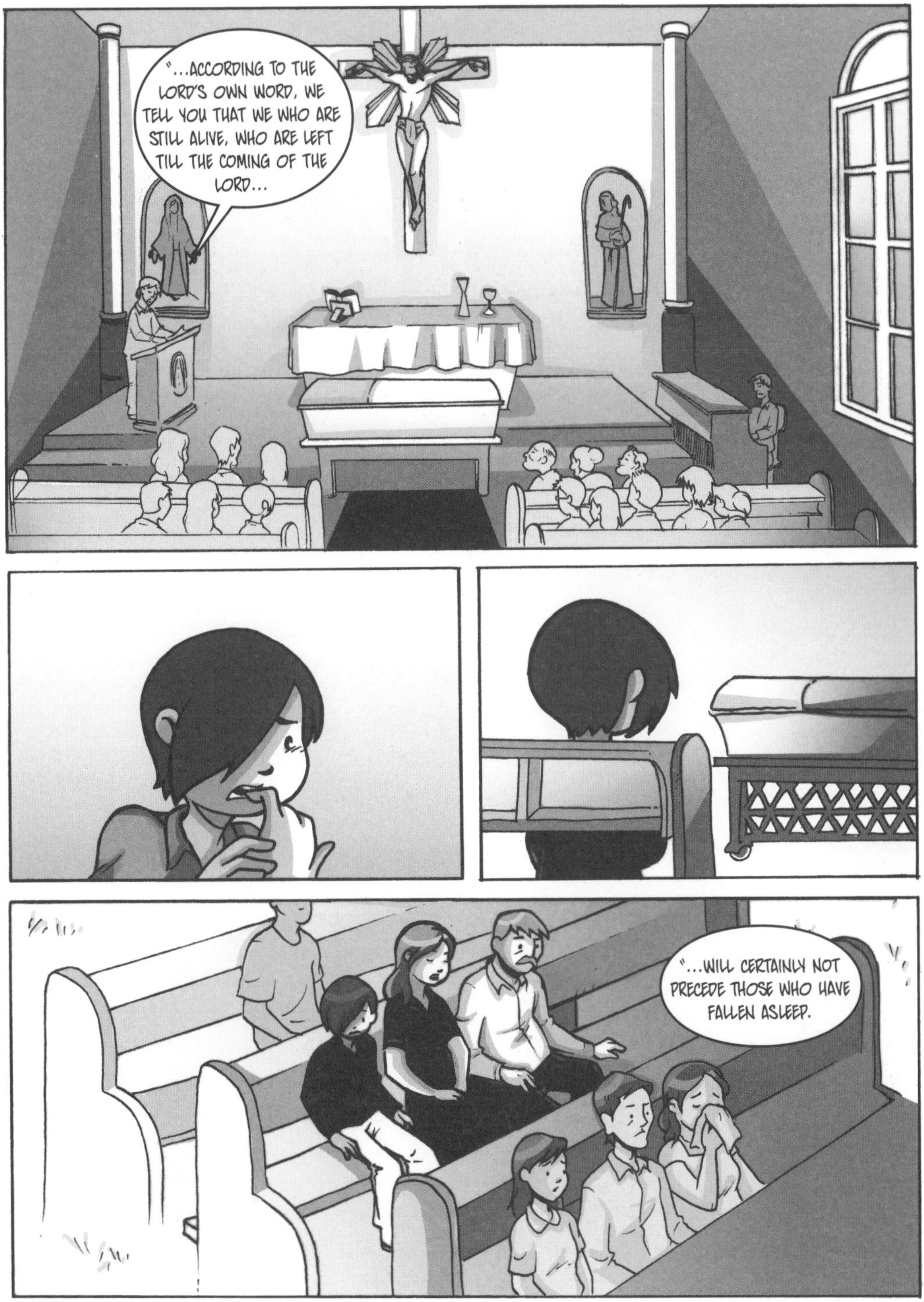
"...ACCORDING TO THE LORD'S OWN WORD, WE TELL YOU THAT WE WHO ARE STILL ALIVE, WHO ARE LEFT TILL THE COMING OF THE LORD...
"...WILL CERTAINLY NOT PRECEDE THOSE WHO HAVE FALLEN ASLEEP.

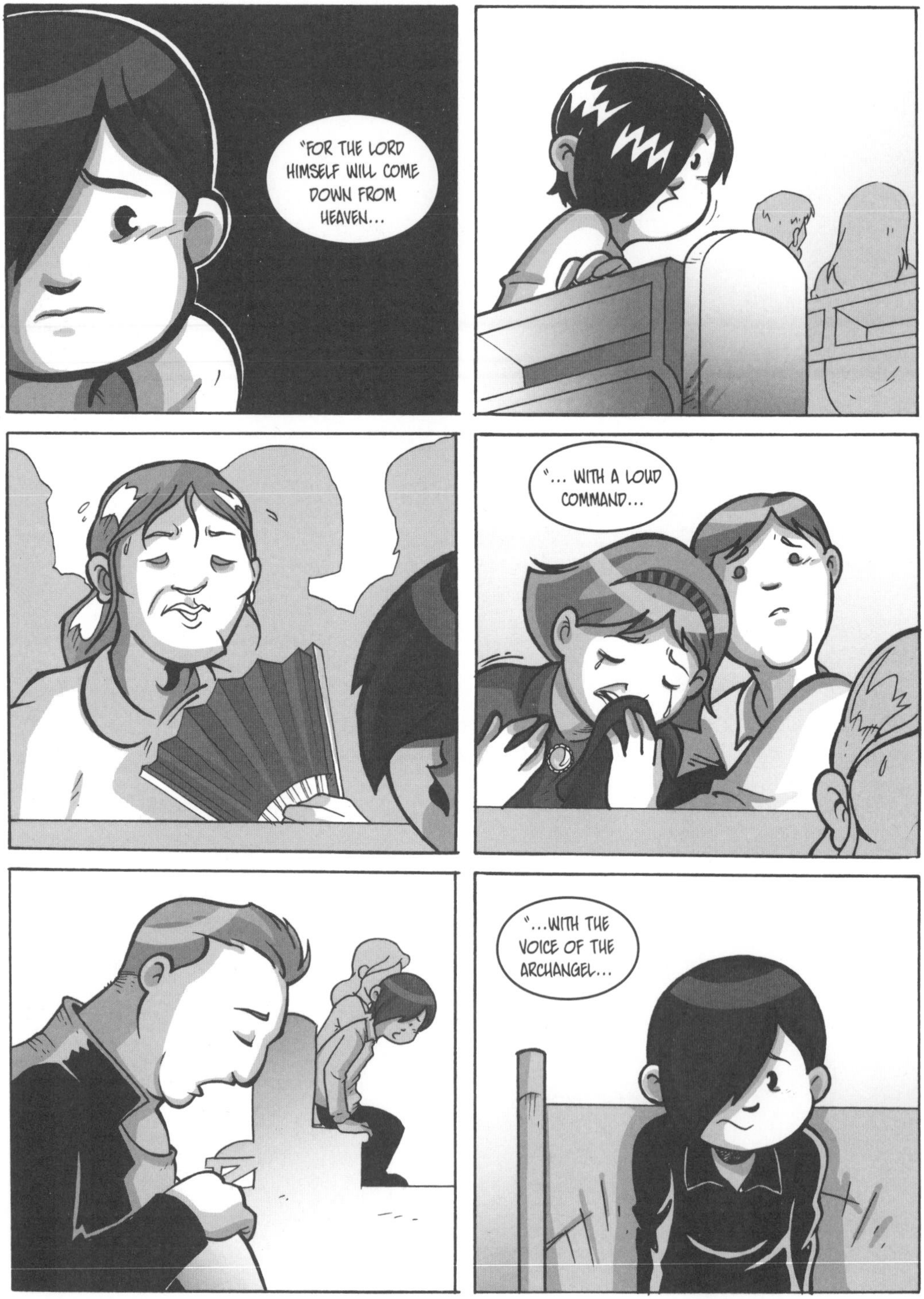
"FOR THE LORD HIMSELF WILL COME DOWN FROM HEAVEN...
"... WITH A LOUD COMMAND...
"...WITH THE VOICE OF THE ARCHANGEL...

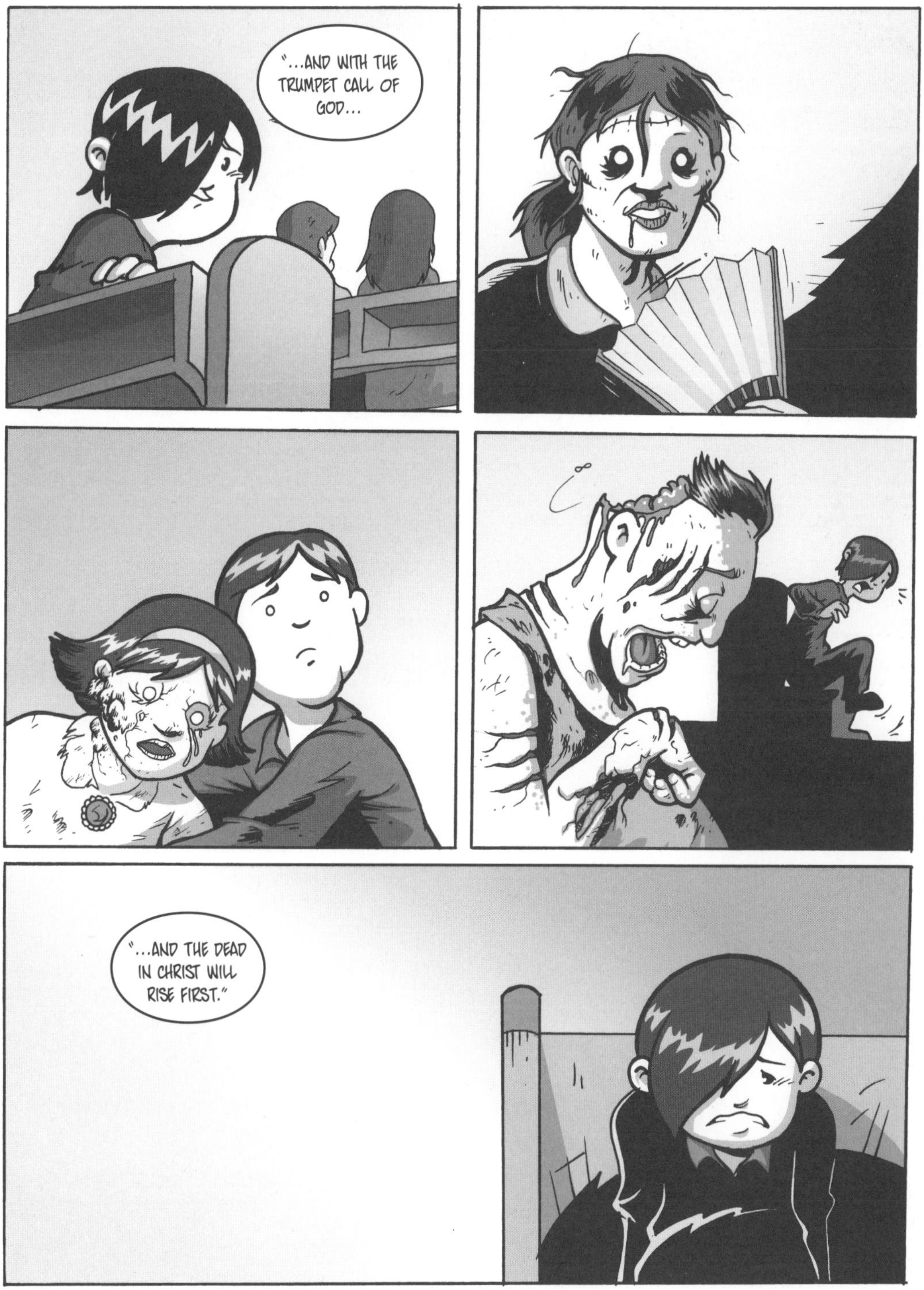
"...AND WITH THE TRUMPET CALL OF GOD...
"...AND THE DEAD IN CHRIST WILL RISE FIRST."

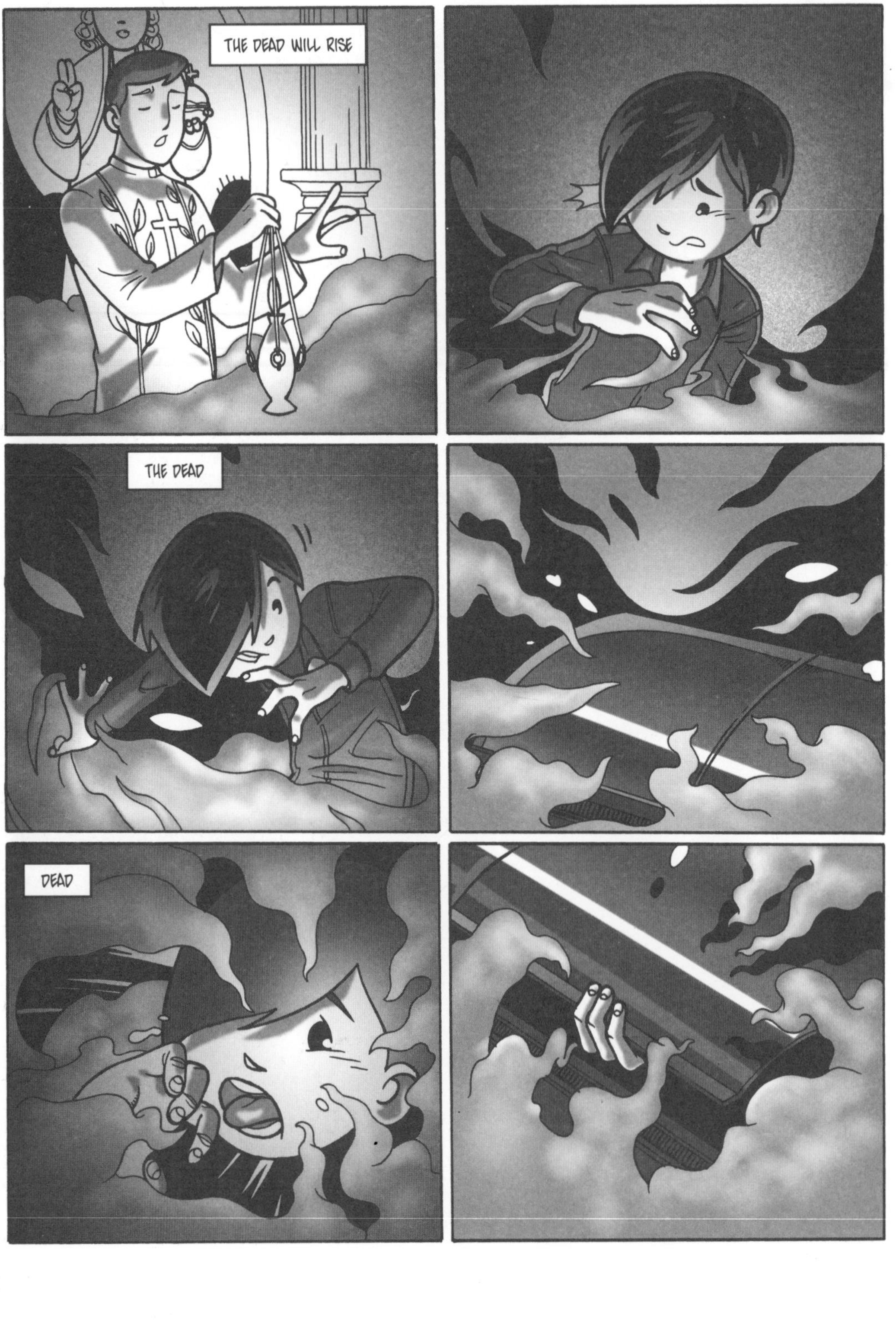
THE DEAD WILL RISE
THE DEAD
DEAD

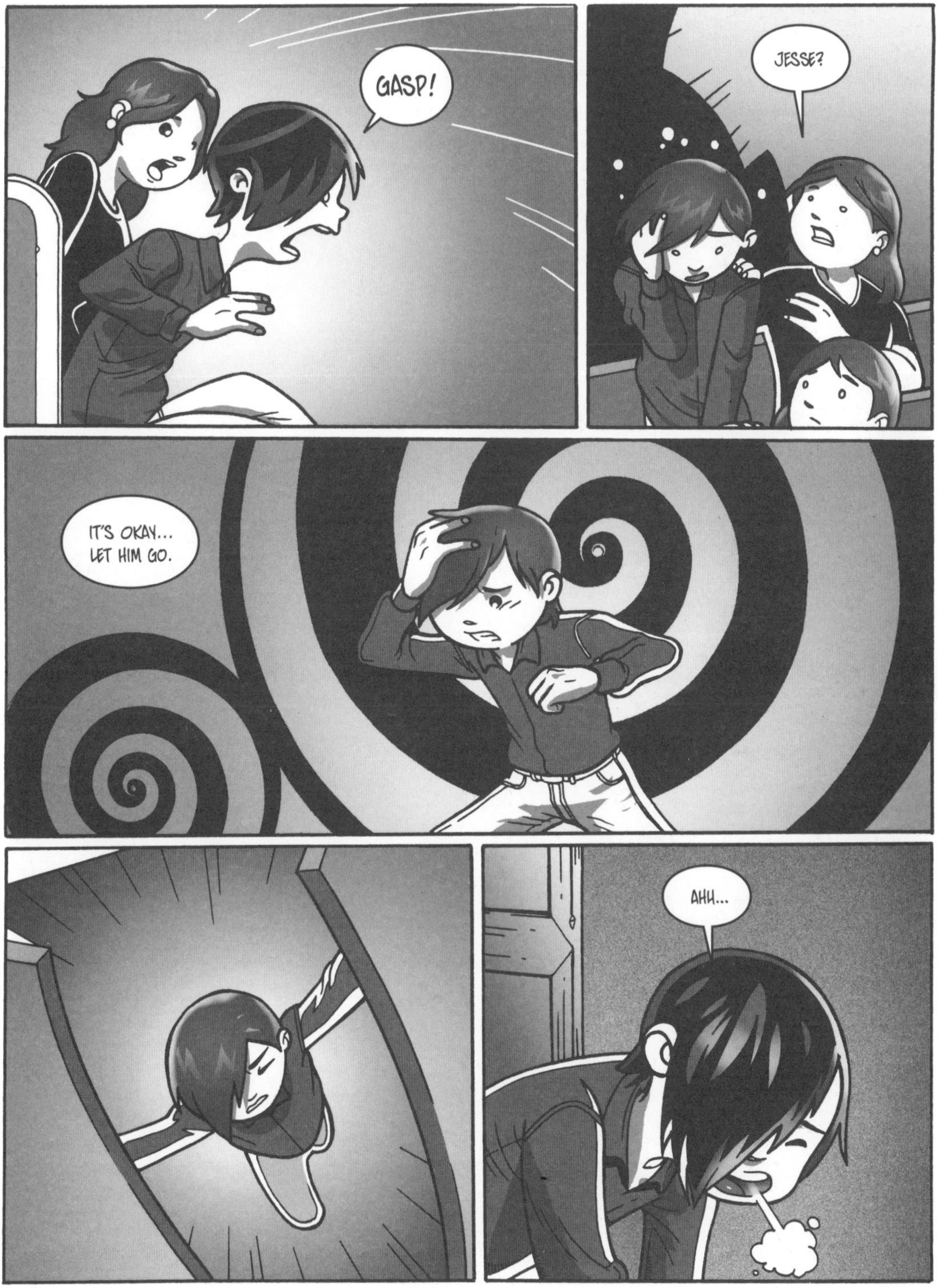
GASP!
JESSE?
IT'S OKAY...
LET HIM GO.
AHH...

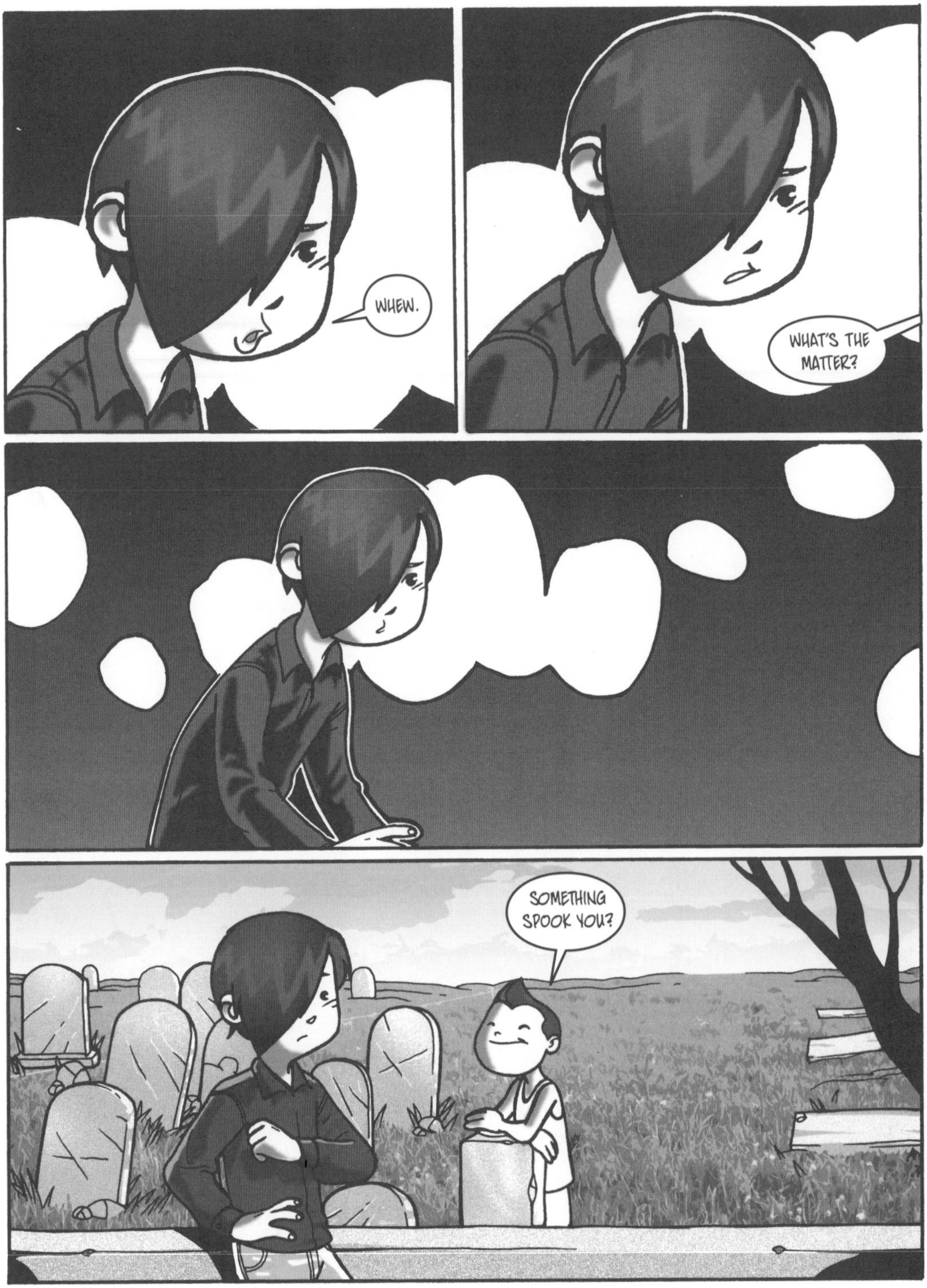
WHEW.
WHAT'S THE MATTER?
SOMETHING SPOOK YOU?

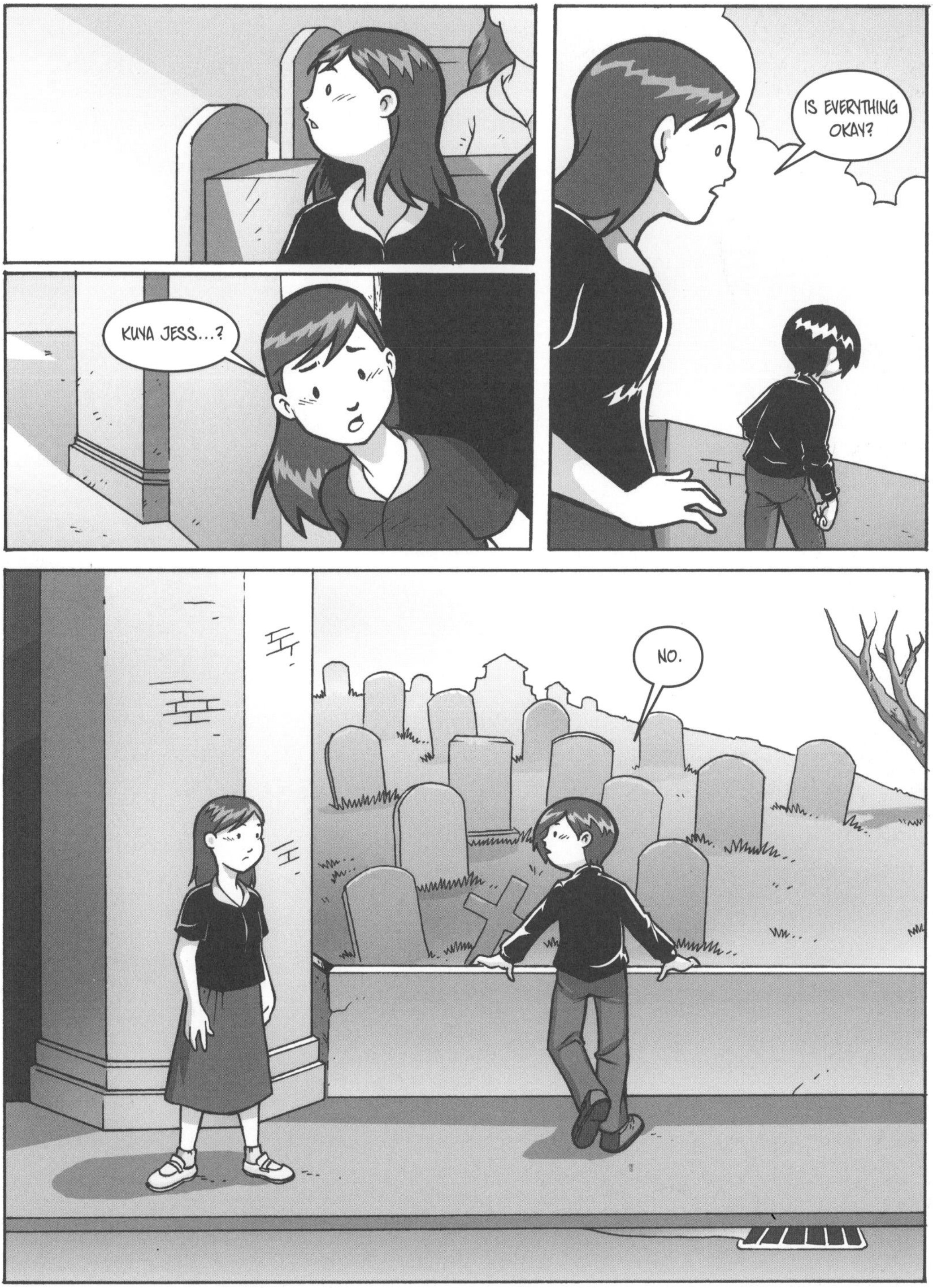
IS EVERYTHING OKAY?
KUYA JESS...?
NO.

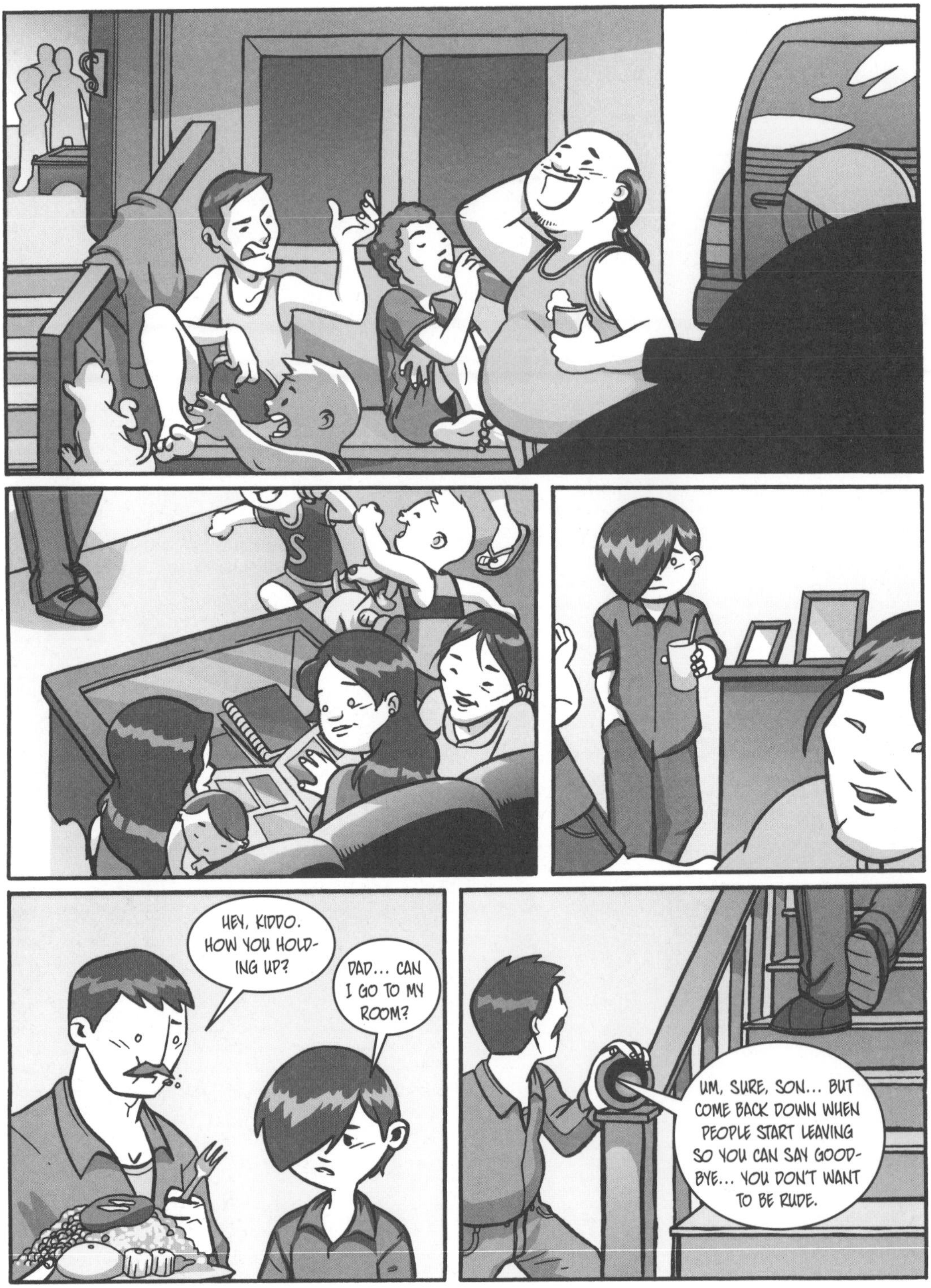
HEY, KIDDO. HOW YOU HOLD-ING UP?
DAD... CAN I GO TO MY ROOM?
UM, SURE, SON... BUT COME BACK DOWN WHEN PEOPLE START LEAVING SO YOU CAN SAY GOOD-BYE... YOU DON'T WANT TO BE RUDE.

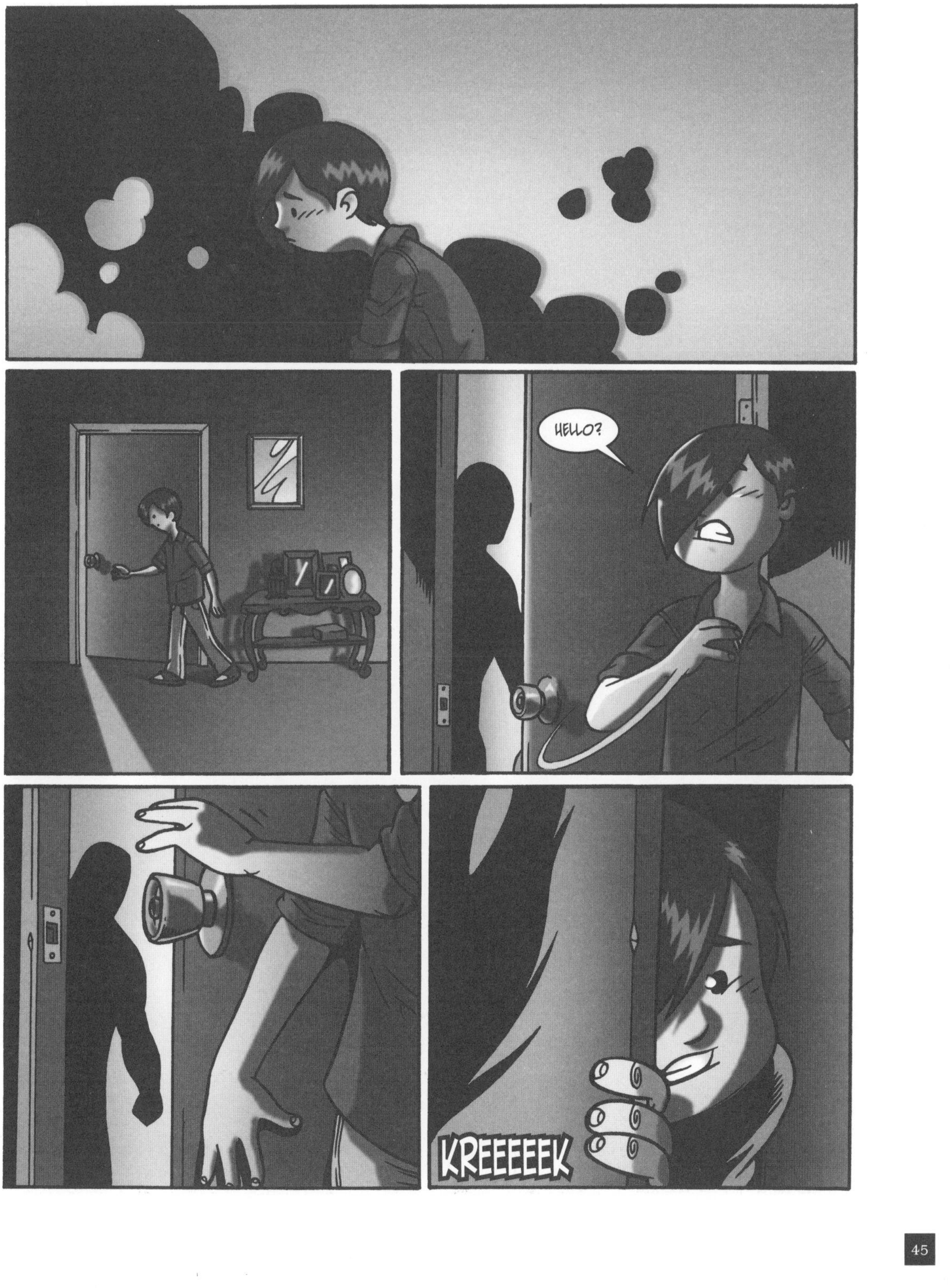
HELLO?
KREEEEEK

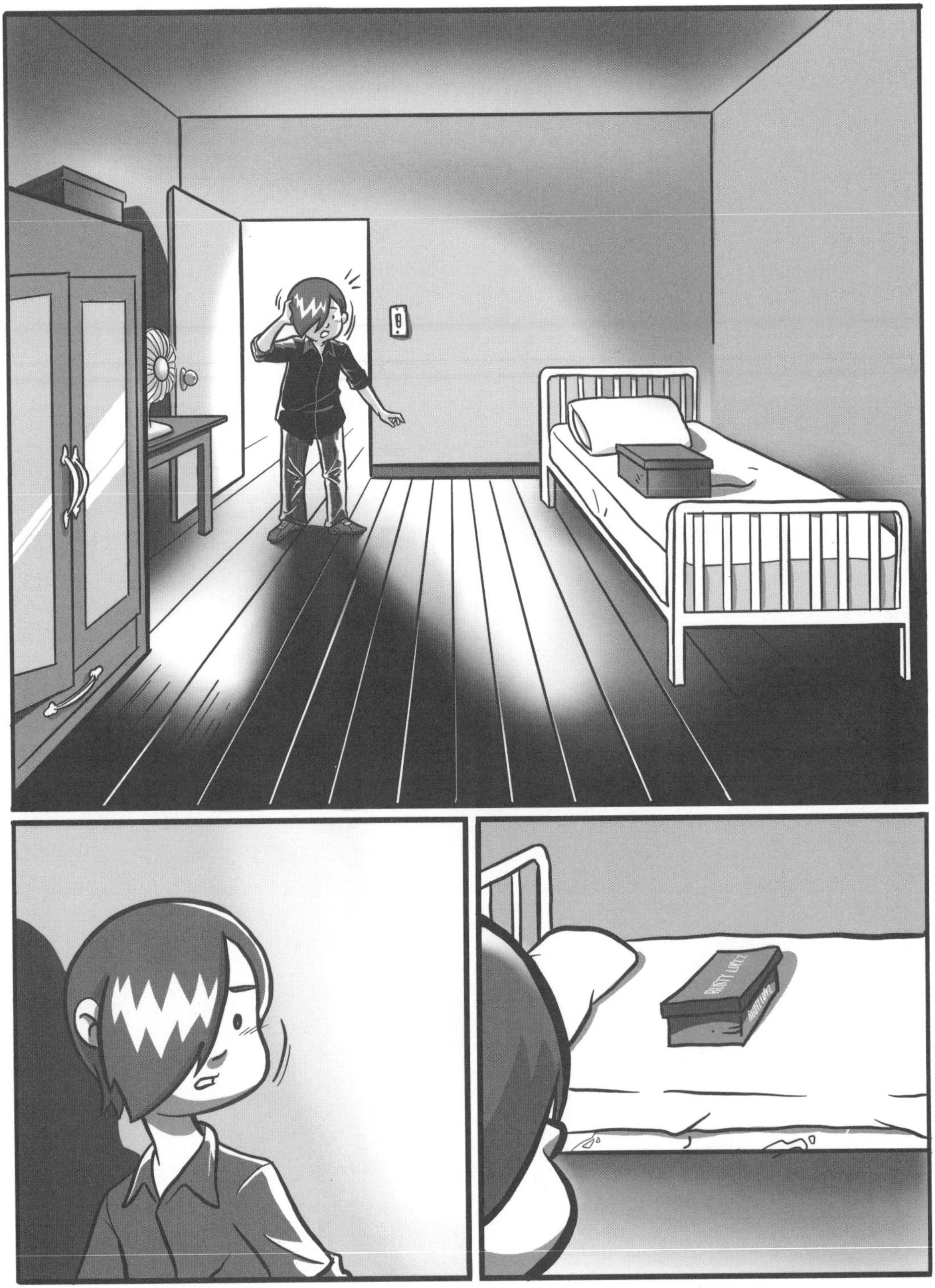
RUSTY LOPEZ
RUSTY LOPEZ

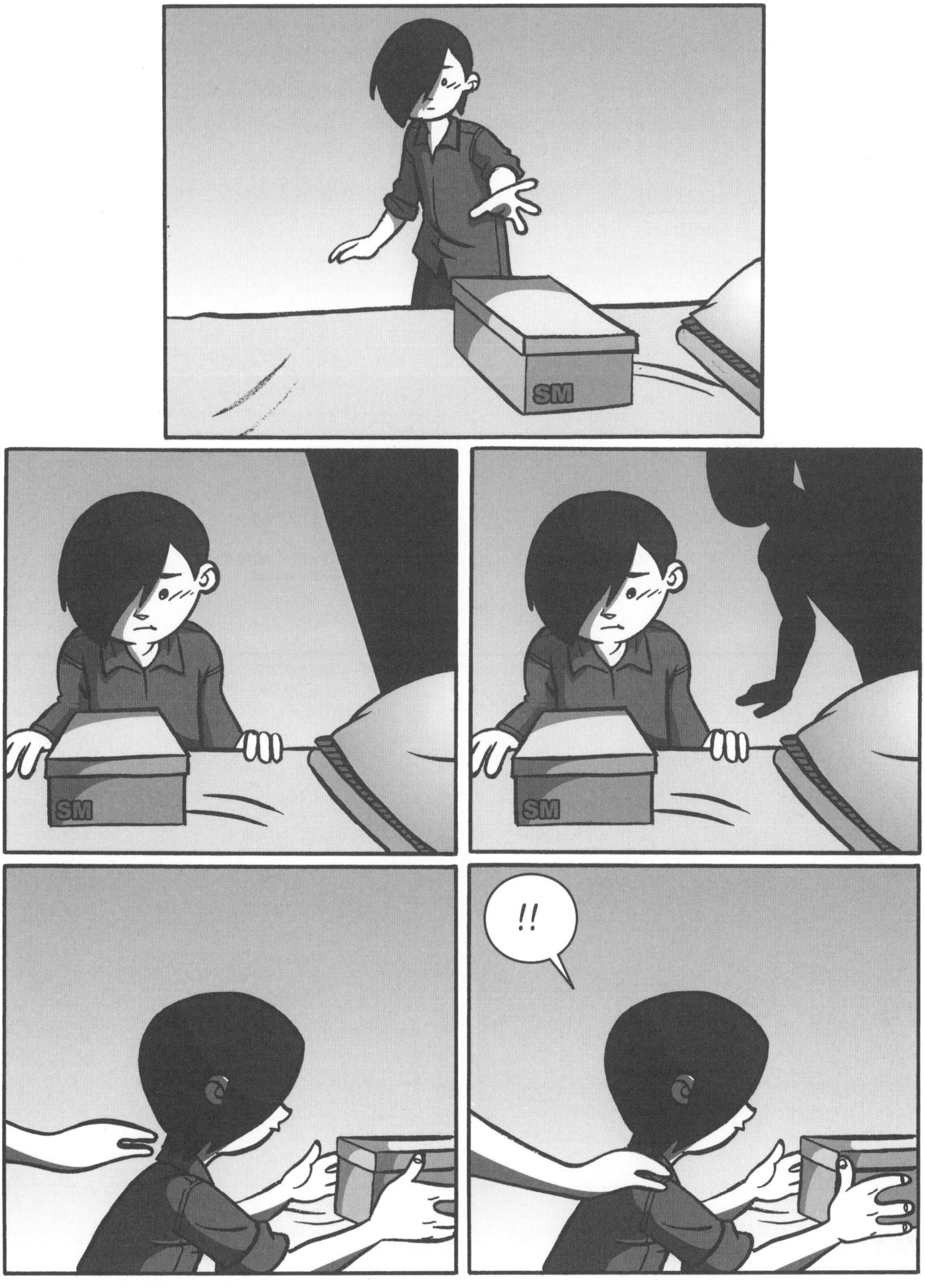
SM
SM
SM
!!

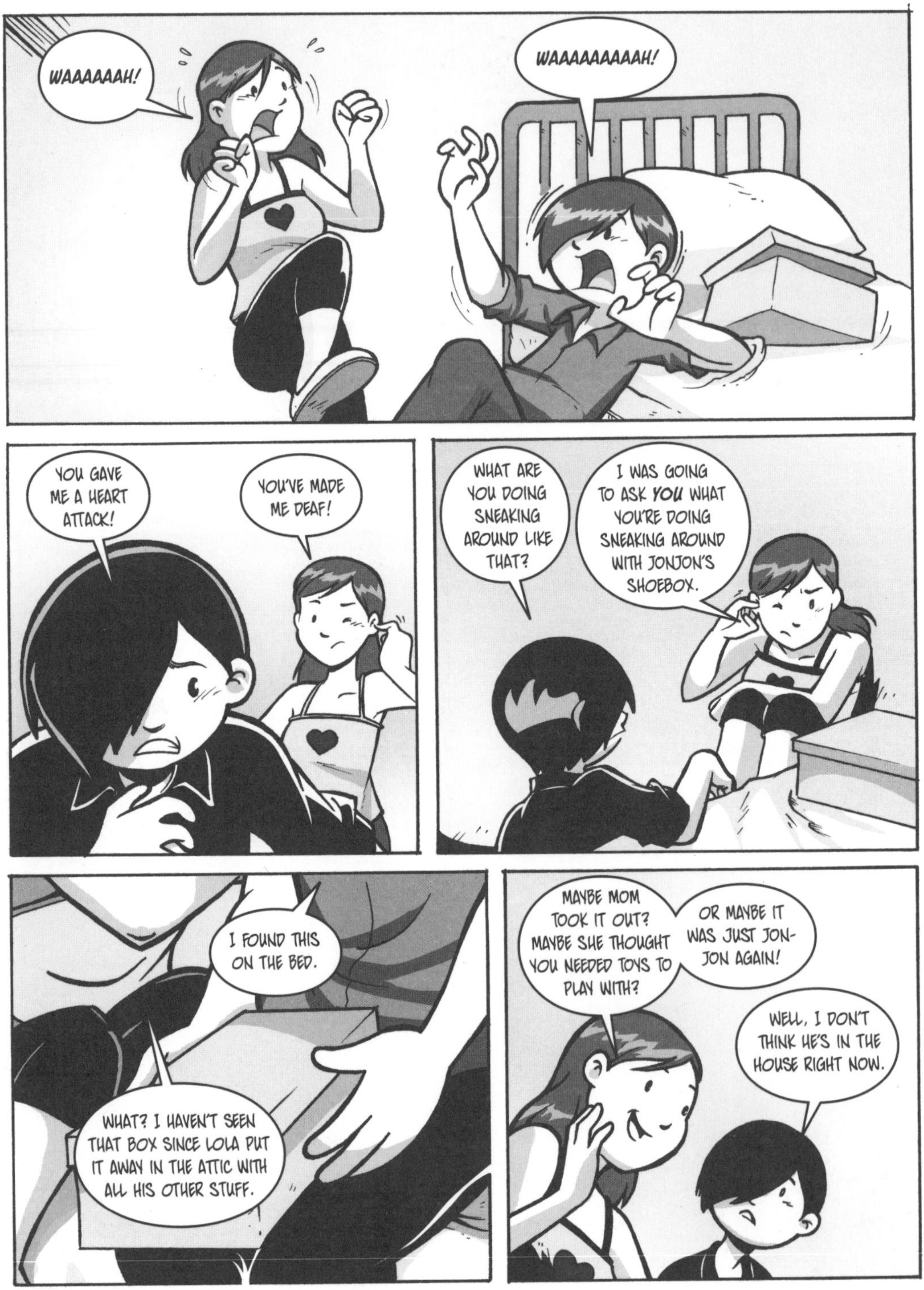
WAAAAAAH!
WAAAAAAAAAH!
YOU GAVE ME A HEART ATTACK!
YOU'VE MADE ME DEAF!
WHAT ARE YOU DOING SNEAKING AROUND LIKE THAT?
I WAS GOING TO ASK ***YOU*** WHAT YOU'RE DOING SNEAKING AROUND WITH JONJON'S SHOEBOX.
I FOUND THIS ON THE BED.
WHAT? I HAVEN'T SEEN THAT BOX SINCE LOLA PUT IT AWAY IN THE ATTIC WITH ALL HIS OTHER STUFF.
MAYBE MOM TOOK IT OUT? MAYBE SHE THOUGHT YOU NEEDED TOYS TO PLAY WITH?
OR MAYBE IT WAS JUST JON-JON AGAIN!
WELL, I DON'T THINK HE'S IN THE HOUSE RIGHT NOW.

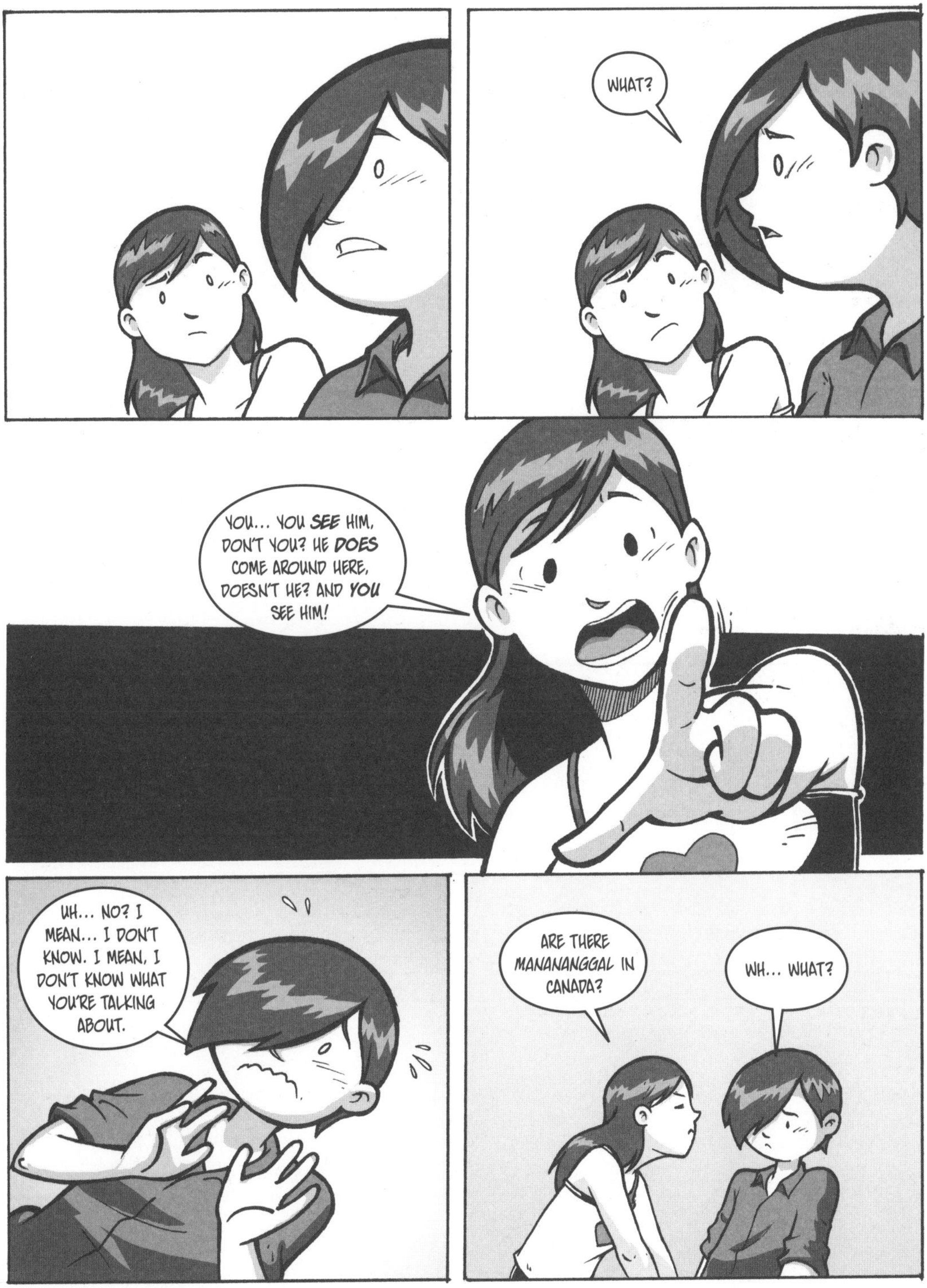
WHAT?
YOU... YOU **SEE** HIM, DON'T YOU? HE **DOES** COME AROUND HERE, DOESN'T HE? AND **YOU** SEE HIM!
UH... NO? I MEAN... I DON'T KNOW. I MEAN, I DON'T KNOW WHAT YOU'RE TALKING ABOUT.
ARE THERE MANANANGGAL IN CANADA?
WH... WHAT?

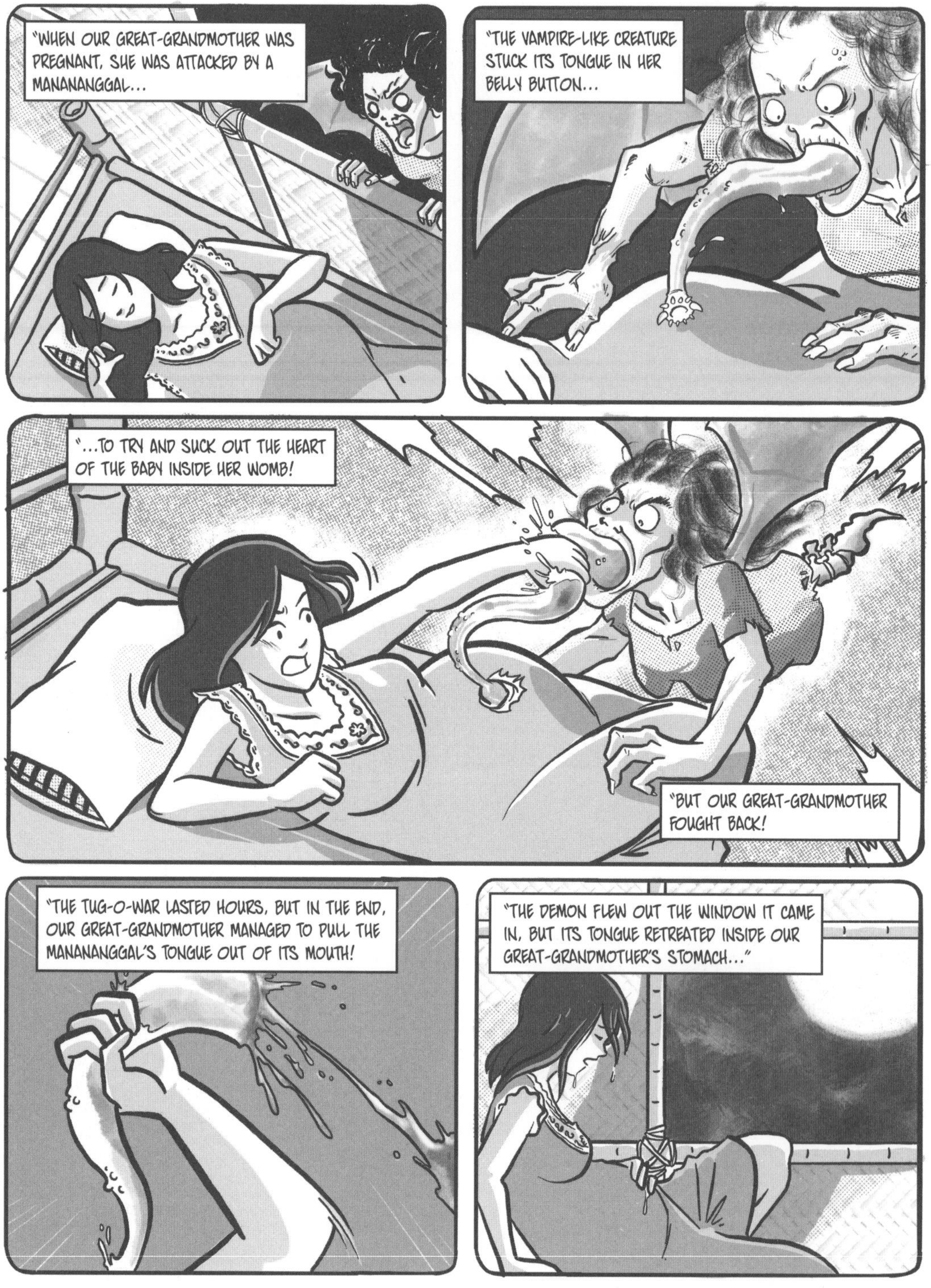
"WHEN OUR GREAT-GRANDMOTHER WAS PREGNANT, SHE WAS ATTACKED BY A MANANANGGAL...
"THE VAMPIRE-LIKE CREATURE STUCK ITS TONGUE IN HER BELLY BUTTON...
"...TO TRY AND SUCK OUT THE HEART OF THE BABY INSIDE HER WOMB!
"BUT OUR GREAT-GRANDMOTHER FOUGHT BACK!
"THE TUG-O-WAR LASTED HOURS, BUT IN THE END, OUR GREAT-GRANDMOTHER MANAGED TO PULL THE MANANANGGAL'S TONGUE OUT OF ITS MOUTH!
"THE DEMON FLEW OUT THE WINDOW IT CAME IN, BUT ITS TONGUE RETREATED INSIDE OUR GREAT-GRANDMOTHER'S STOMACH..."

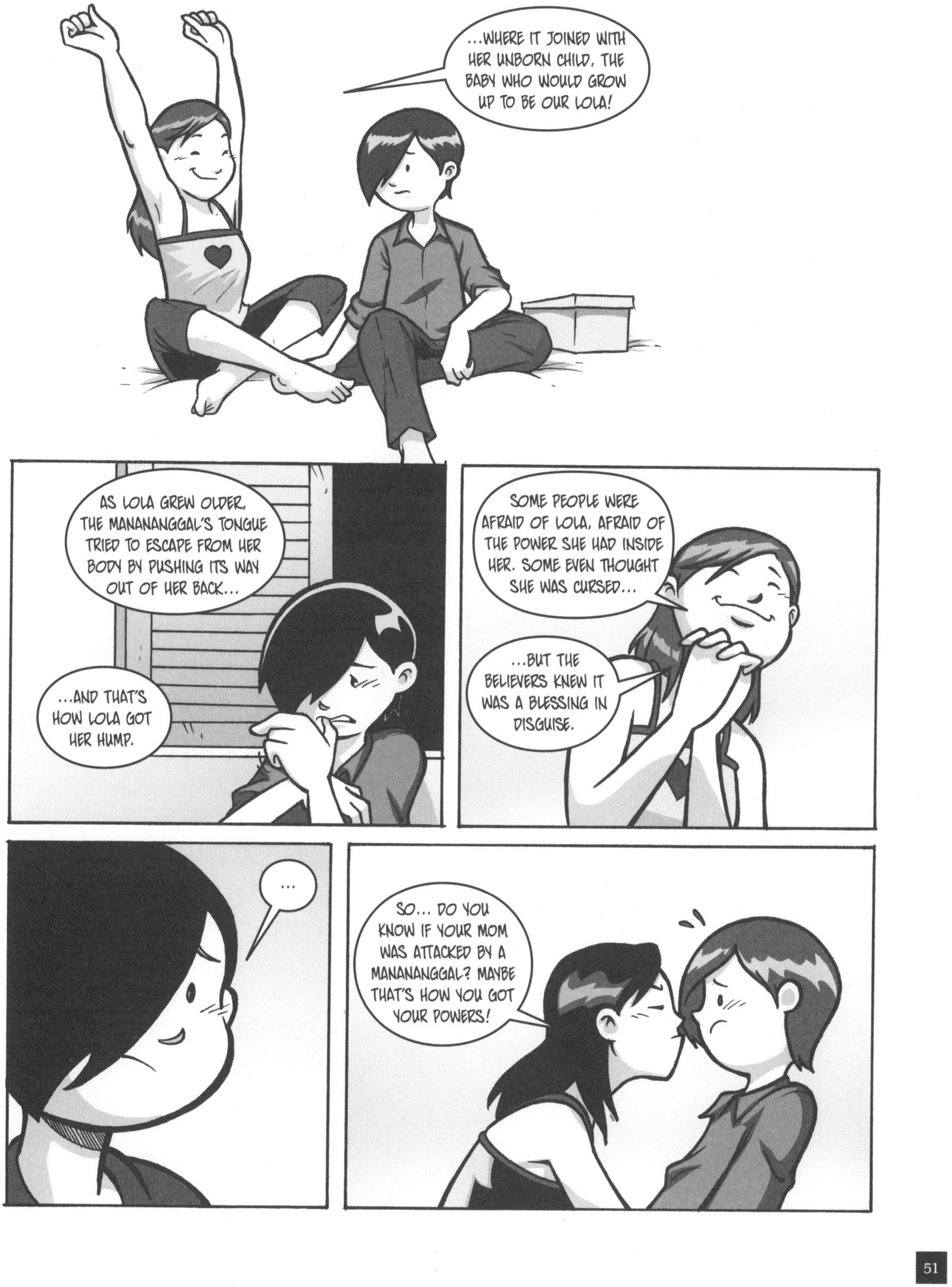
...WHERE IT JOINED WITH HER UNBORN CHILD, THE BABY WHO WOULD GROW UP TO BE OUR LOLA!
AS LOLA GREW OLDER, THE MANANANGGAL'S TONGUE TRIED TO ESCAPE FROM HER BODY BY PUSHING ITS WAY OUT OF HER BACK...
...AND THAT'S HOW LOLA GOT HER HUMP.
SOME PEOPLE WERE AFRAID OF LOLA, AFRAID OF THE POWER SHE HAD INSIDE HER. SOME EVEN THOUGHT SHE WAS CURSED...
...BUT THE BELIEVERS KNEW IT WAS A BLESSING IN DISGUISE.
...
SO... DO YOU KNOW IF YOUR MOM WAS ATTACKED BY A MANANANGGAL? MAYBE THAT'S HOW YOU GOT YOUR POWERS!

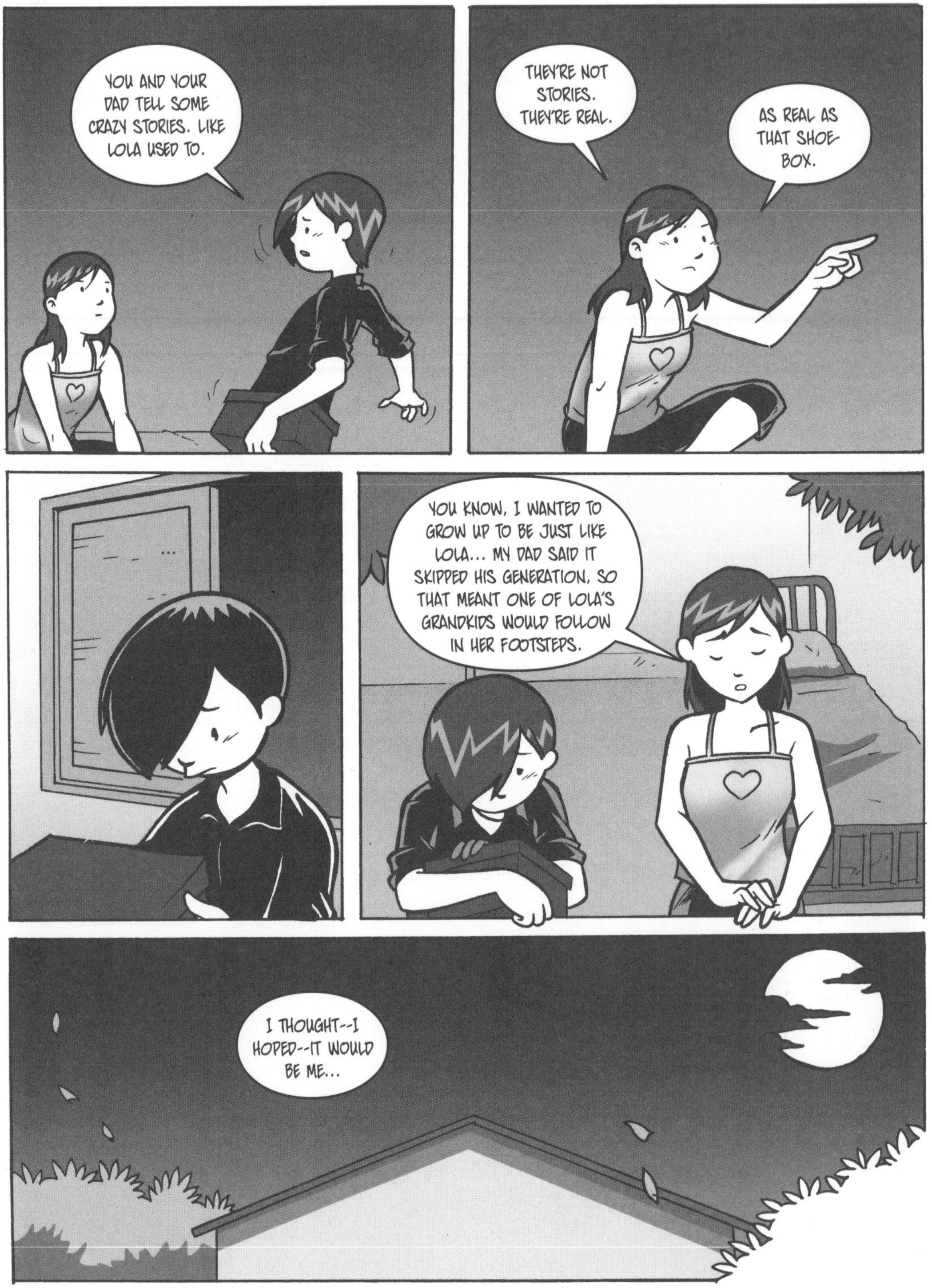
YOU AND YOUR DAD TELL SOME CRAZY STORIES. LIKE LOLA USED TO.
THEY'RE NOT STORIES. THEY'RE REAL.
AS REAL AS THAT SHOE-BOX.
...
YOU KNOW, I WANTED TO GROW UP TO BE JUST LIKE LOLA... MY DAD SAID IT SKIPPED HIS GENERATION, SO THAT MEANT ONE OF LOLA'S GRANDKIDS WOULD FOLLOW IN HER FOOTSTEPS.
I THOUGHT--I HOPED--IT WOULD BE ME...

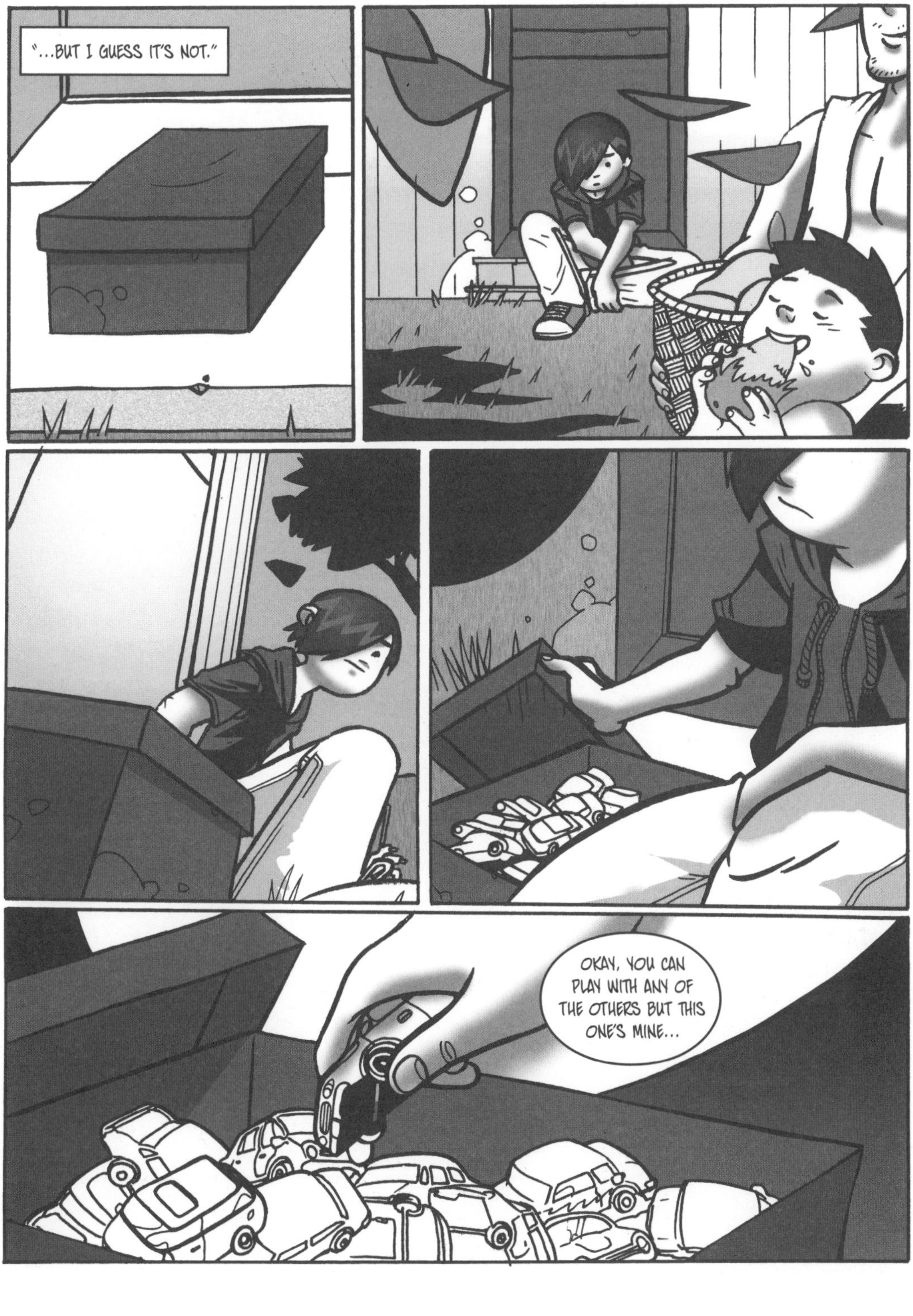
"...BUT I GUESS IT'S NOT."
OKAY, YOU CAN PLAY WITH ANY OF THE OTHERS BUT THIS ONE'S MINE...

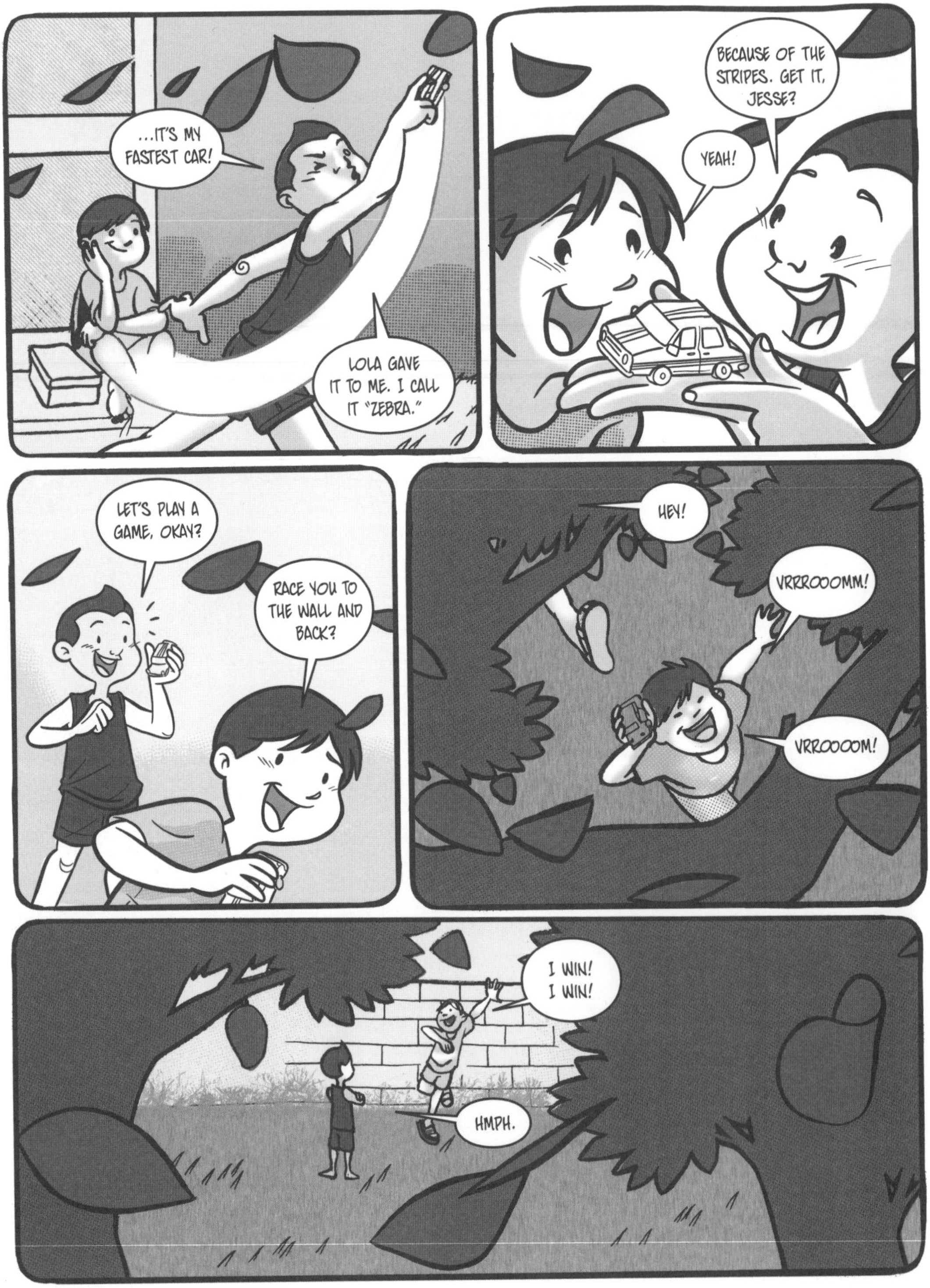
...IT'S MY FASTEST CAR!
LOLA GAVE IT TO ME. I CALL IT "ZEBRA."
BECAUSE OF THE STRIPES. GET IT, JESSE?
YEAH!
LET'S PLAY A GAME, OKAY?
RACE YOU TO THE WALL AND BACK?
HEY!
VRRROOOMM!
VRROOOOM!
I WIN! I WIN!
HMPH.

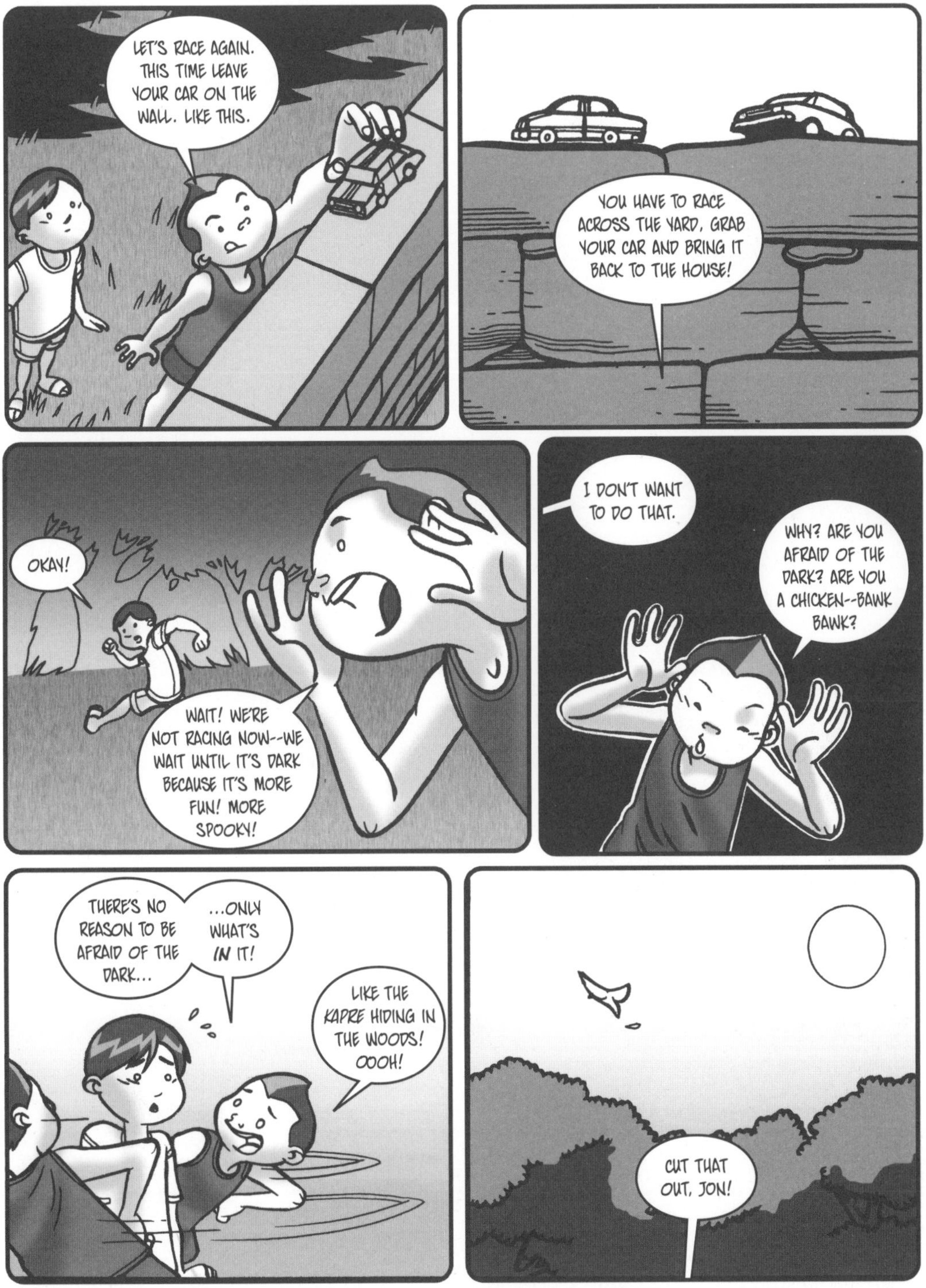
LET'S RACE AGAIN. THIS TIME LEAVE YOUR CAR ON THE WALL. LIKE THIS.
YOU HAVE TO RACE ACROSS THE YARD, GRAB YOUR CAR AND BRING IT BACK TO THE HOUSE!
OKAY!
WAIT! WE'RE NOT RACING NOW--WE WAIT UNTIL IT'S DARK BECAUSE IT'S MORE FUN! MORE SPOOKY!
I DON'T WANT TO DO THAT.
WHY? ARE YOU AFRAID OF THE DARK? ARE YOU A CHICKEN--BAWK BAWK?
THERE'S NO REASON TO BE AFRAID OF THE DARK...
...ONLY WHAT'S IN IT!
LIKE THE KAPRE HIDING IN THE WOODS! OOOH!
CUT THAT OUT, JON!

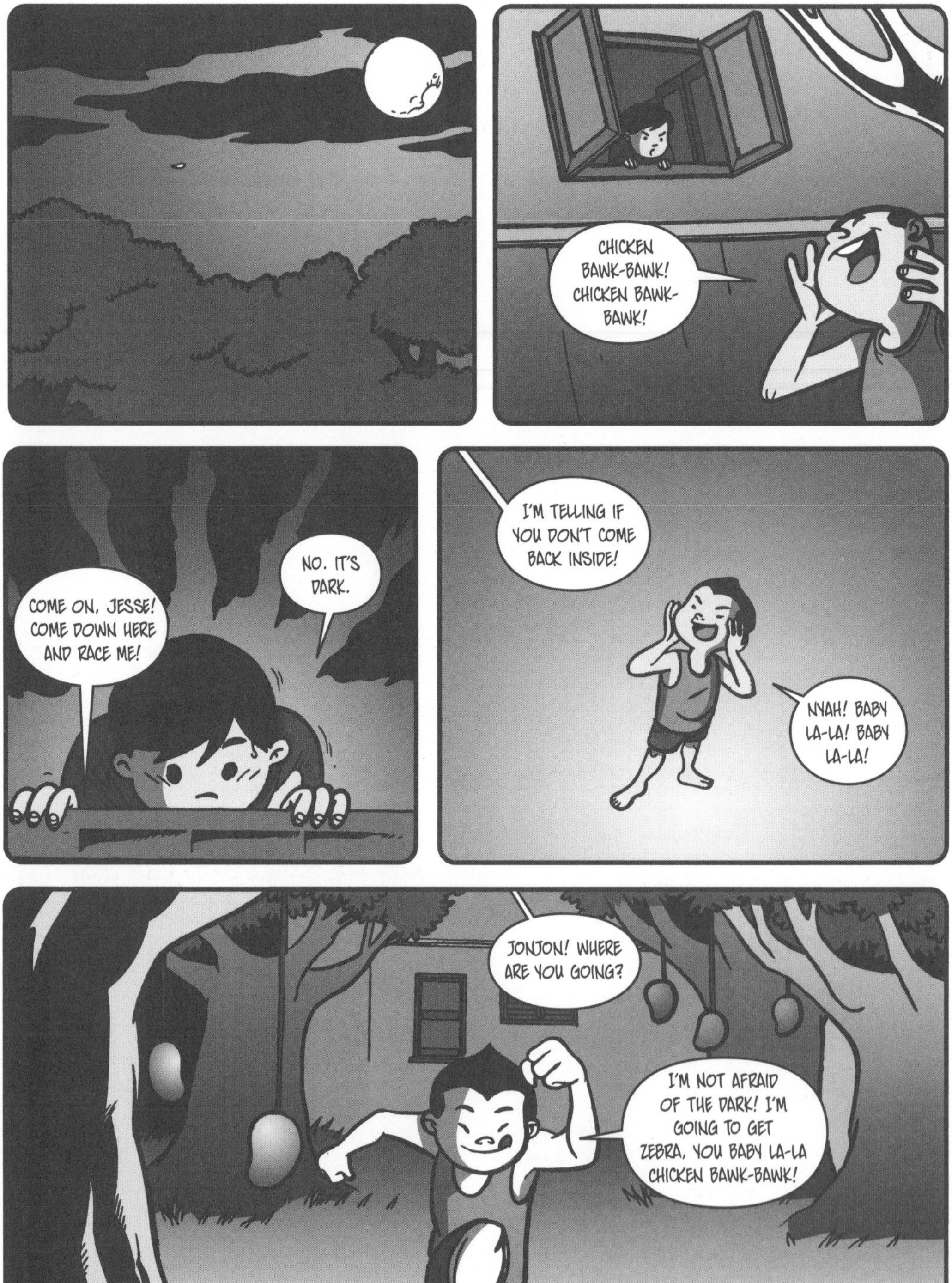
CHICKEN BAWK-BAWK! CHICKEN BAWK-BAWK!
COME ON, JESSE! COME DOWN HERE AND RACE ME!
NO. IT'S DARK.
I'M TELLING IF YOU DON'T COME BACK INSIDE!
NYAH! BABY LA-LA! BABY LA-LA!
JONJON! WHERE ARE YOU GOING?
I'M NOT AFRAID OF THE DARK! I'M GOING TO GET ZEBRA, YOU BABY LA-LA CHICKEN BAWK-BAWK!

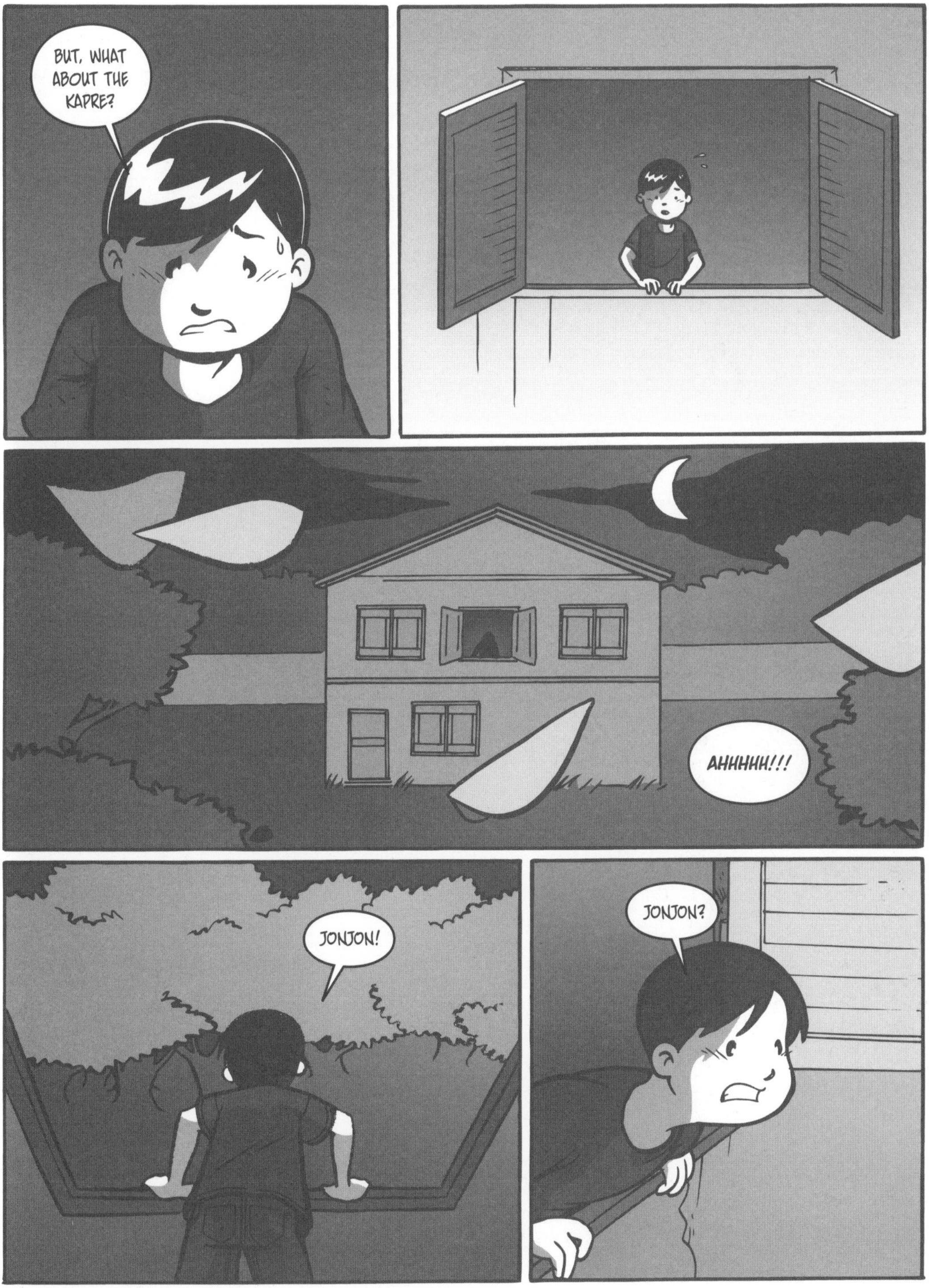
BUT, WHAT ABOUT THE KAPRE?
AHHHHH!!!
JONJON!
JONJON?

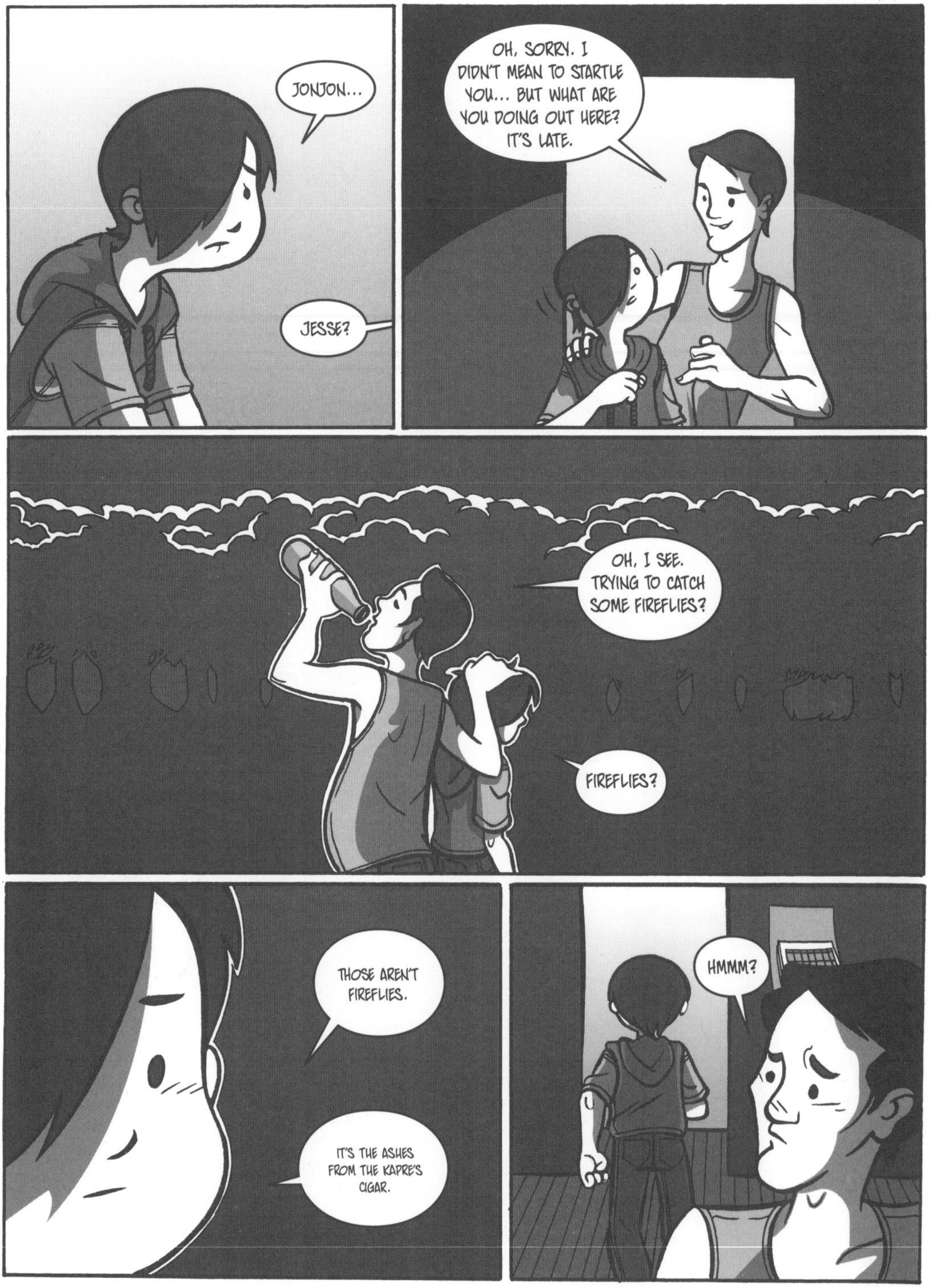
JONJON...
JESSE?
OH, SORRY. I DIDN'T MEAN TO STARTLE YOU... BUT WHAT ARE YOU DOING OUT HERE? IT'S LATE.
OH, I SEE. TRYING TO CATCH SOME FIREFLIES?
FIREFLIES?
THOSE AREN'T FIREFLIES.
IT'S THE ASHES FROM THE KAPRE'S CIGAR.
HMMM?

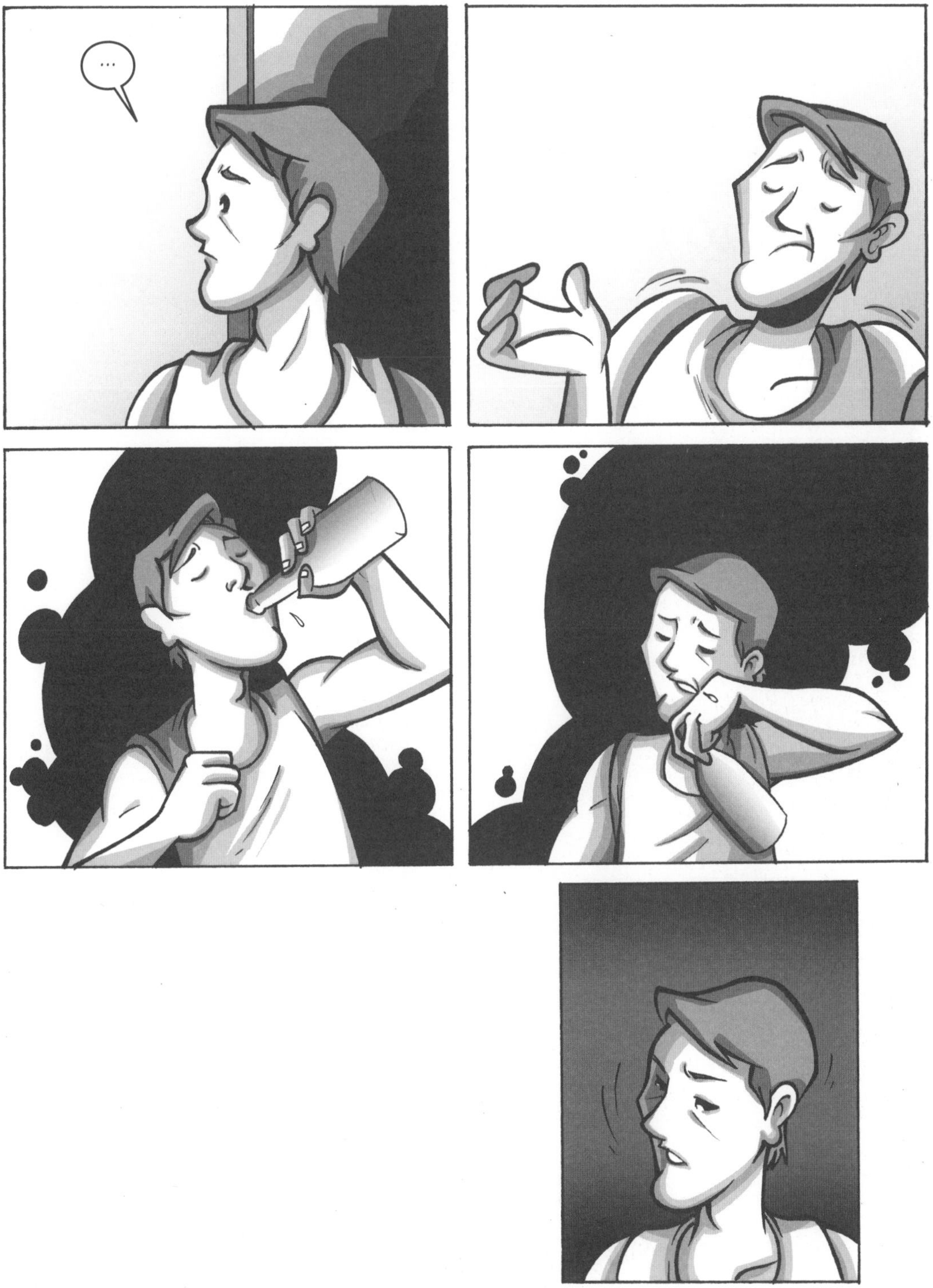
...

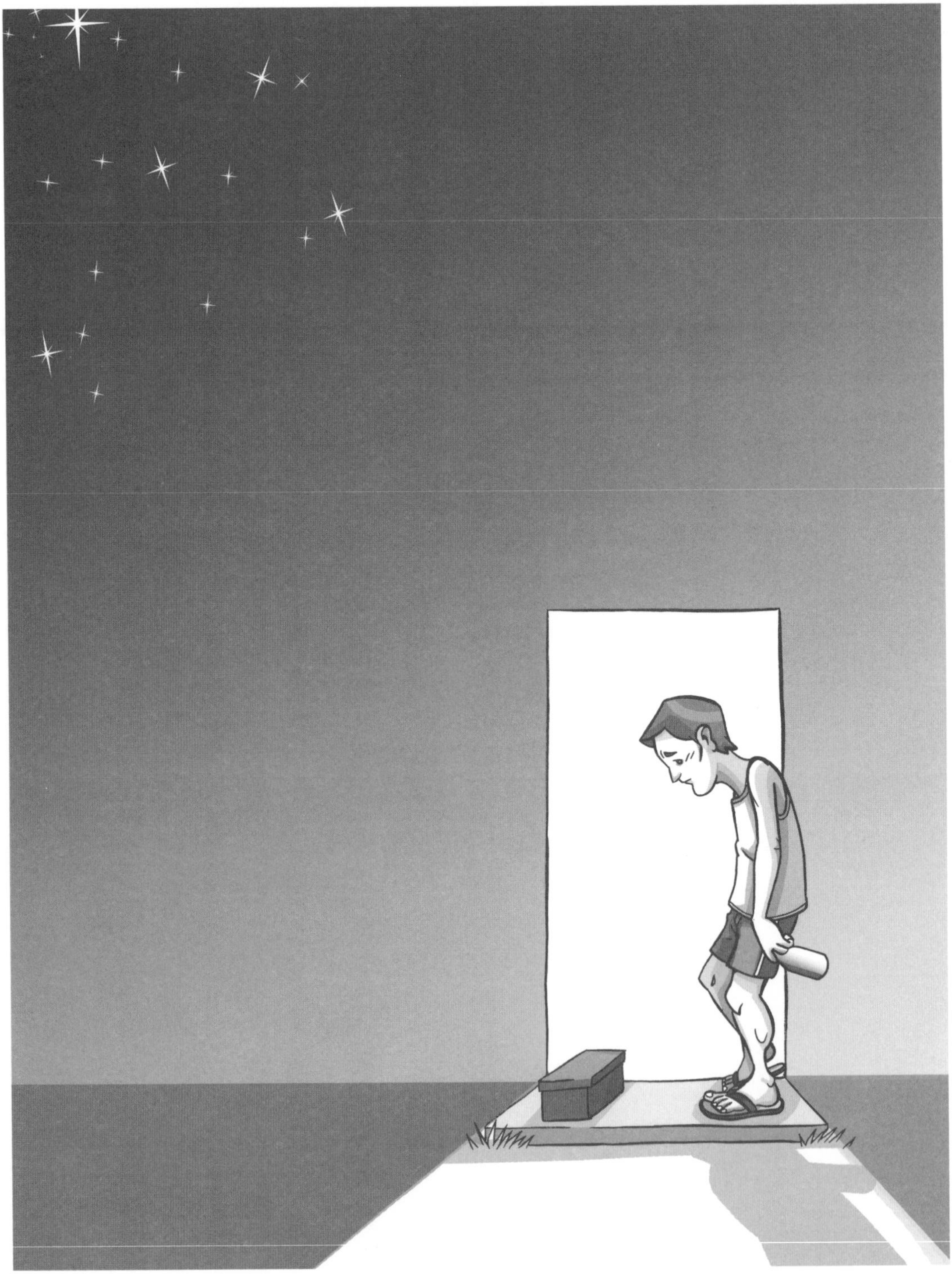

ACT

III

LOLA

A Ghost Story

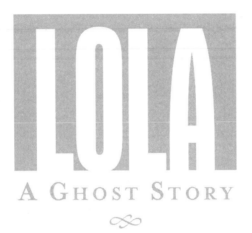

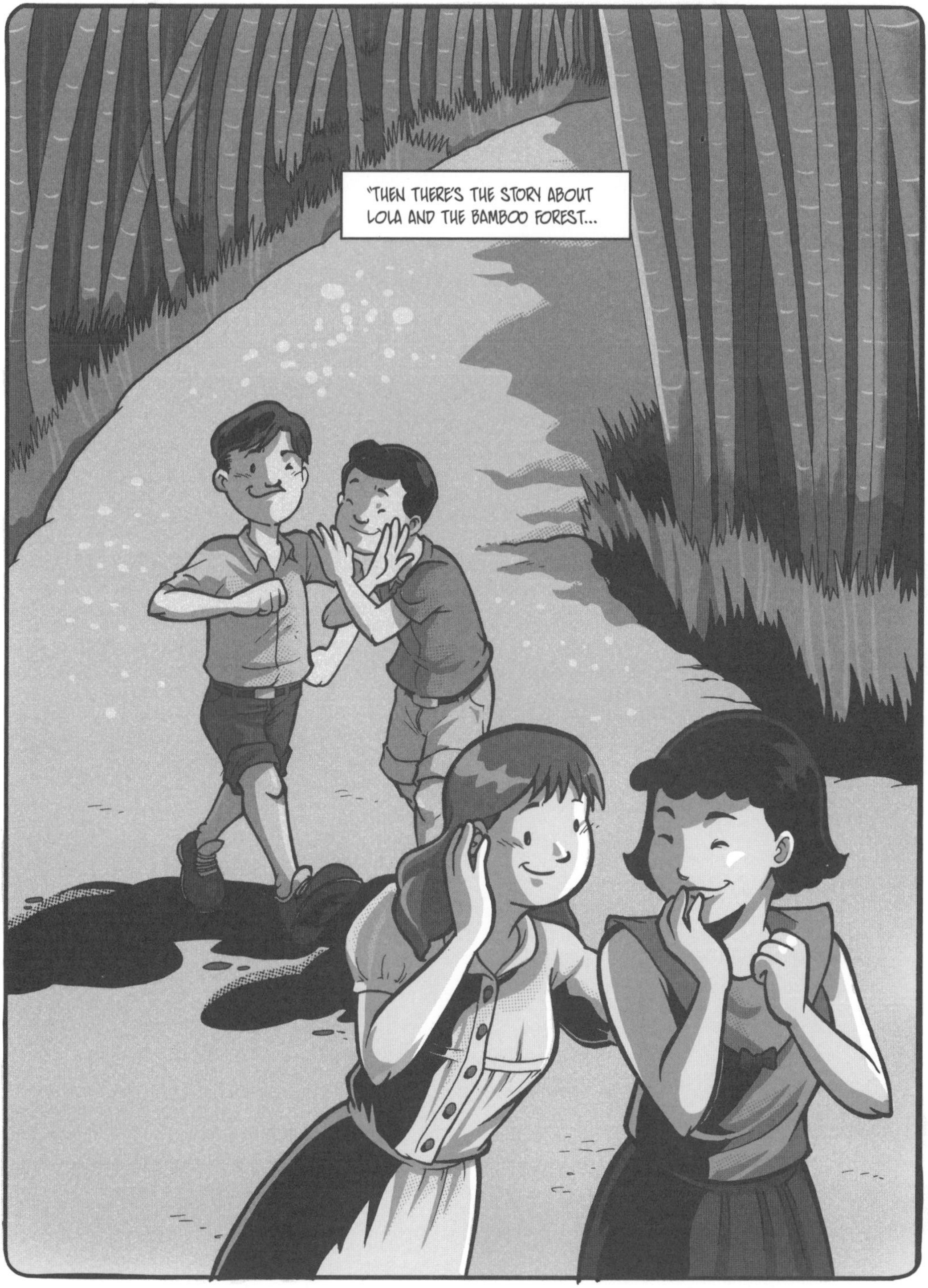
"THEN THERE'S THE STORY ABOUT LOLA AND THE BAMBOO FOREST...

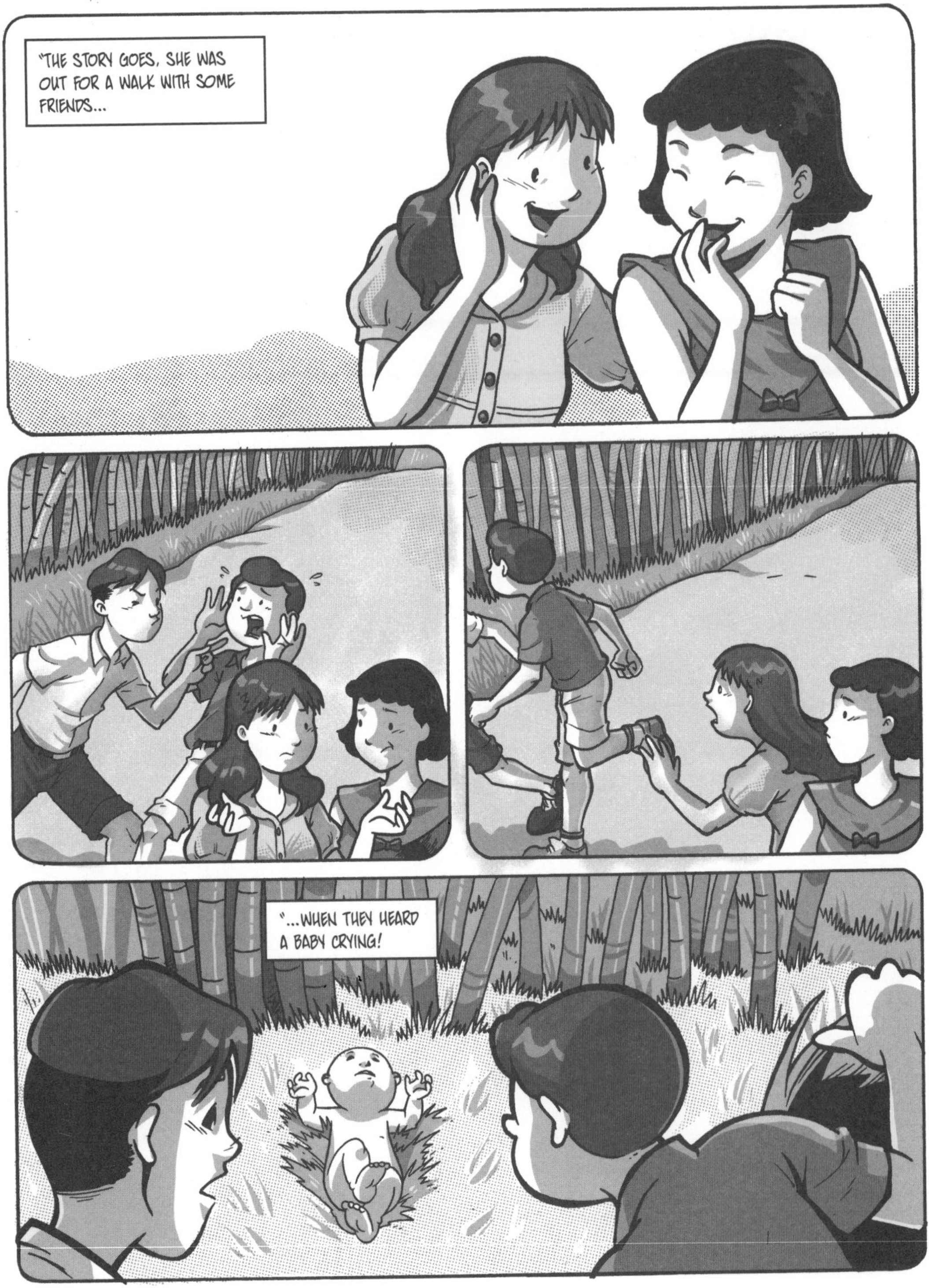
"THE STORY GOES, SHE WAS OUT FOR A WALK WITH SOME FRIENDS...
"...WHEN THEY HEARD A BABY CRYING!

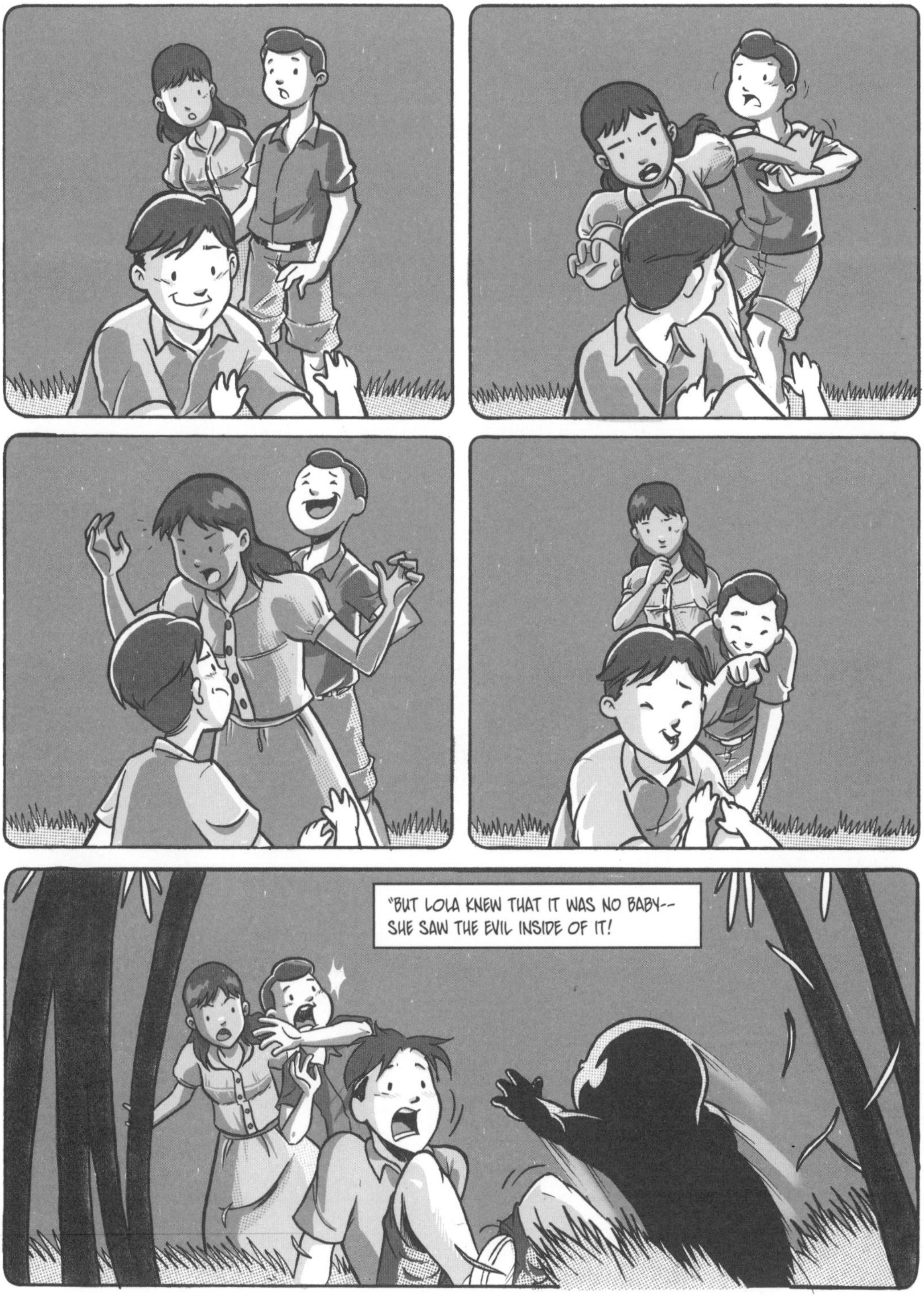
"BUT LOLA KNEW THAT IT WAS NO BABY--
SHE SAW THE EVIL INSIDE OF IT!

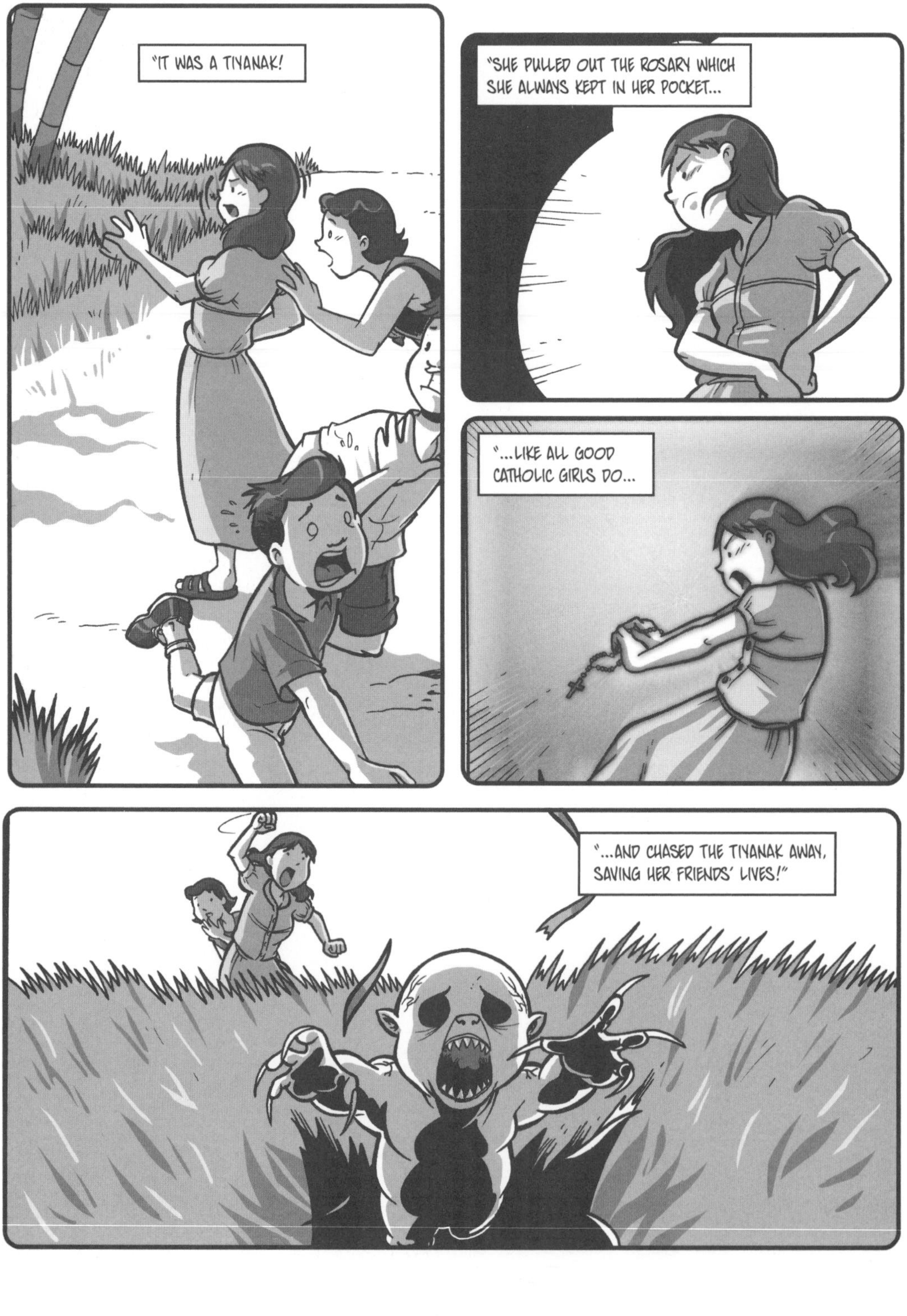
"IT WAS A TIYANAK!
"SHE PULLED OUT THE ROSARY WHICH SHE ALWAYS KEPT IN HER POCKET...
"...LIKE ALL GOOD CATHOLIC GIRLS DO...
"...AND CHASED THE TIYANAK AWAY, SAVING HER FRIENDS' LIVES!"

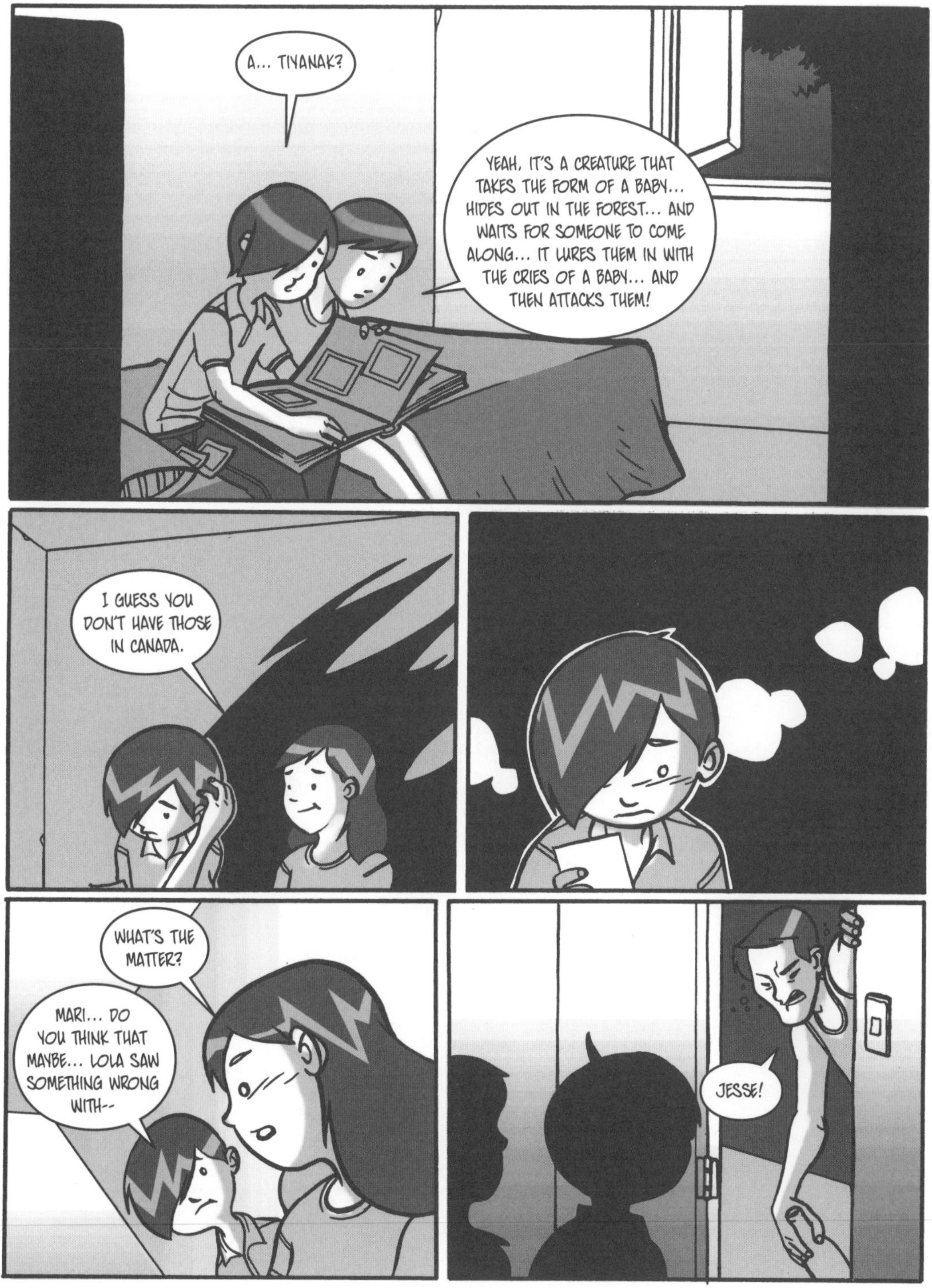
A... TIYANAK?
YEAH, IT'S A CREATURE THAT TAKES THE FORM OF A BABY... HIDES OUT IN THE FOREST... AND WAITS FOR SOMEONE TO COME ALONG... IT LURES THEM IN WITH THE CRIES OF A BABY... AND THEN ATTACKS THEM!
I GUESS YOU DON'T HAVE THOSE IN CANADA.
WHAT'S THE MATTER?
MARI... DO YOU THINK THAT MAYBE... LOLA SAW SOMETHING WRONG WITH--
JESSE!

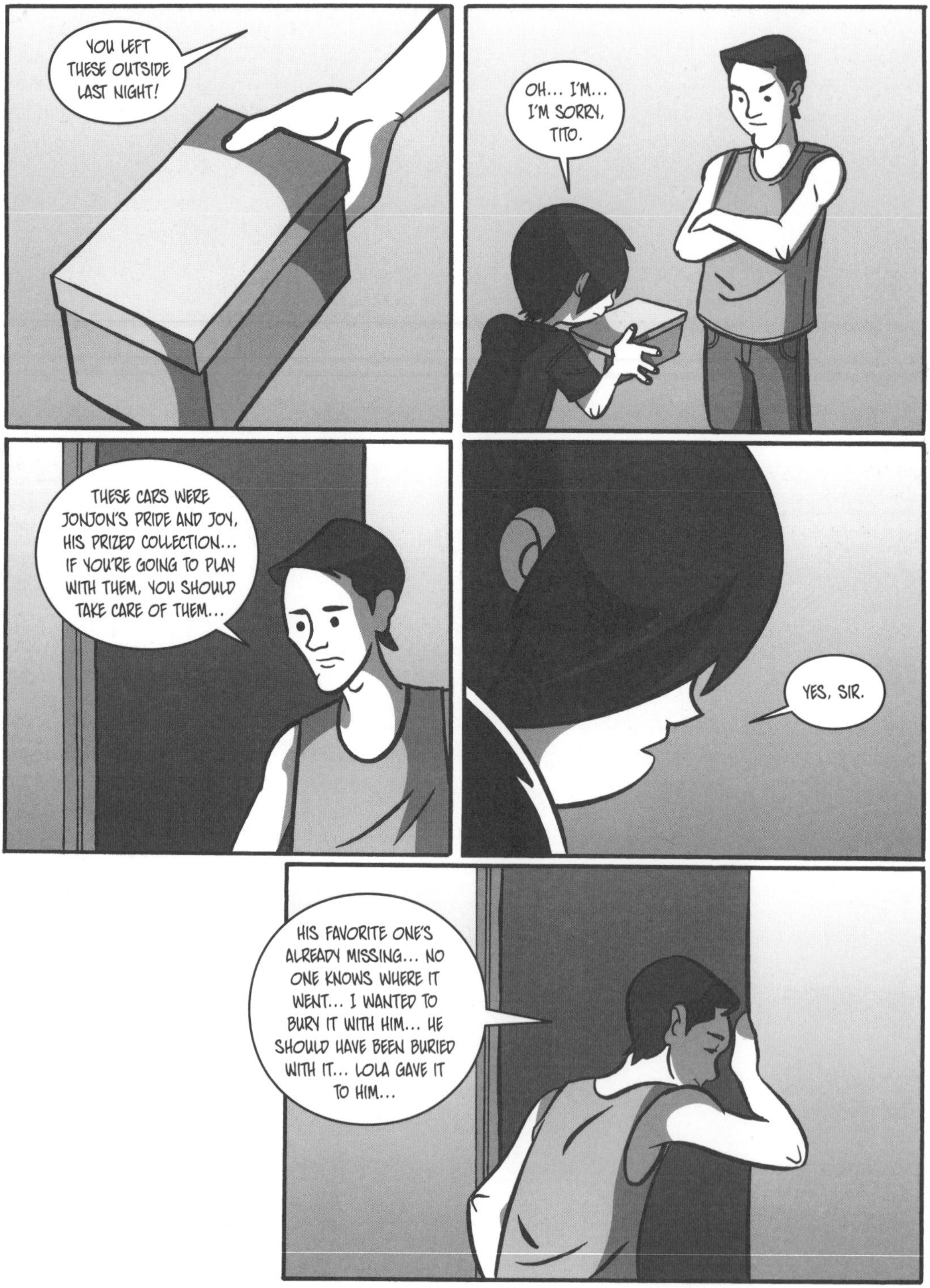
YOU LEFT THESE OUTSIDE LAST NIGHT!
OH... I'M... I'M SORRY, TITO.
THESE CARS WERE JONJON'S PRIDE AND JOY, HIS PRIZED COLLECTION... IF YOU'RE GOING TO PLAY WITH THEM, YOU SHOULD TAKE CARE OF THEM...
YES, SIR.
HIS FAVORITE ONE'S ALREADY MISSING... NO ONE KNOWS WHERE IT WENT... I WANTED TO BURY IT WITH HIM... HE SHOULD HAVE BEEN BURIED WITH IT... LOLA GAVE IT TO HIM...

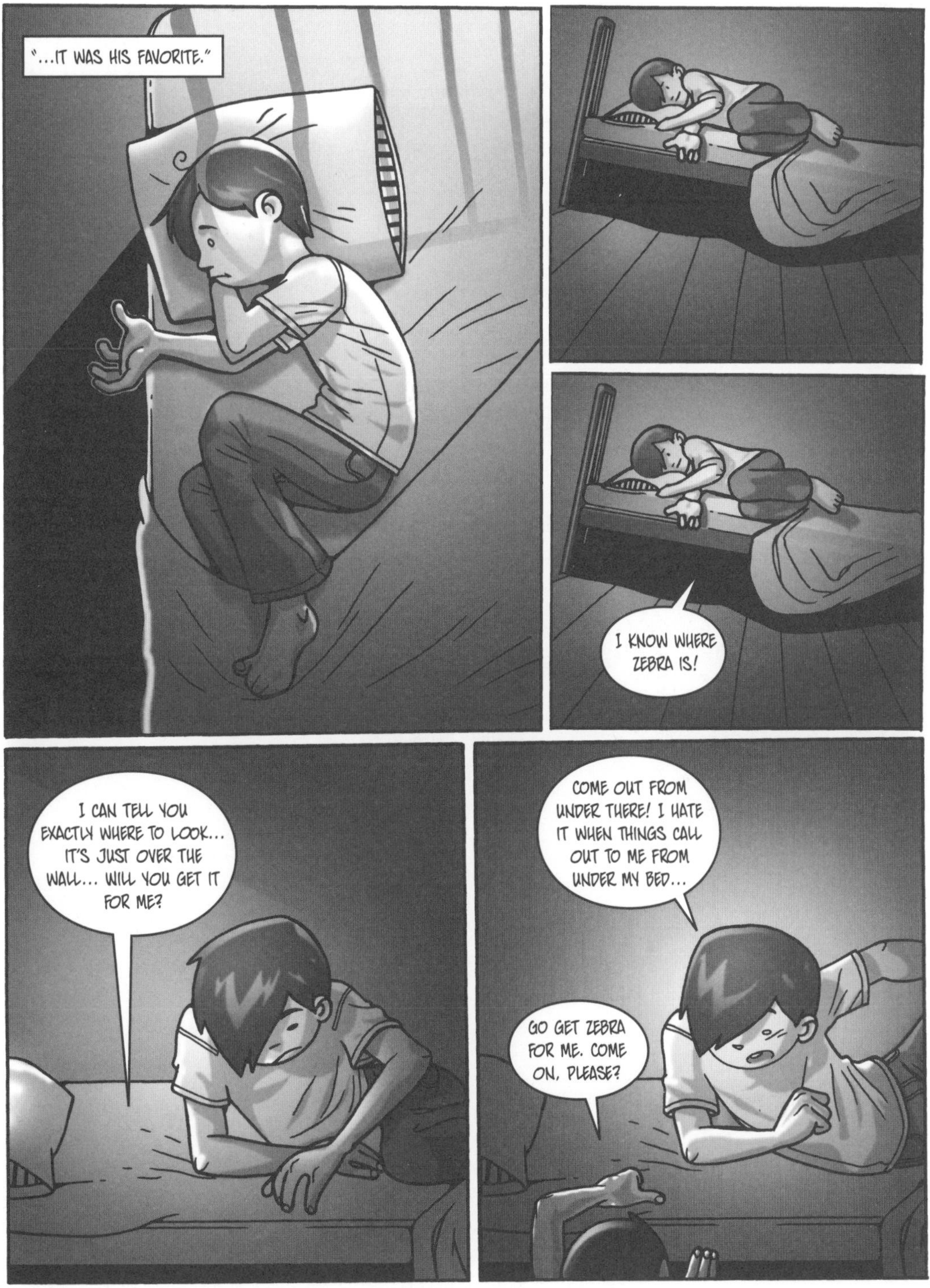
"...IT WAS HIS FAVORITE."
I KNOW WHERE ZEBRA IS!
I CAN TELL YOU EXACTLY WHERE TO LOOK... IT'S JUST OVER THE WALL... WILL YOU GET IT FOR ME?
COME OUT FROM UNDER THERE! I HATE IT WHEN THINGS CALL OUT TO ME FROM UNDER MY BED...
GO GET ZEBRA FOR ME. COME ON, PLEASE?

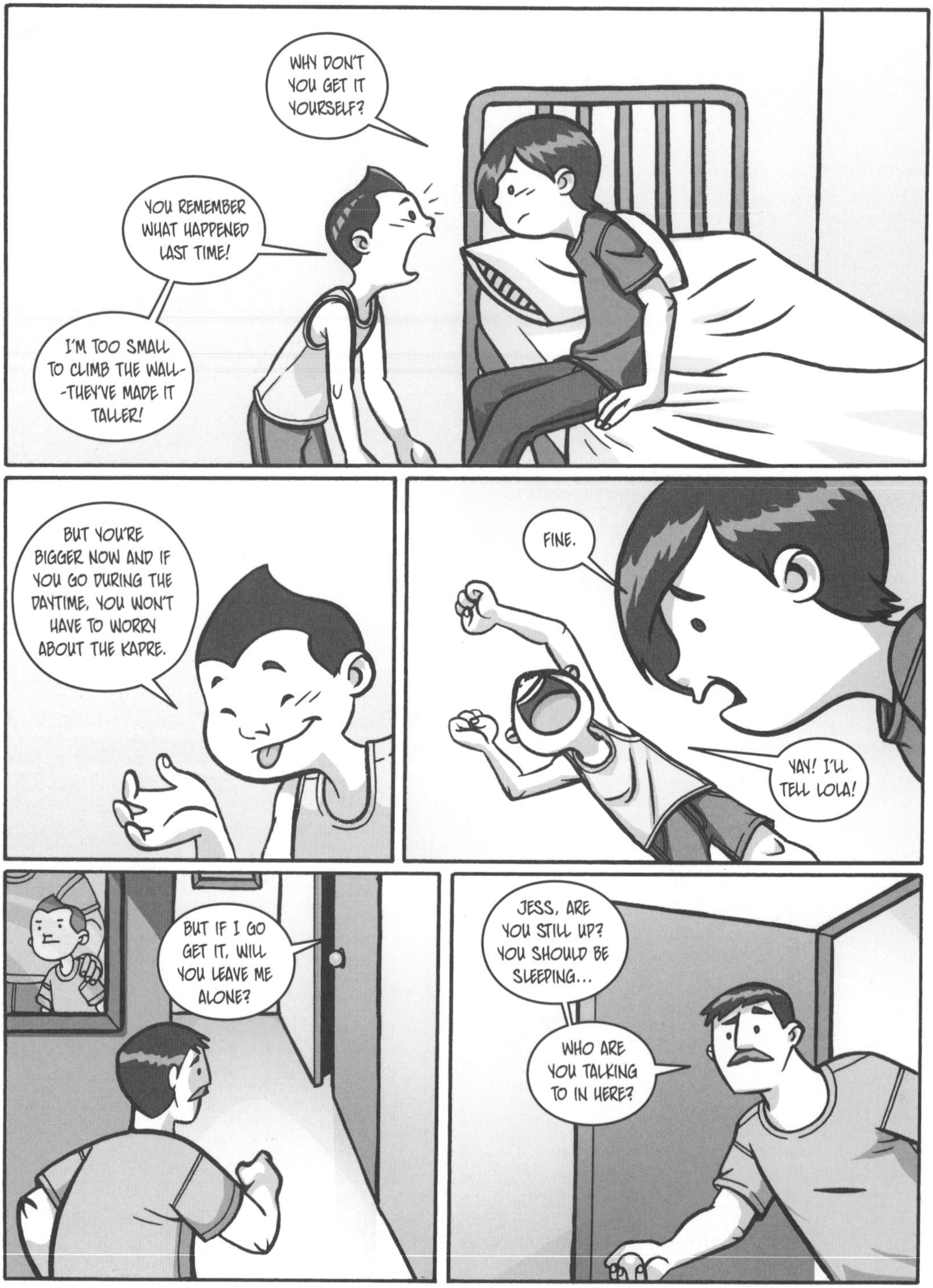
WHY DON'T YOU GET IT YOURSELF?
YOU REMEMBER WHAT HAPPENED LAST TIME!
I'M TOO SMALL TO CLIMB THE WALL--THEY'VE MADE IT TALLER!
BUT YOU'RE BIGGER NOW AND IF YOU GO DURING THE DAYTIME, YOU WON'T HAVE TO WORRY ABOUT THE KAPRE.
FINE.
YAY! I'LL TELL LOLA!
BUT IF I GO GET IT, WILL YOU LEAVE ME ALONE?
JESS, ARE YOU STILL UP? YOU SHOULD BE SLEEPING...
WHO ARE YOU TALKING TO IN HERE?

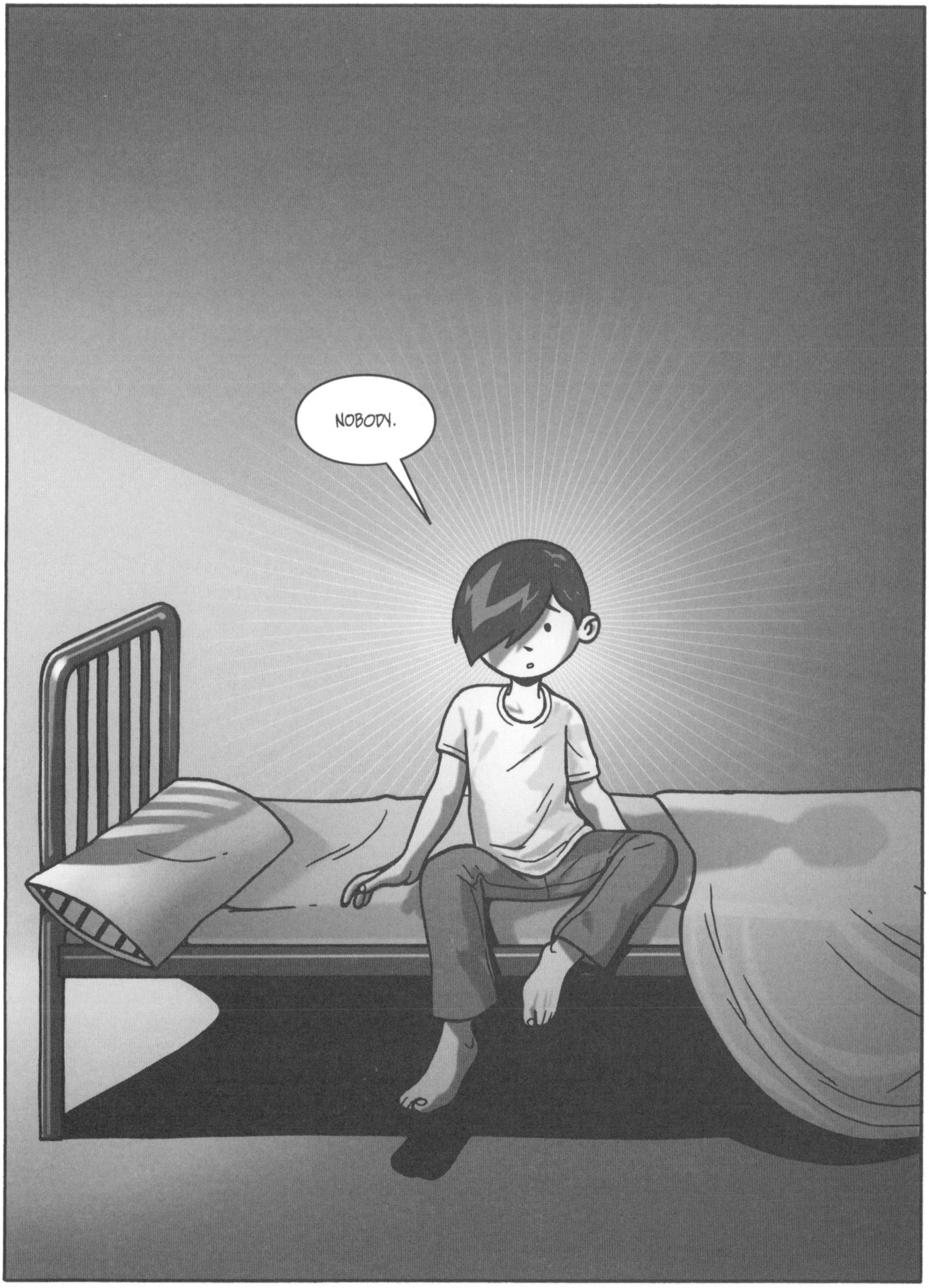
NOBODY.

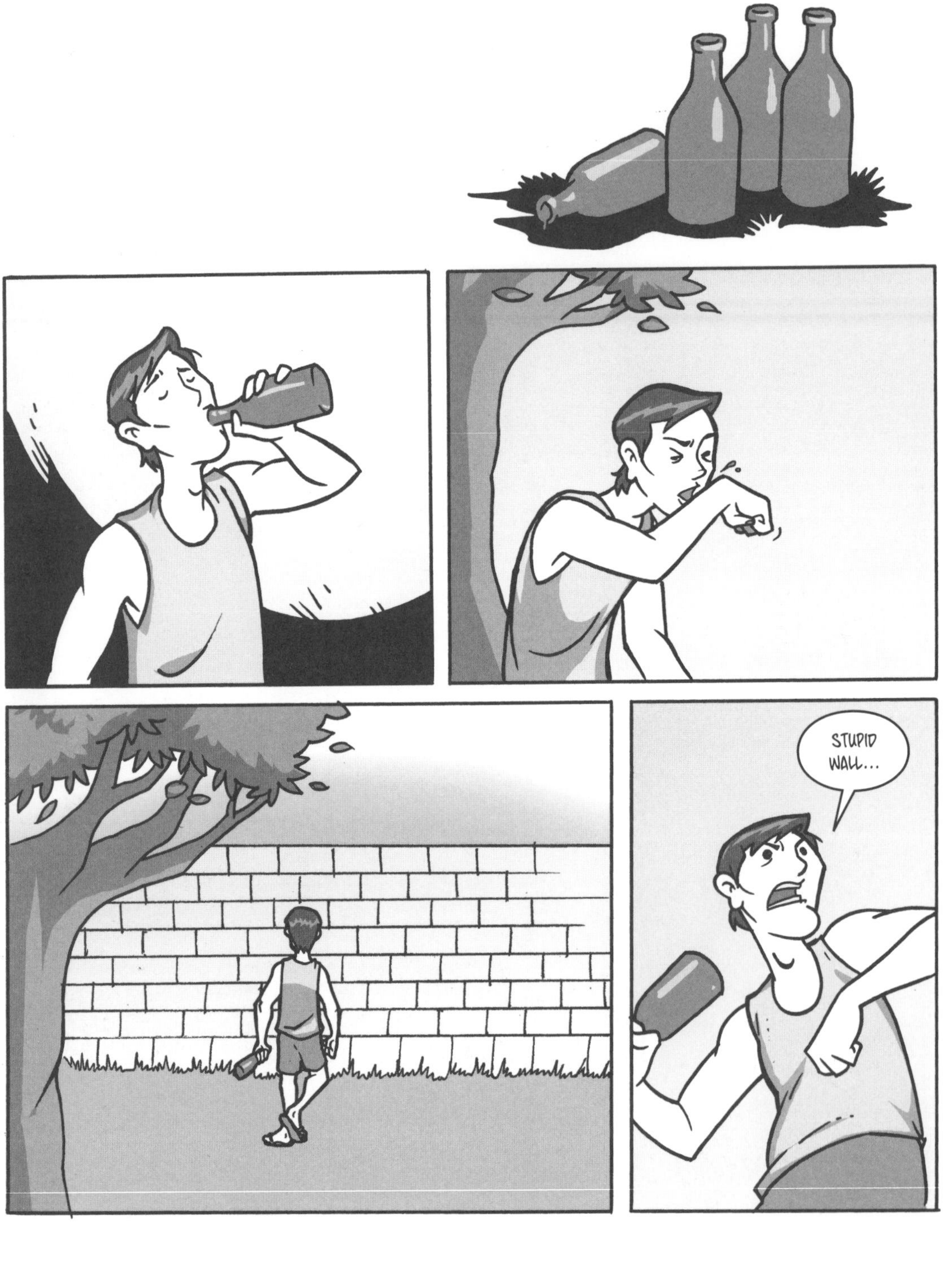
STUPID WALL...

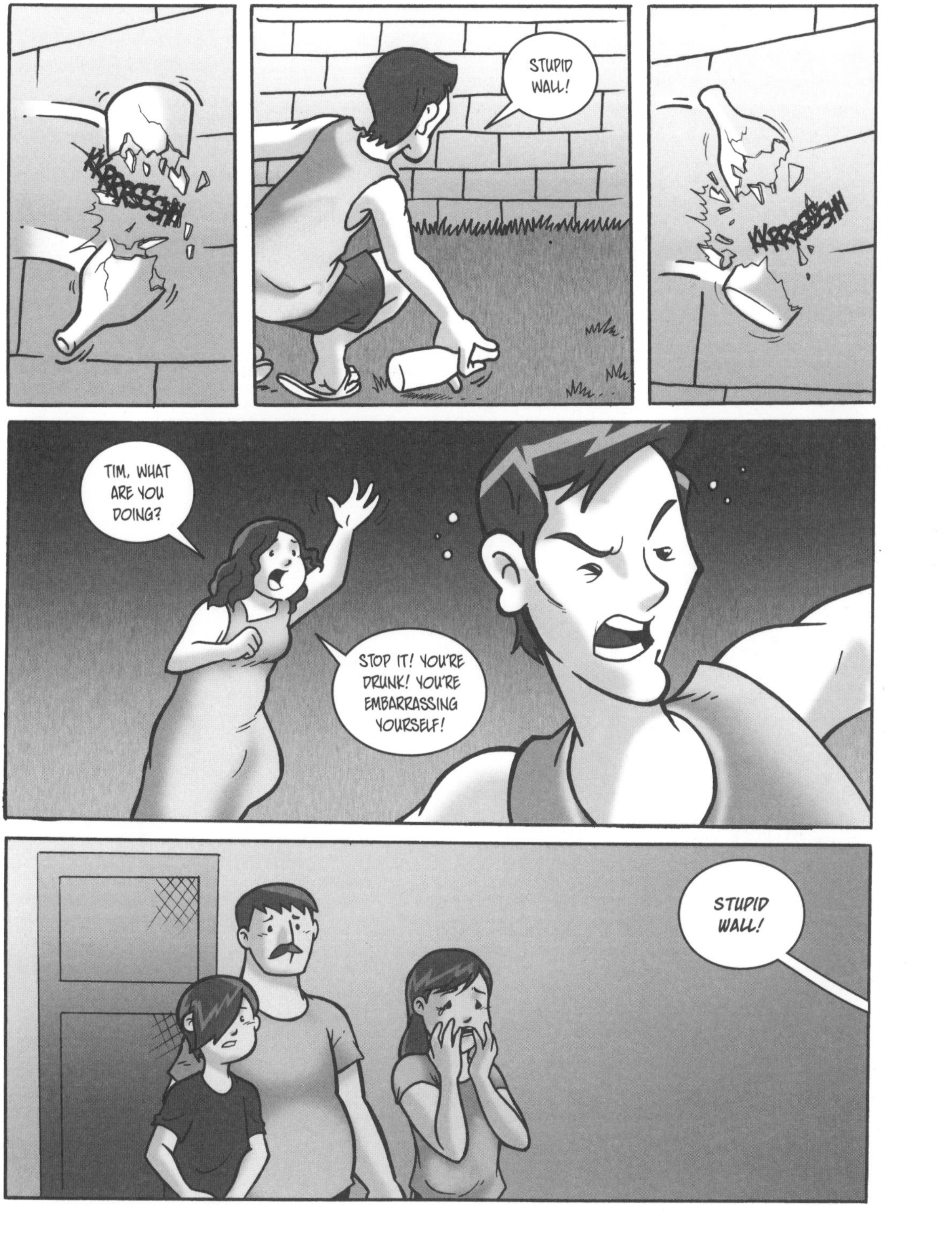
KKRRRSSSHH
STUPID WALL!
KKRRRSSSHH
TIM, WHAT ARE YOU DOING?
STOP IT! YOU'RE DRUNK! YOU'RE EMBARRASSING YOURSELF!
STUPID WALL!

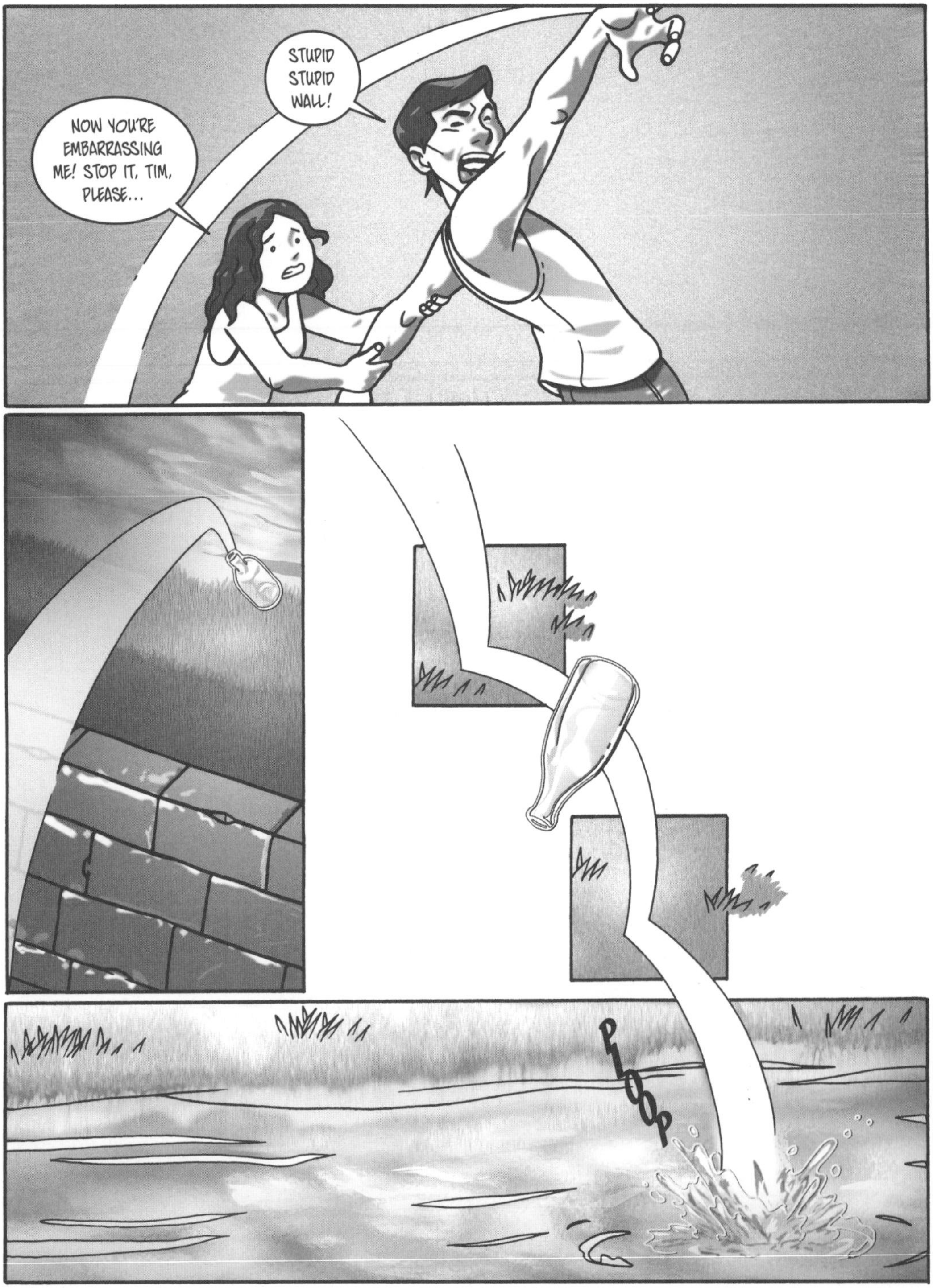
STUPID STUPID WALL!
NOW YOU'RE EMBARRASSING ME! STOP IT, TIM, PLEASE...
PLOOP

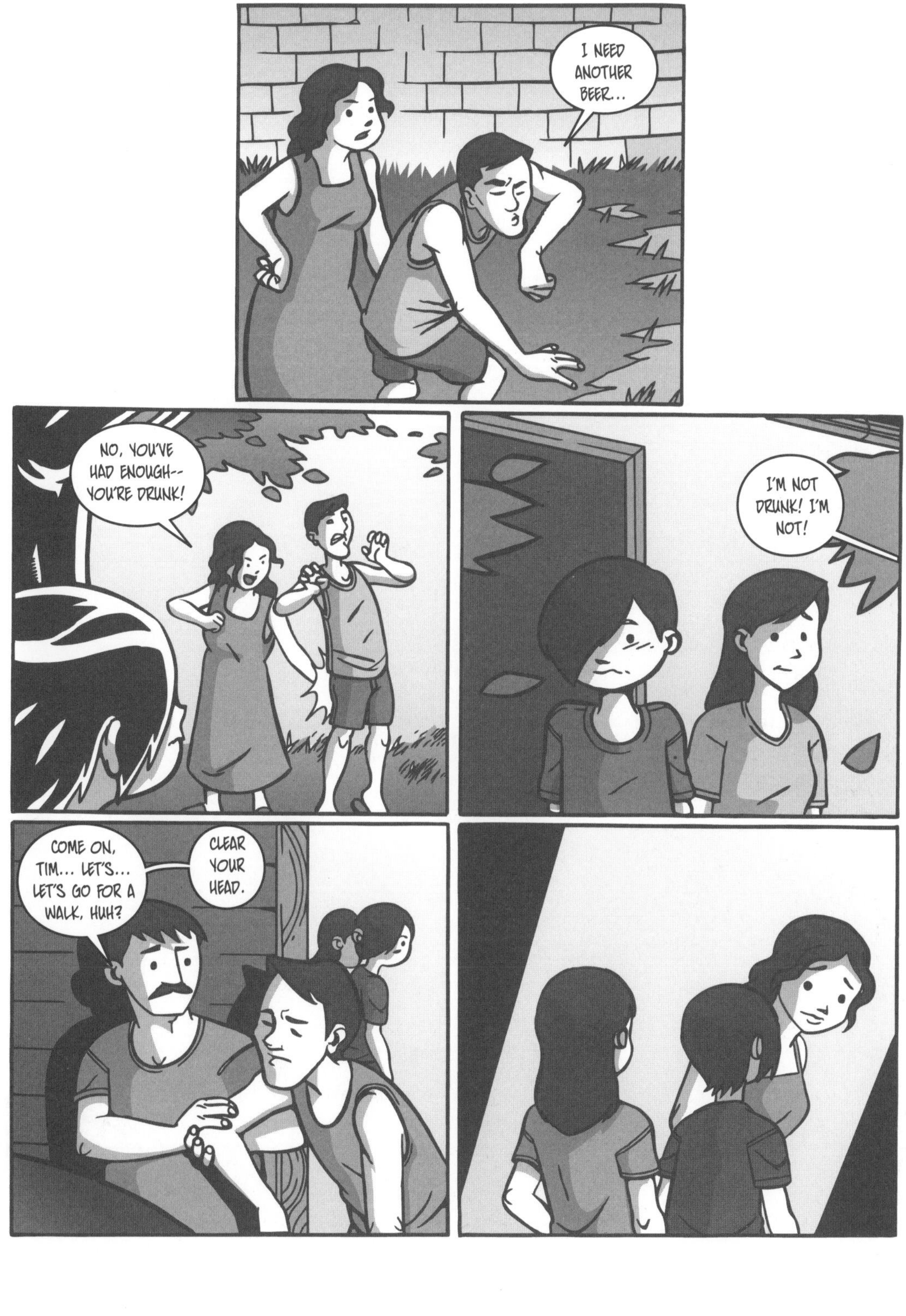
I NEED ANOTHER BEER...
NO, YOU'VE HAD ENOUGH-- YOU'RE DRUNK!
I'M NOT DRUNK! I'M NOT!
COME ON, TIM... LET'S... LET'S GO FOR A WALK, HUH?
CLEAR YOUR HEAD.

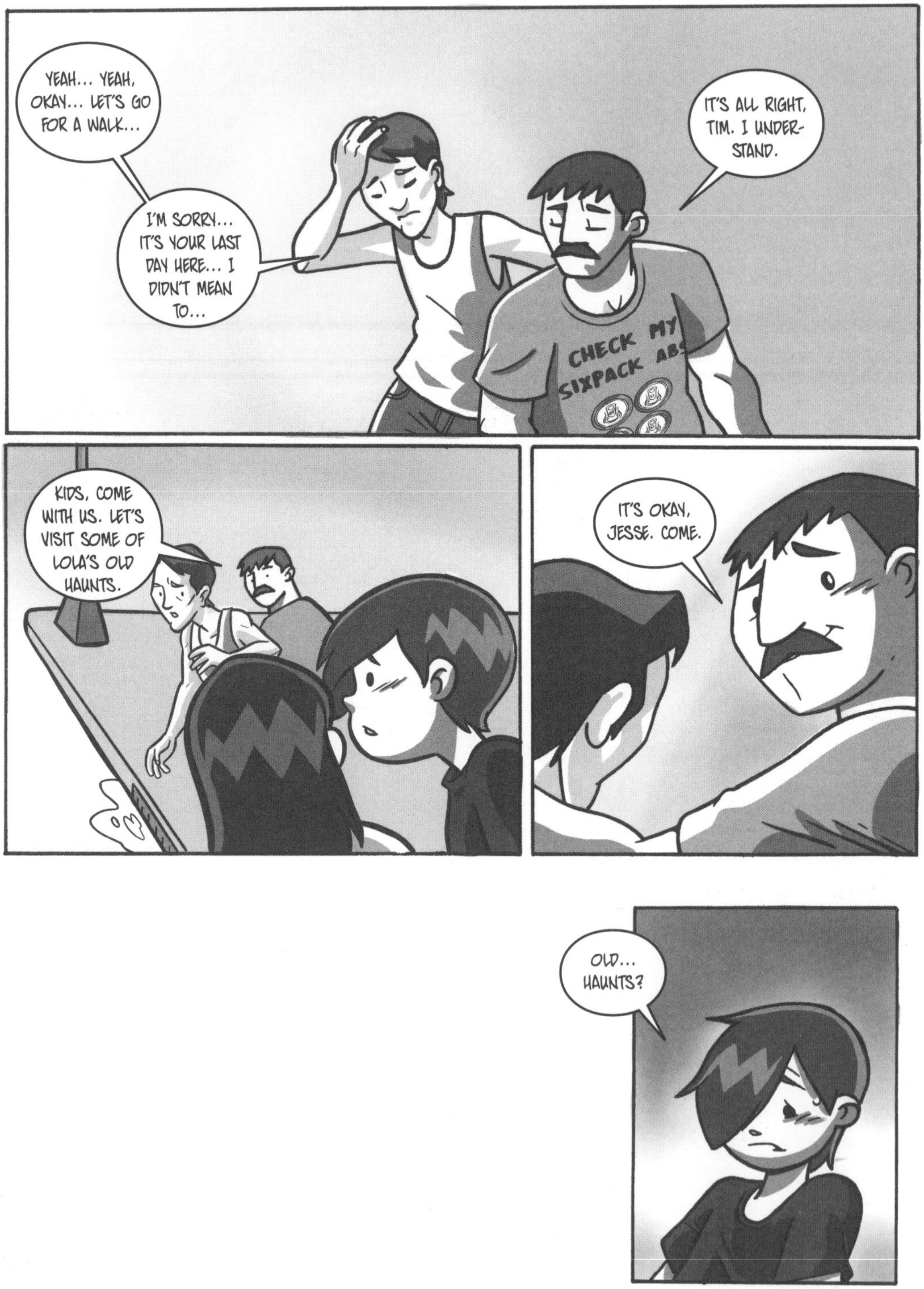
YEAH... YEAH, OKAY... LET'S GO FOR A WALK...
I'M SORRY... IT'S YOUR LAST DAY HERE... I DIDN'T MEAN TO...
IT'S ALL RIGHT, TIM. I UNDER-STAND.
CHECK MY SIXPACK ABS
KIDS, COME WITH US. LET'S VISIT SOME OF LOLA'S OLD HAUNTS.
IT'S OKAY, JESSE. COME.
OLD... HAUNTS?

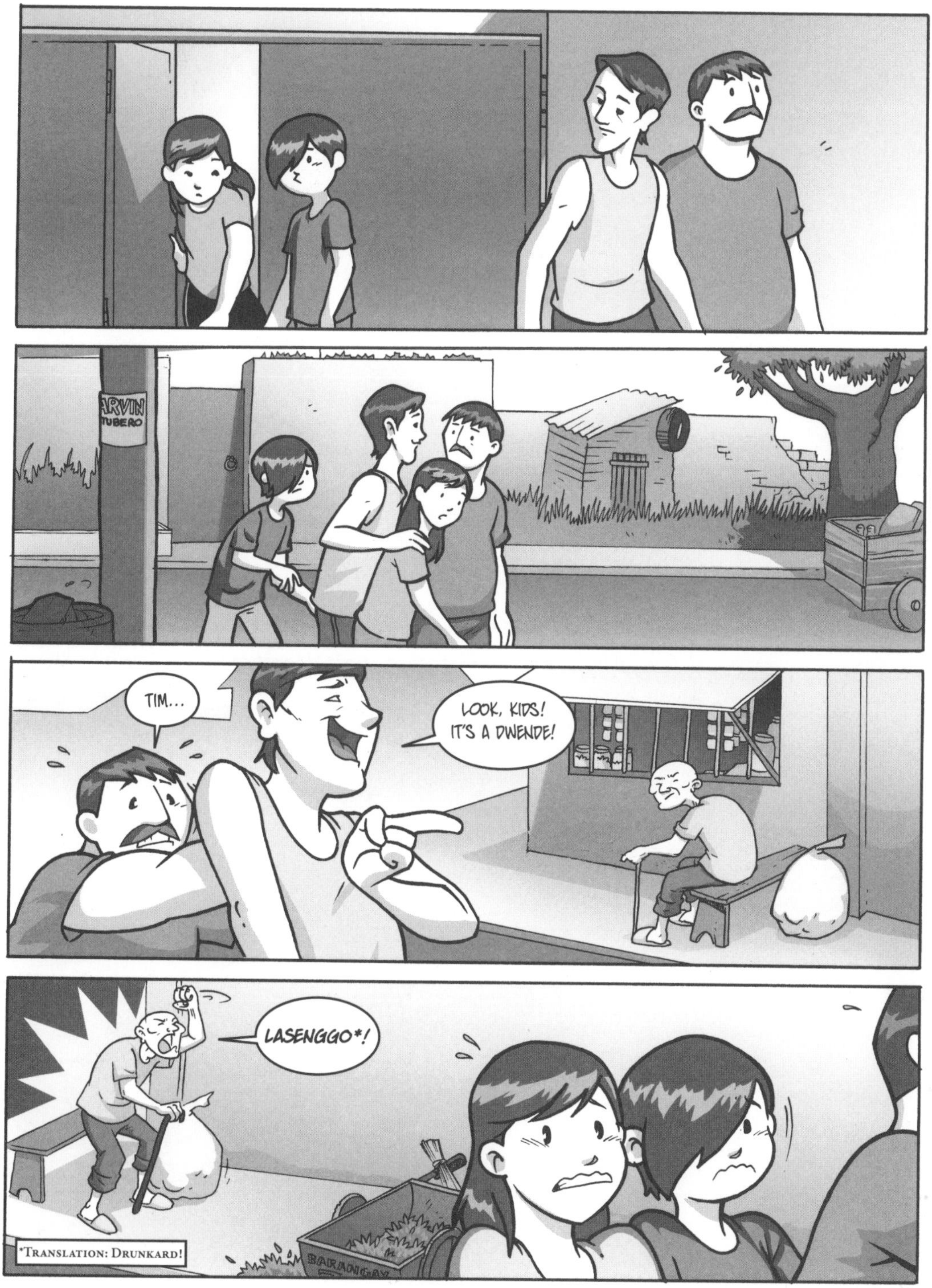
ARVIN
TUBERO
TIM...
LOOK, KIDS! IT'S A DWENDE!
LASENGGO*!
*Translation: Drunkard!
BARANGAY

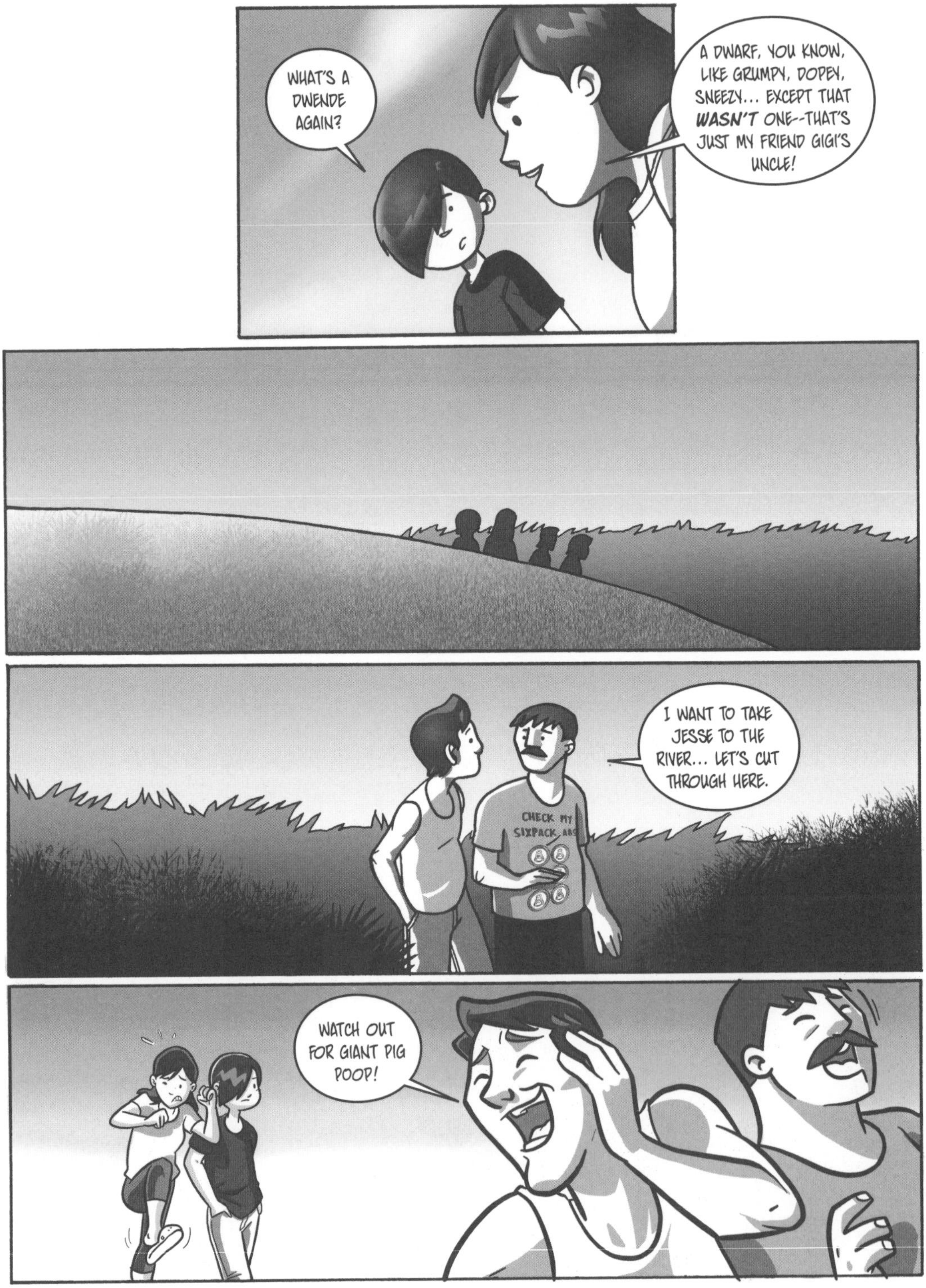
WHAT'S A DWENDE AGAIN?
A DWARF, YOU KNOW, LIKE GRUMPY, DOPEY, SNEEZY... EXCEPT THAT **WASN'T** ONE--THAT'S JUST MY FRIEND GIGI'S UNCLE!
I WANT TO TAKE JESSE TO THE RIVER... LET'S CUT THROUGH HERE.
CHECK MY SIXPACK ABS
WATCH OUT FOR GIANT PIG POOP!

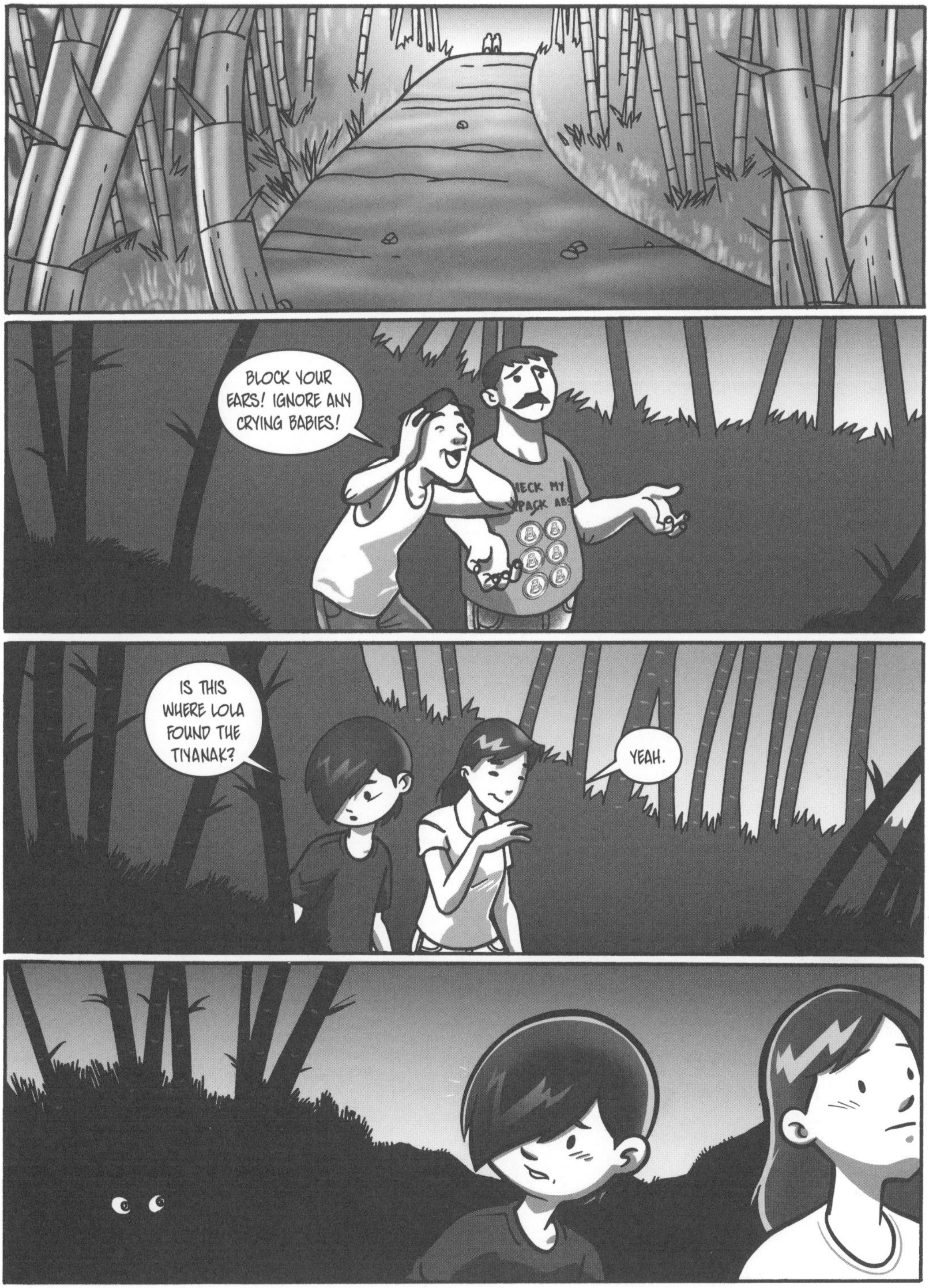
BLOCK YOUR EARS! IGNORE ANY CRYING BABIES!
IS THIS WHERE LOLA FOUND THE TIYANAK?
YEAH.

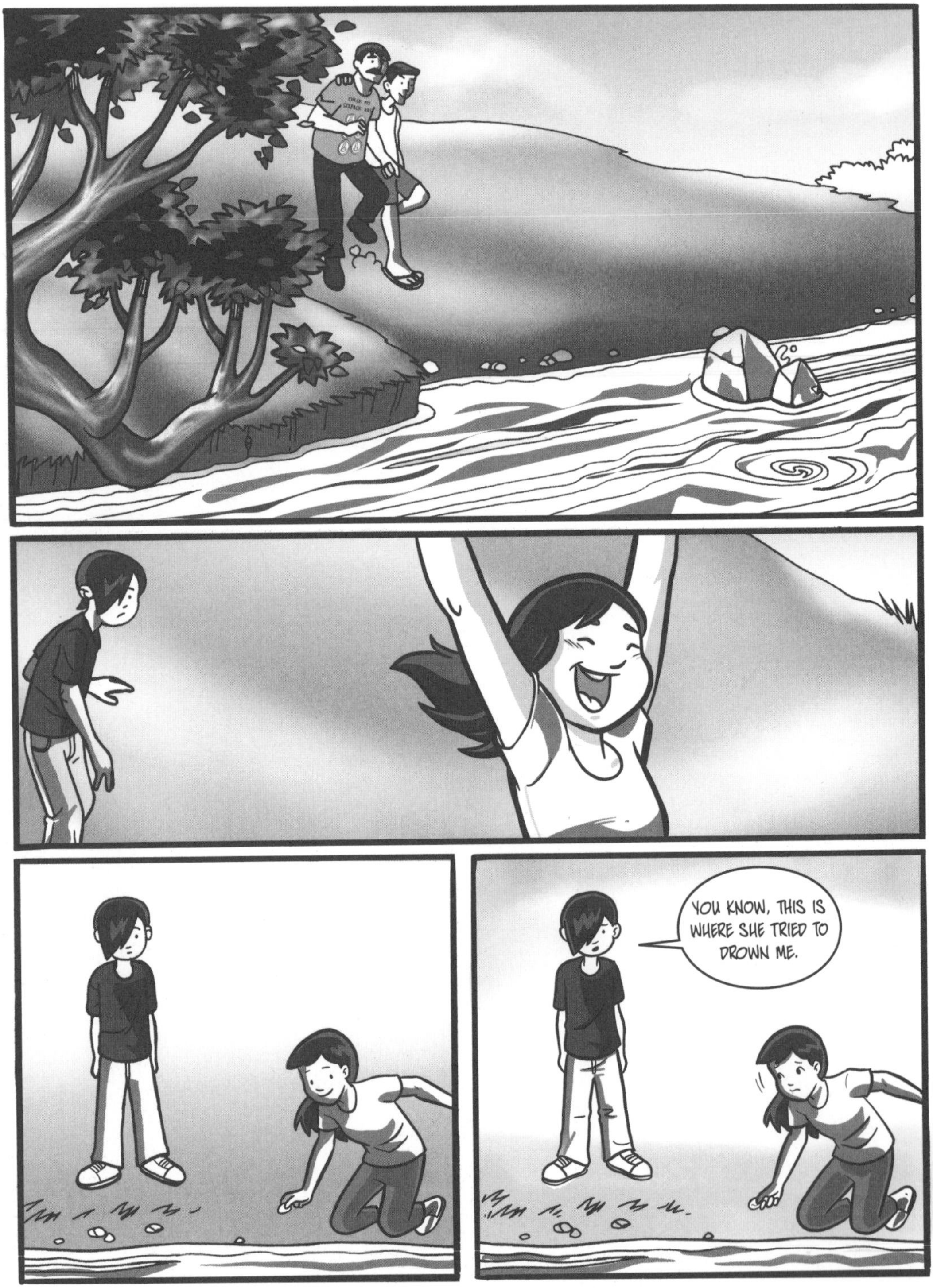
YOU KNOW, THIS IS WHERE SHE TRIED TO DROWN ME.

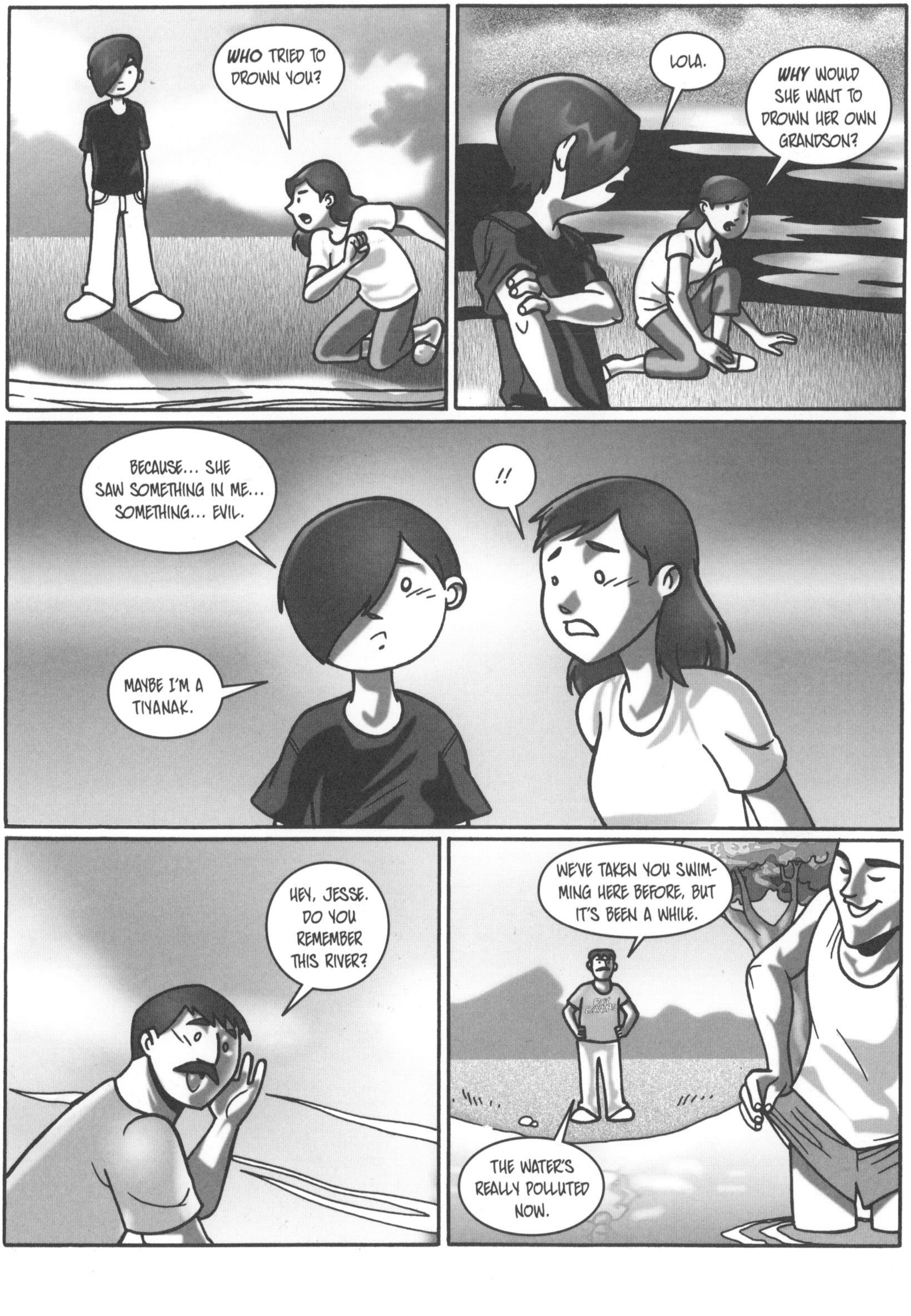
WHO TRIED TO DROWN YOU?
LOLA.
WHY WOULD SHE WANT TO DROWN HER OWN GRANDSON?
BECAUSE... SHE SAW SOMETHING IN ME... SOMETHING... EVIL.
MAYBE I'M A TIYANAK.
!!
HEY, JESSE. DO YOU REMEMBER THIS RIVER?
WE'VE TAKEN YOU SWIM-MING HERE BEFORE, BUT IT'S BEEN A WHILE.
THE WATER'S REALLY POLLUTED NOW.

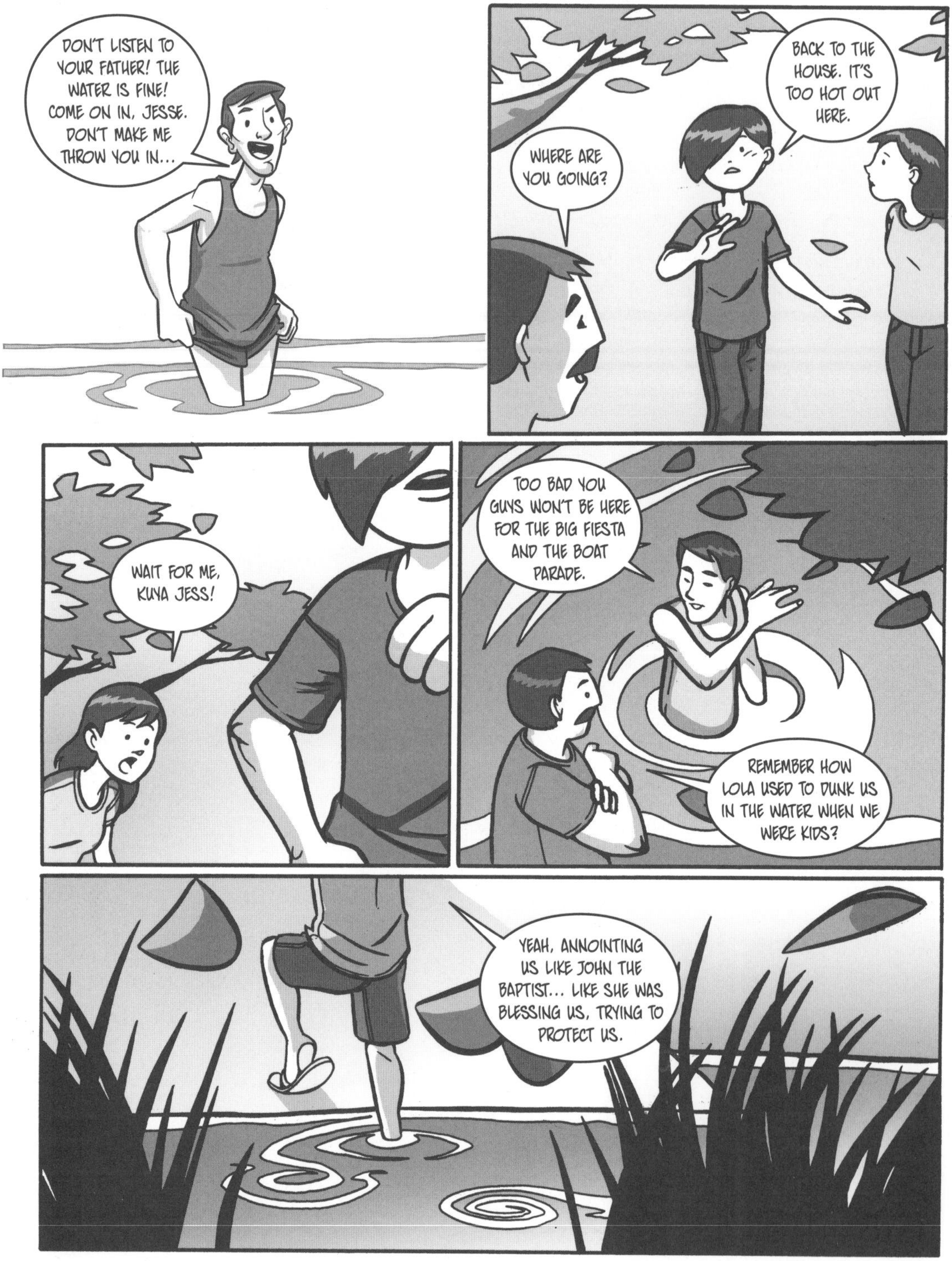
DON'T LISTEN TO YOUR FATHER! THE WATER IS FINE! COME ON IN, JESSE. DON'T MAKE ME THROW YOU IN...
WHERE ARE YOU GOING?
BACK TO THE HOUSE. IT'S TOO HOT OUT HERE.
WAIT FOR ME, KUYA JESS!
TOO BAD YOU GUYS WON'T BE HERE FOR THE BIG FIESTA AND THE BOAT PARADE.
REMEMBER HOW LOLA USED TO DUNK US IN THE WATER WHEN WE WERE KIDS?
YEAH, ANNOINTING US LIKE JOHN THE BAPTIST... LIKE SHE WAS BLESSING US, TRYING TO PROTECT US.

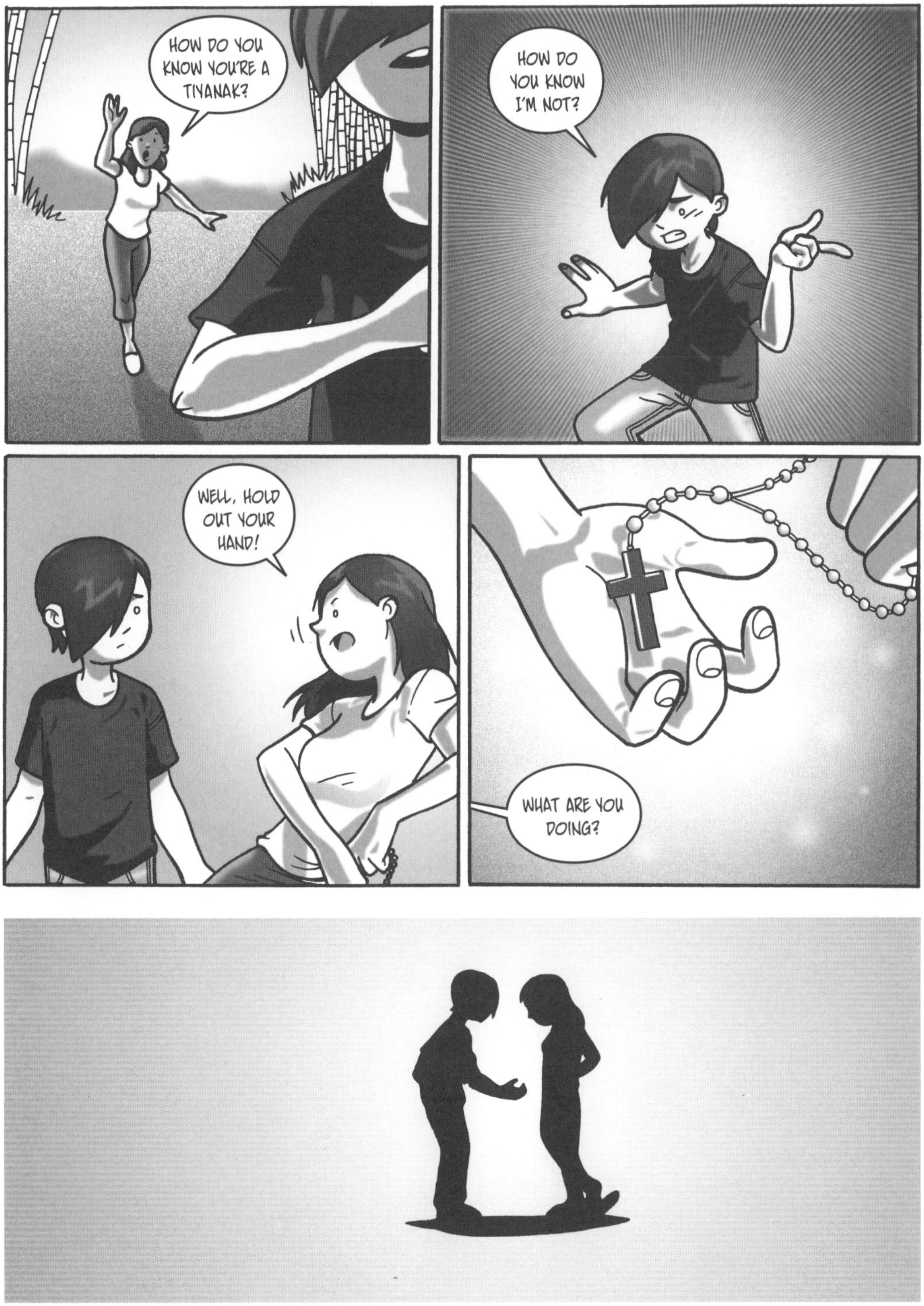
HOW DO YOU KNOW YOU'RE A TIYANAK?
HOW DO YOU KNOW I'M NOT?
WELL, HOLD OUT YOUR HAND!
WHAT ARE YOU DOING?

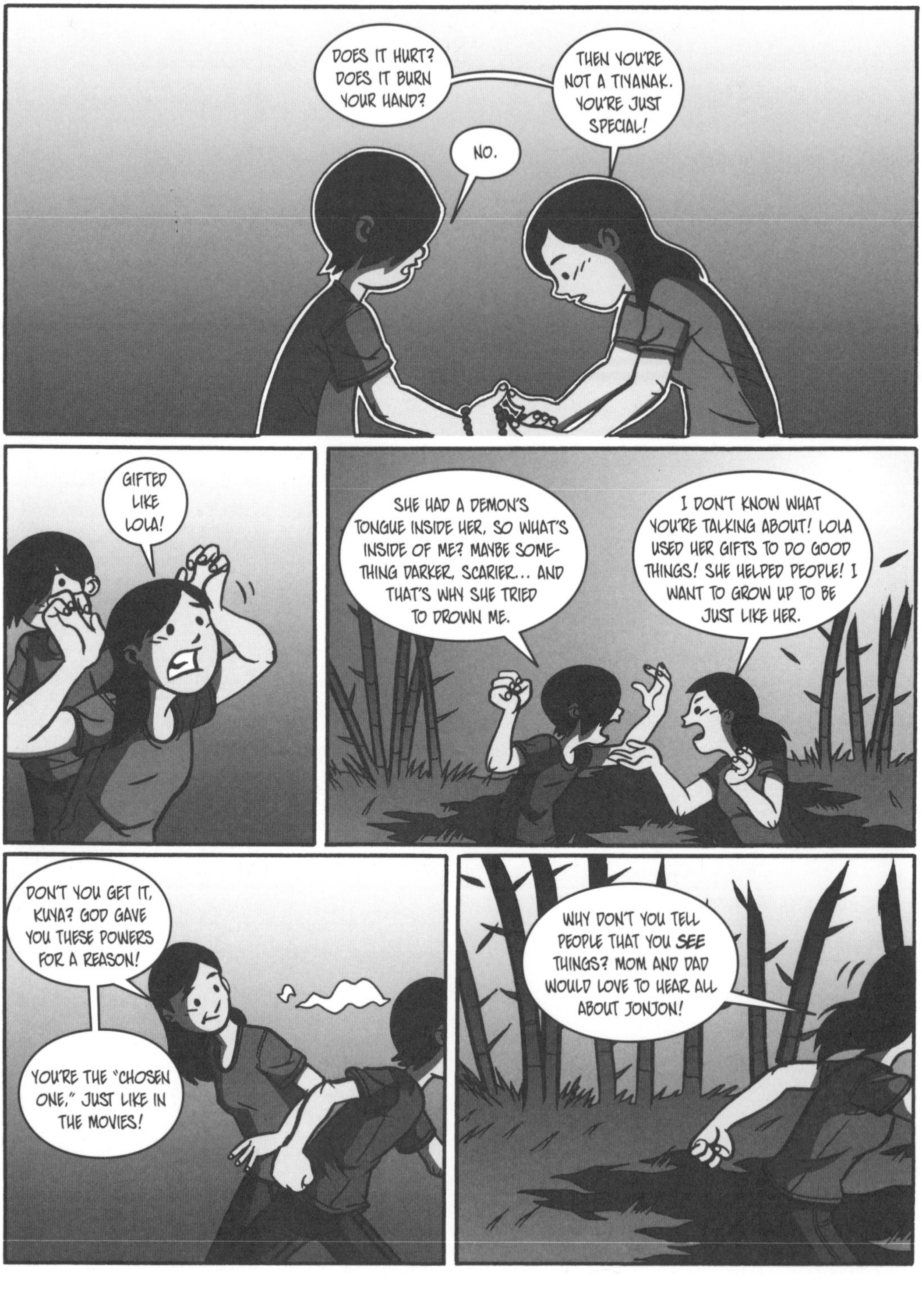
DOES IT HURT? DOES IT BURN YOUR HAND?
NO.
THEN YOU'RE NOT A TIYANAK. YOU'RE JUST SPECIAL!
GIFTED LIKE LOLA!
SHE HAD A DEMON'S TONGUE INSIDE HER, SO WHAT'S INSIDE OF ME? MAYBE SOME-THING DARKER, SCARIER... AND THAT'S WHY SHE TRIED TO DROWN ME.
I DON'T KNOW WHAT YOU'RE TALKING ABOUT! LOLA USED HER GIFTS TO DO GOOD THINGS! SHE HELPED PEOPLE! I WANT TO GROW UP TO BE JUST LIKE HER.
DON'T YOU GET IT, KUYA? GOD GAVE YOU THESE POWERS FOR A REASON!
YOU'RE THE "CHOSEN ONE," JUST LIKE IN THE MOVIES!
WHY DON'T YOU TELL PEOPLE THAT YOU SEE THINGS? MOM AND DAD WOULD LOVE TO HEAR ALL ABOUT JONJON!

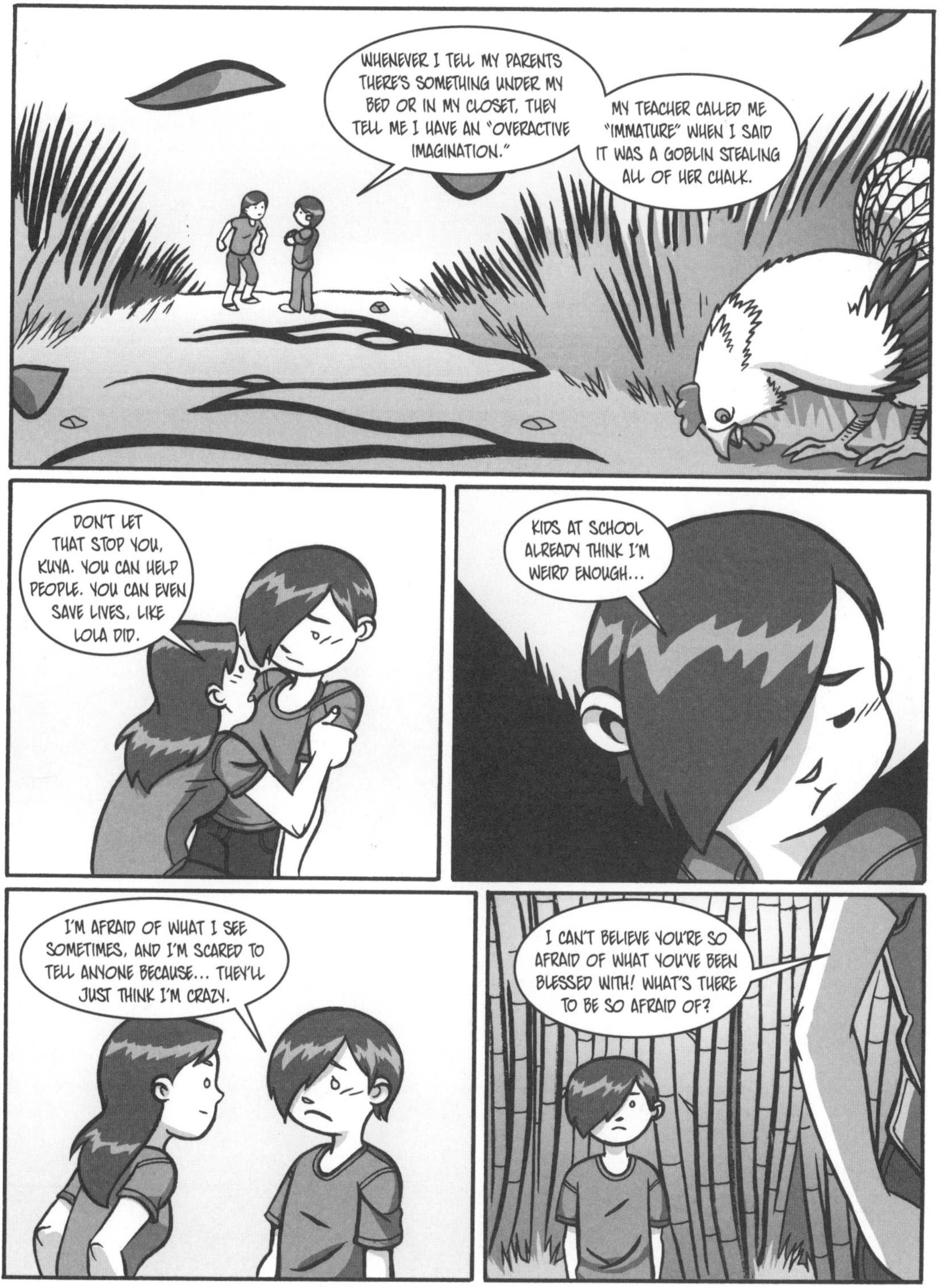
WHENEVER I TELL MY PARENTS THERE'S SOMETHING UNDER MY BED OR IN MY CLOSET, THEY TELL ME I HAVE AN "OVERACTIVE IMAGINATION."
MY TEACHER CALLED ME "IMMATURE" WHEN I SAID IT WAS A GOBLIN STEALING ALL OF HER CHALK.
DON'T LET THAT STOP YOU, KUYA. YOU CAN HELP PEOPLE. YOU CAN EVEN SAVE LIVES, LIKE LOLA DID.
KIDS AT SCHOOL ALREADY THINK I'M WEIRD ENOUGH...
I'M AFRAID OF WHAT I SEE SOMETIMES, AND I'M SCARED TO TELL ANYONE BECAUSE... THEY'LL JUST THINK I'M CRAZY.
I CAN'T BELIEVE YOU'RE SO AFRAID OF WHAT YOU'VE BEEN BLESSED WITH! WHAT'S THERE TO BE SO AFRAID OF?

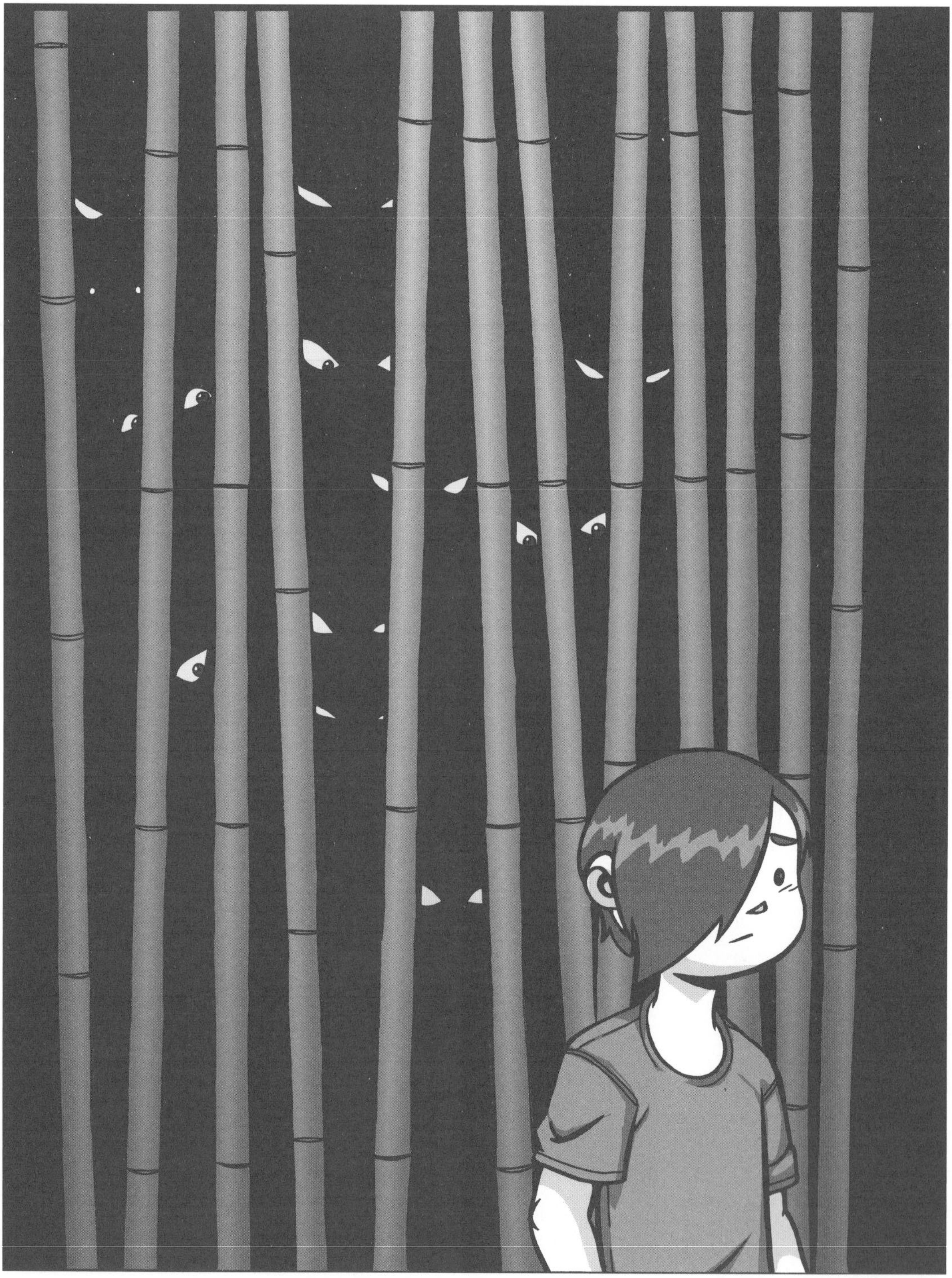

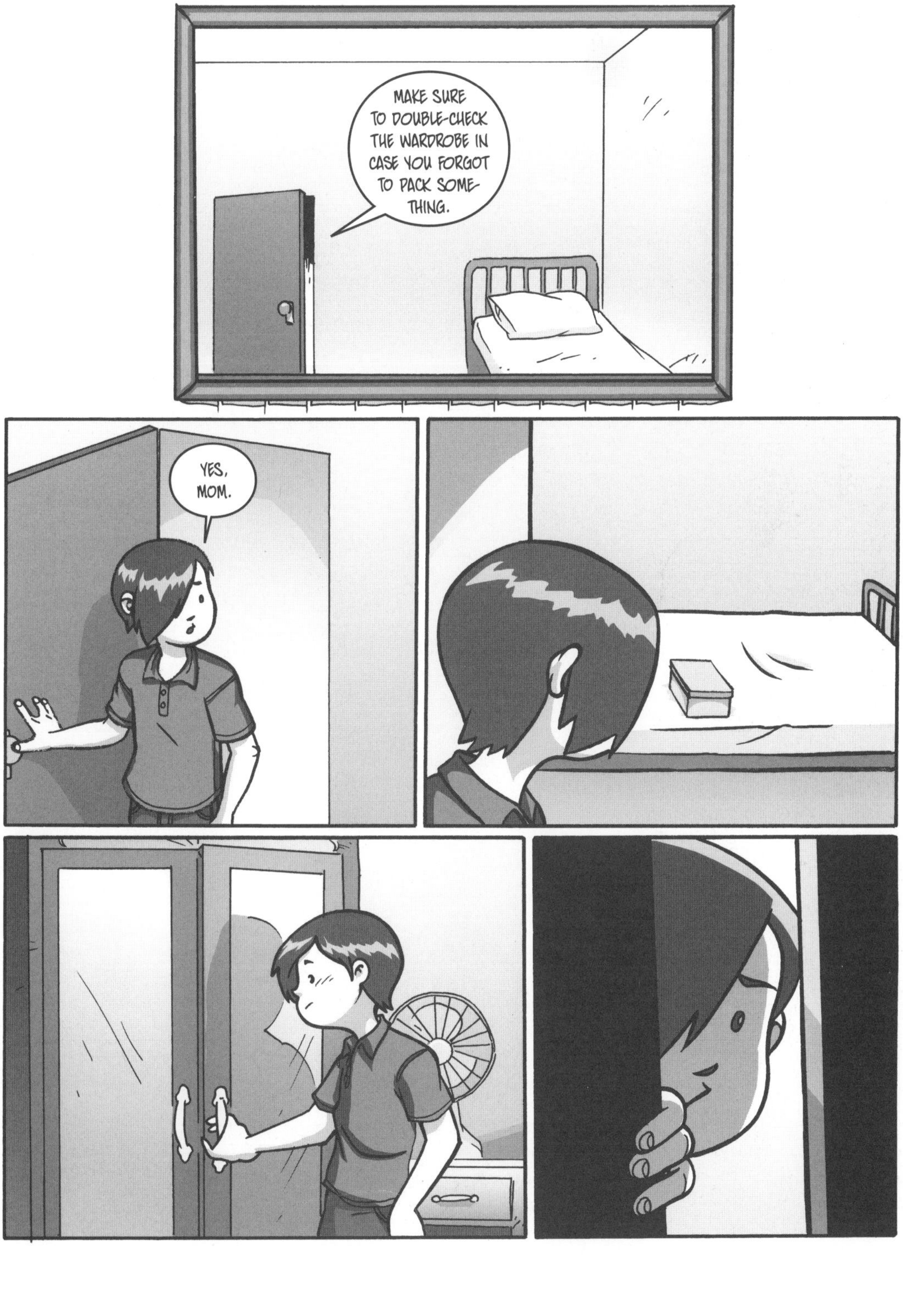
MAKE SURE TO DOUBLE-CHECK THE WARDROBE IN CASE YOU FORGOT TO PACK SOME-THING.
YES, MOM.

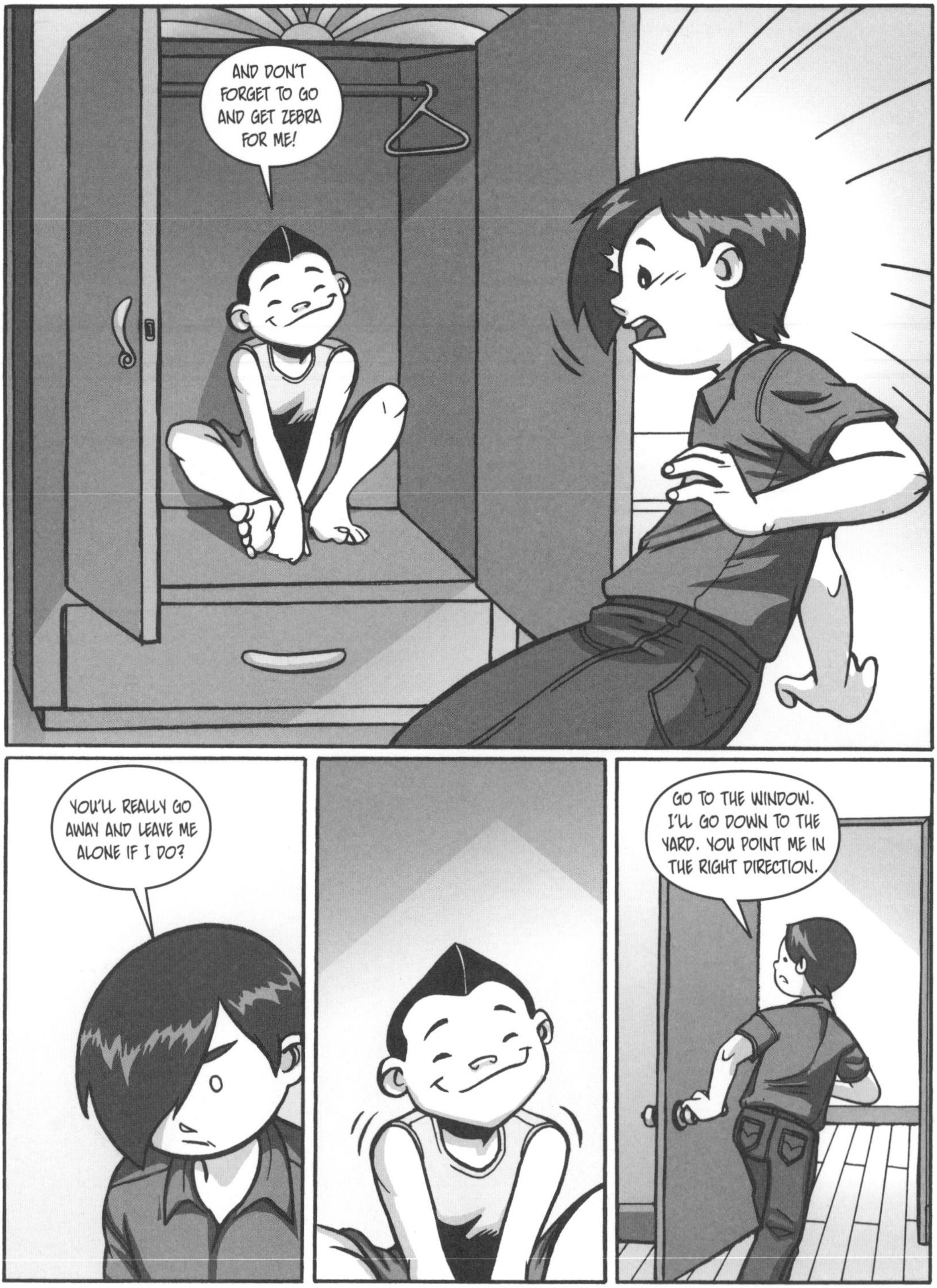
AND DON'T FORGET TO GO AND GET ZEBRA FOR ME!
YOU'LL REALLY GO AWAY AND LEAVE ME ALONE IF I DO?
GO TO THE WINDOW. I'LL GO DOWN TO THE YARD. YOU POINT ME IN THE RIGHT DIRECTION.

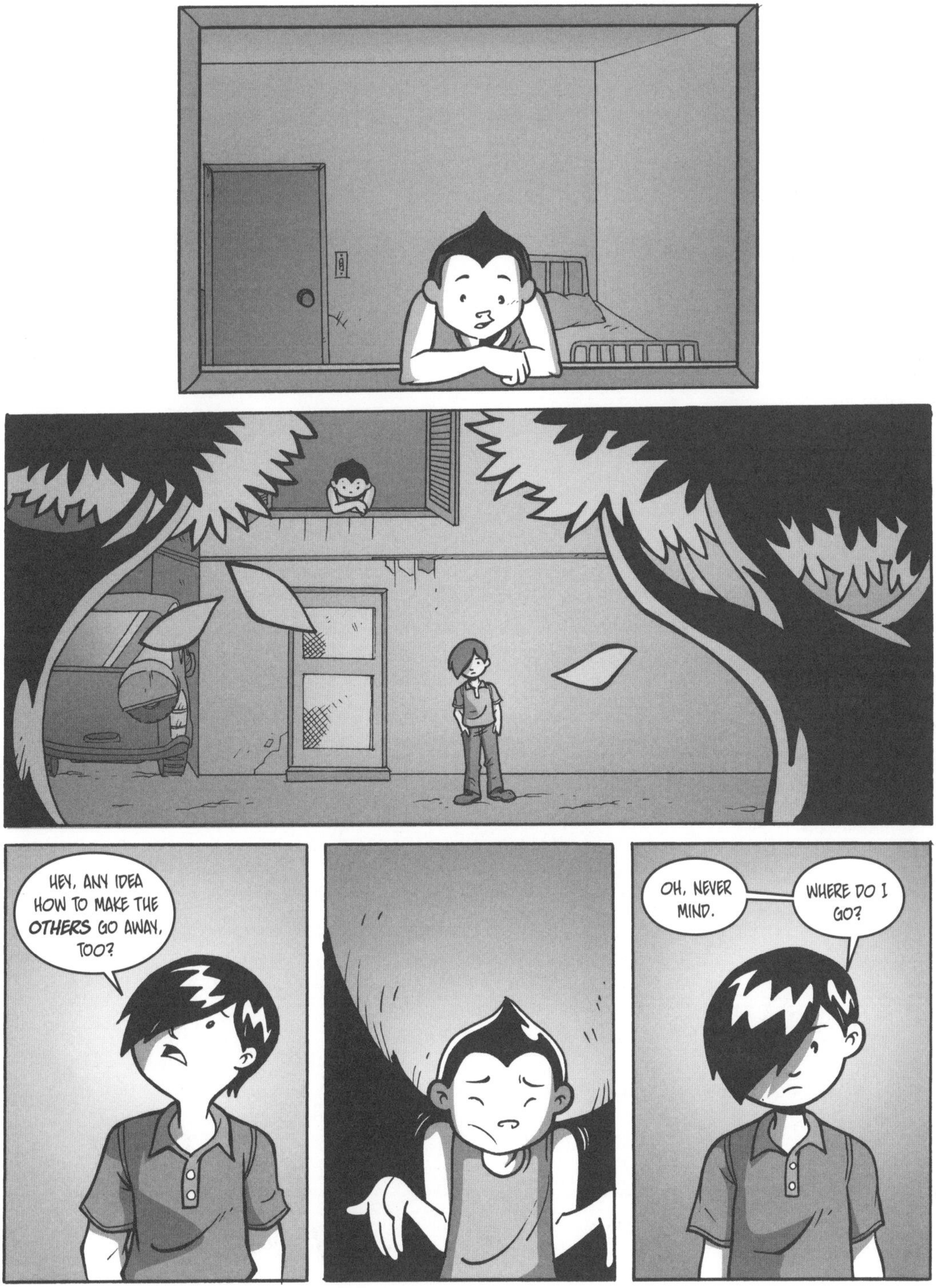
HEY, ANY IDEA HOW TO MAKE THE **OTHERS** GO AWAY, TOO?
OH, NEVER MIND.
WHERE DO I GO?

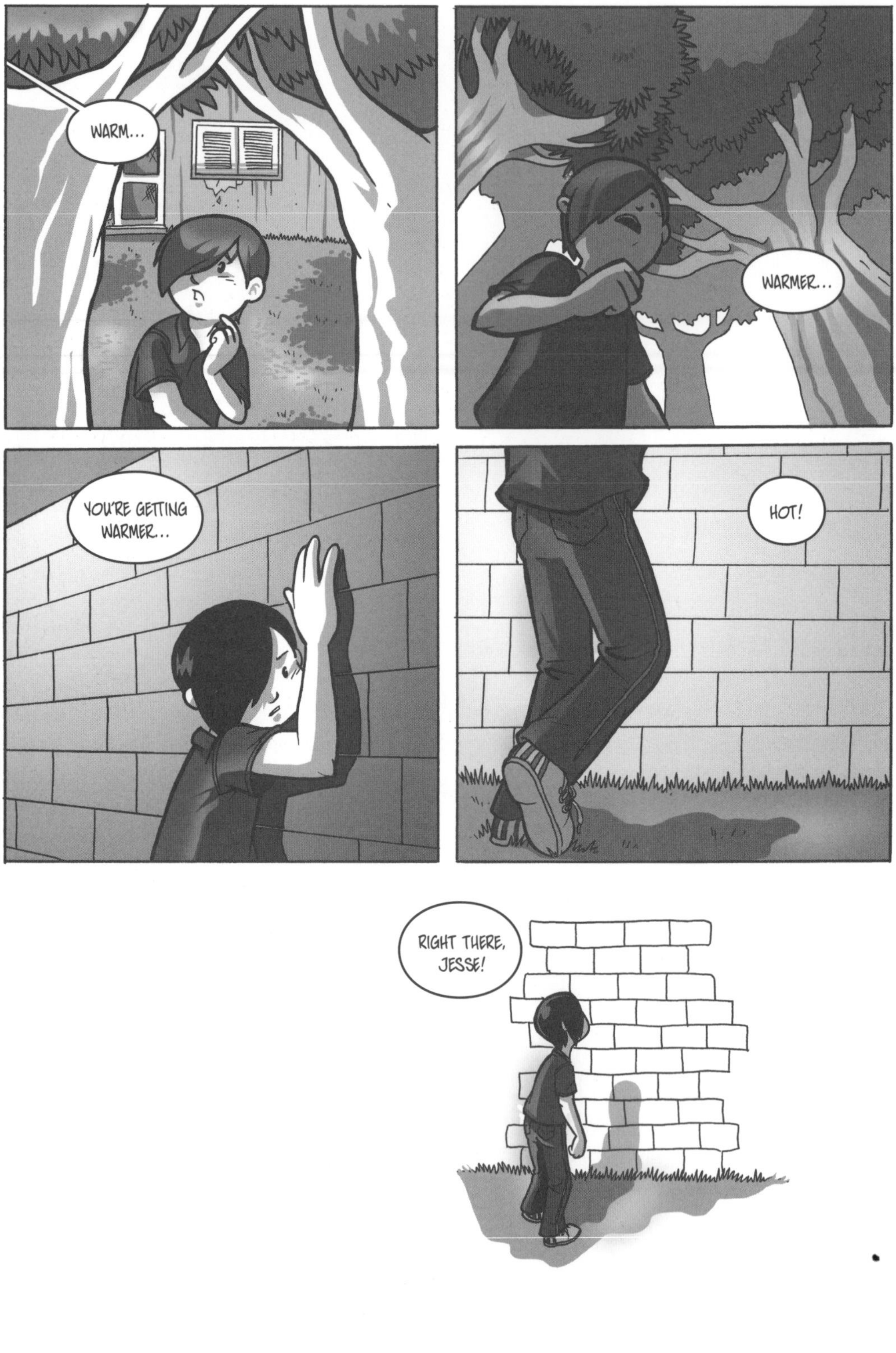
WARM...
WARMER...
YOU'RE GETTING WARMER...
HOT!
RIGHT THERE, JESSE!

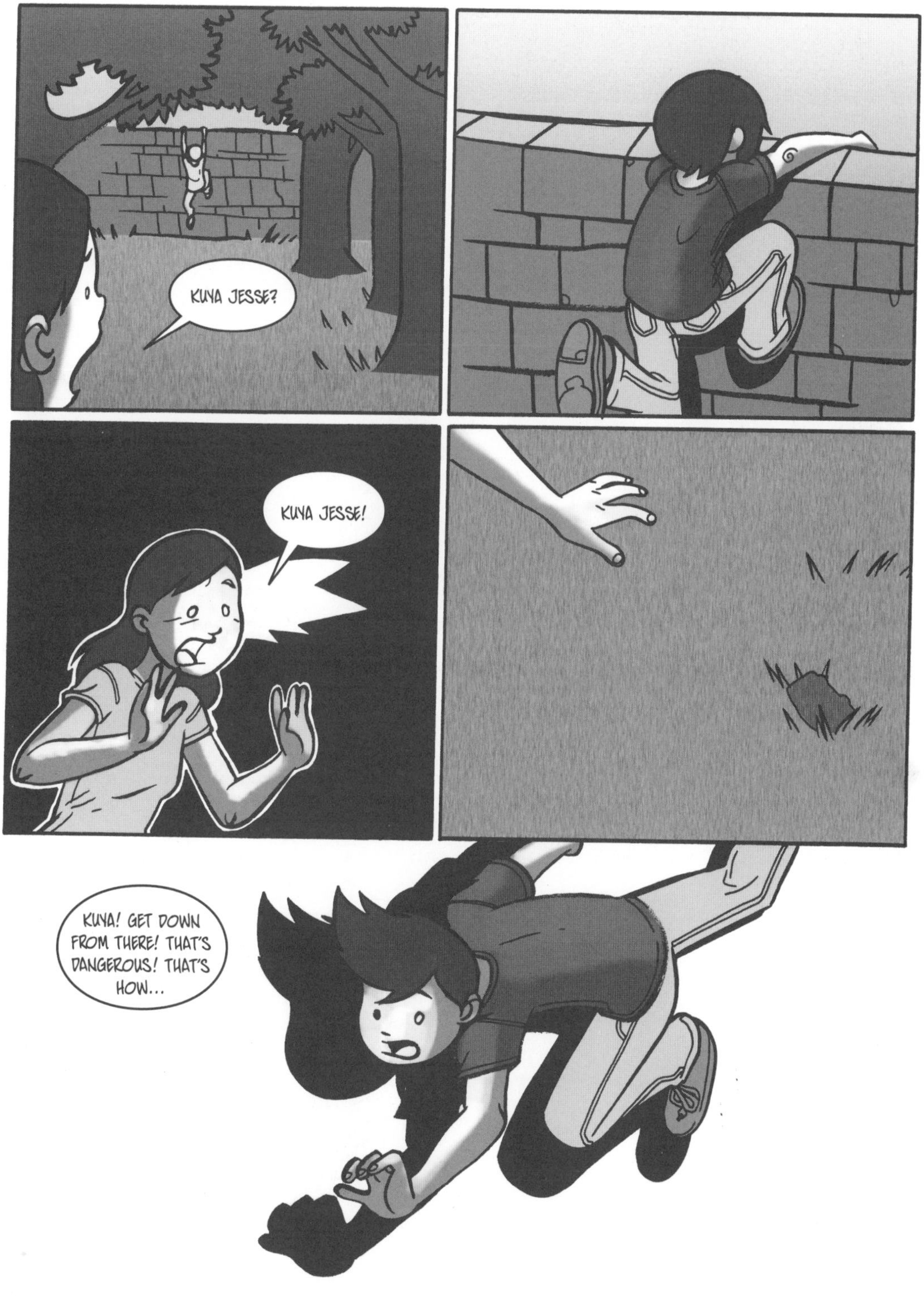
KUYA JESSE?
KUYA JESSE!
KUYA! GET DOWN FROM THERE! THAT'S DANGEROUS! THAT'S HOW...

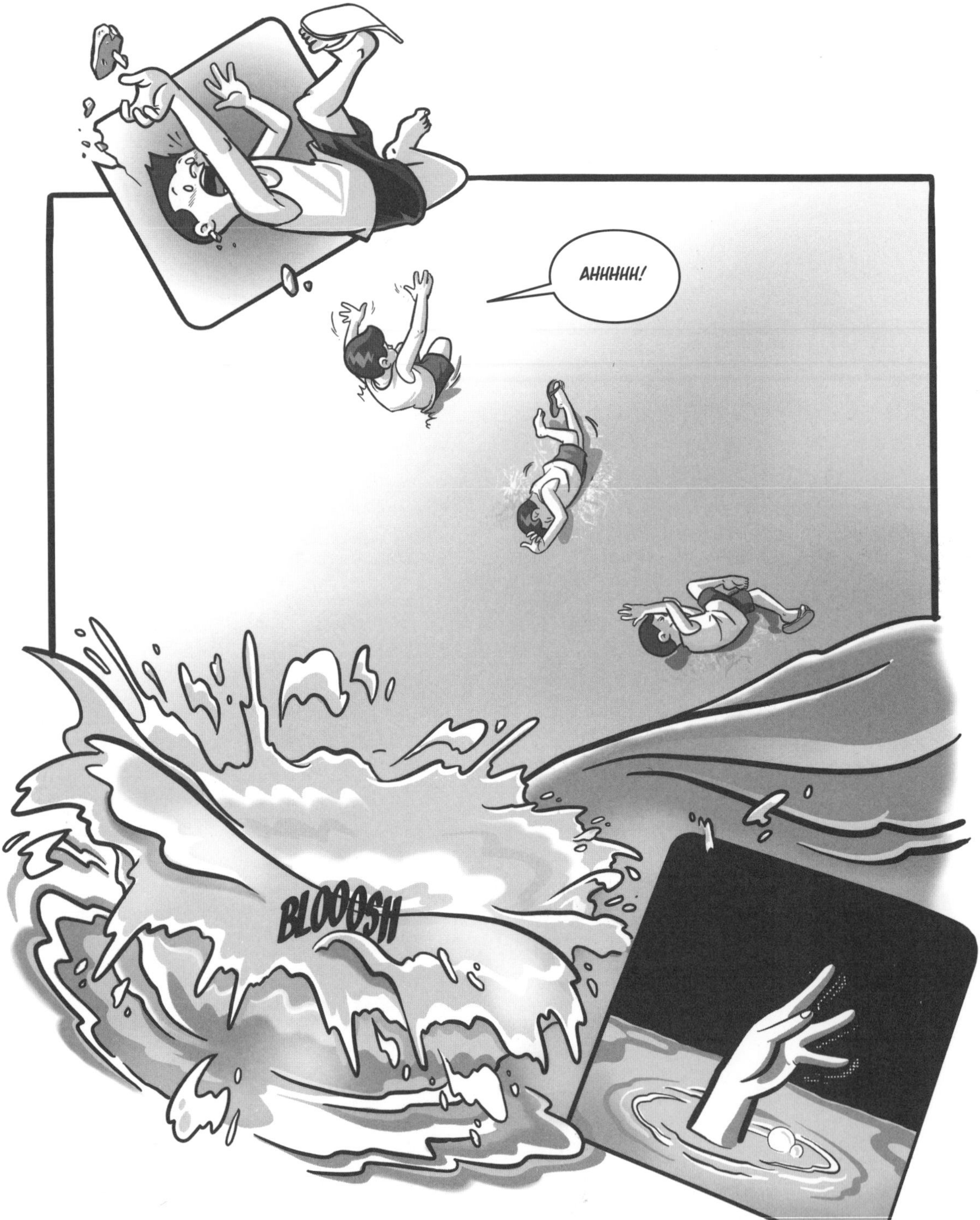
AHHHHH!
BLOOOSH

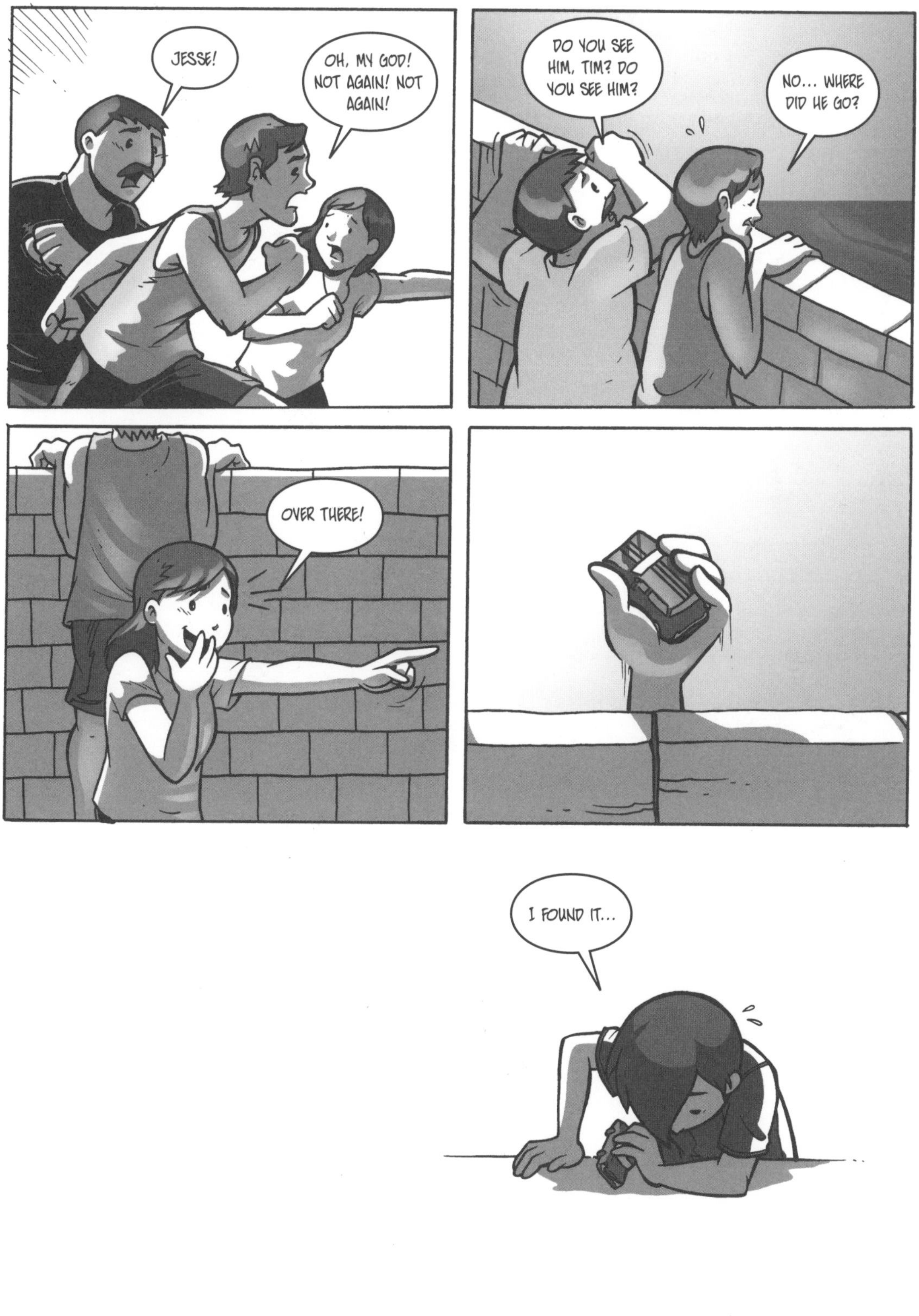
JESSE!
OH, MY GOD! NOT AGAIN! NOT AGAIN!
DO YOU SEE HIM, TIM? DO YOU SEE HIM?
NO... WHERE DID HE GO?
OVER THERE!
I FOUND IT...

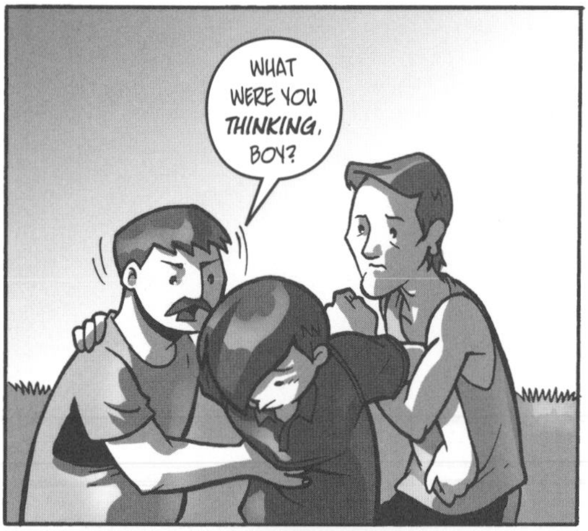
WHAT WERE YOU *THINKING*, BOY?

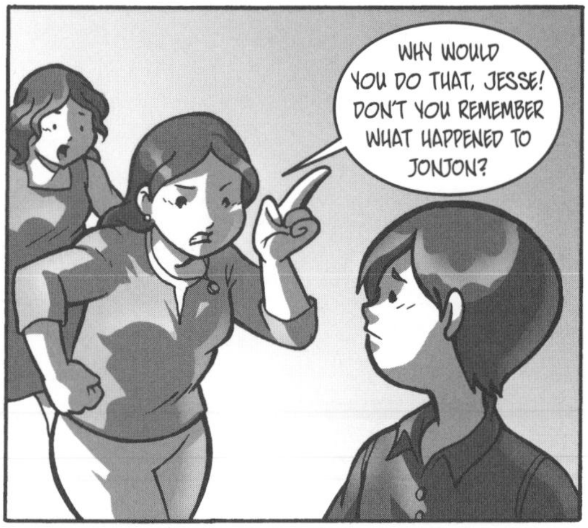
WHY WOULD YOU DO THAT, JESSE! DON'T YOU REMEMBER WHAT HAPPENED TO JONJON?

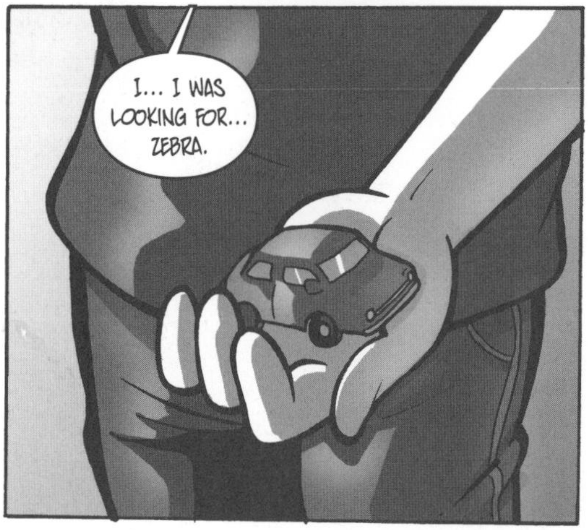
I... I WAS LOOKING FOR... ZEBRA.

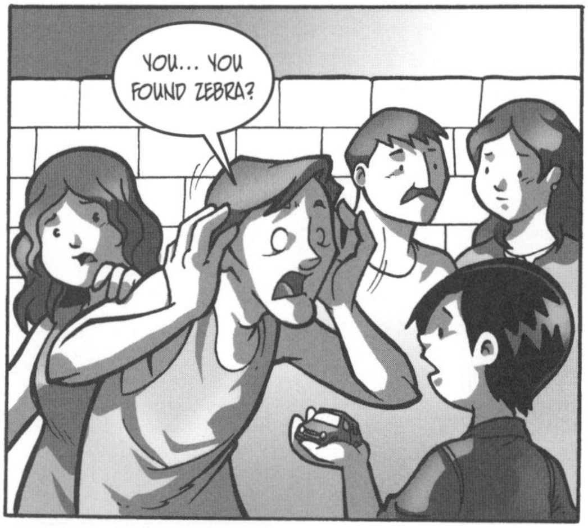
YOU... YOU FOUND ZEBRA?

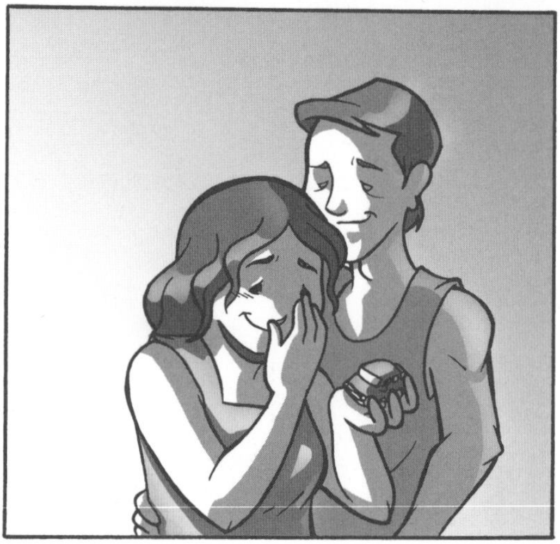

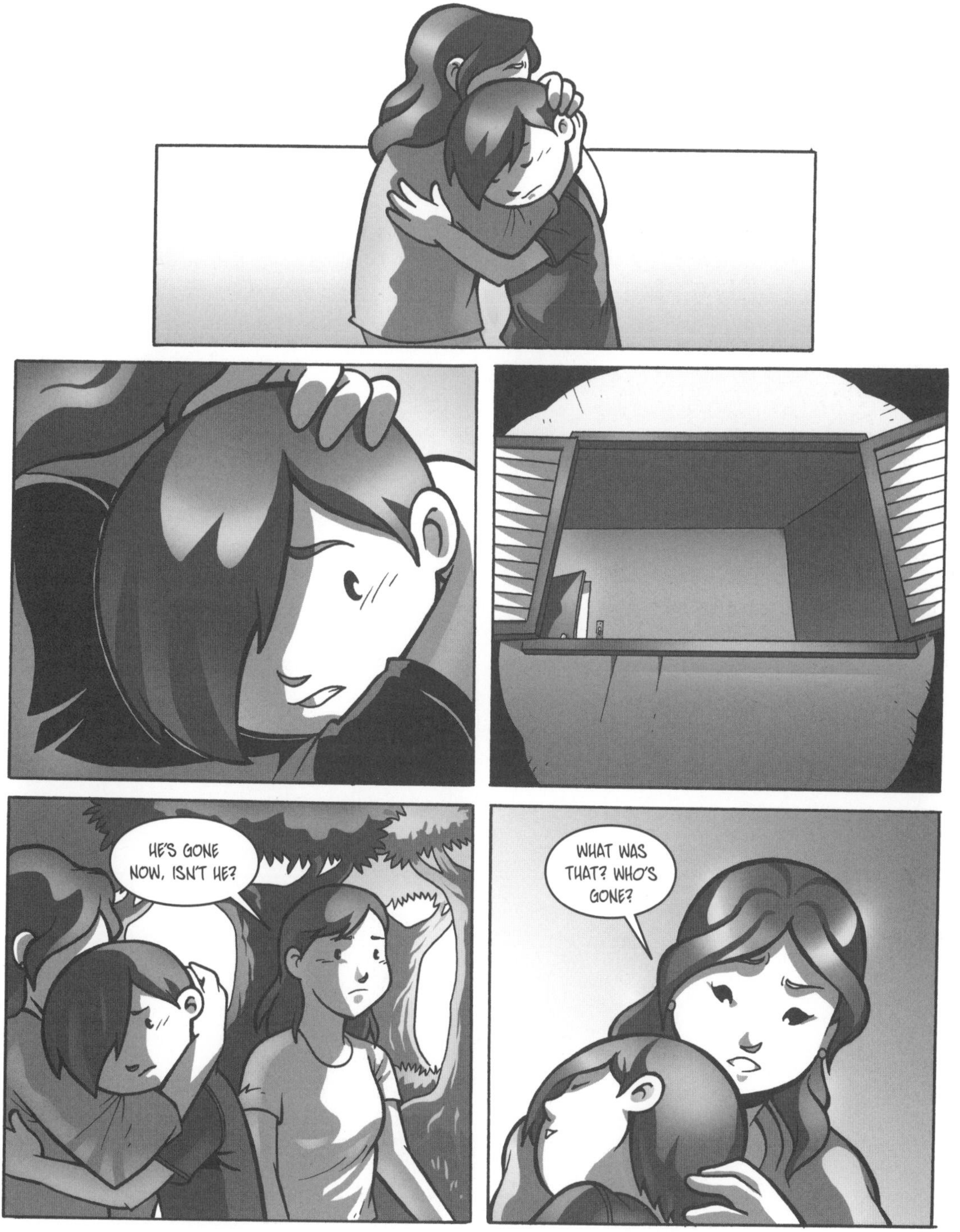
HE'S GONE NOW, ISN'T HE?
WHAT WAS THAT? WHO'S GONE?

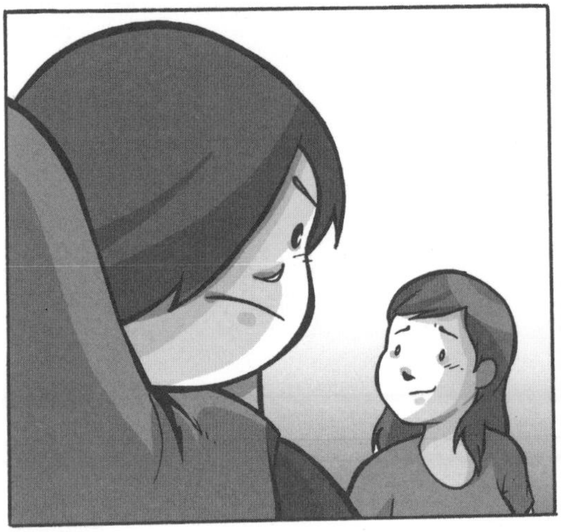

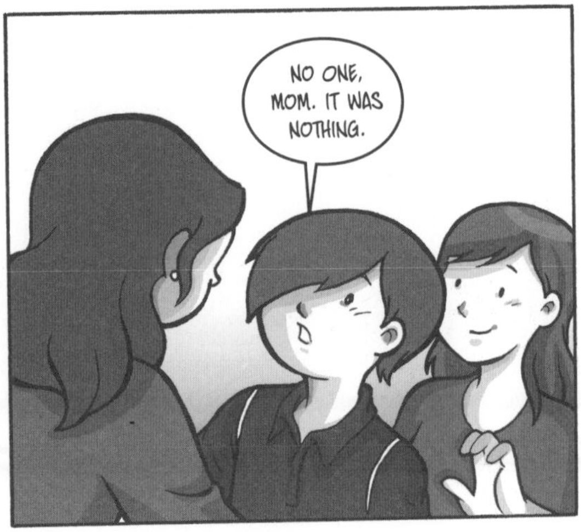
NO ONE, MOM. IT WAS NOTHING.

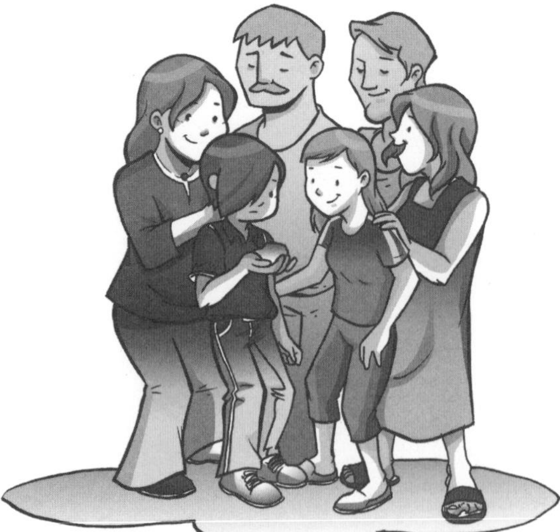

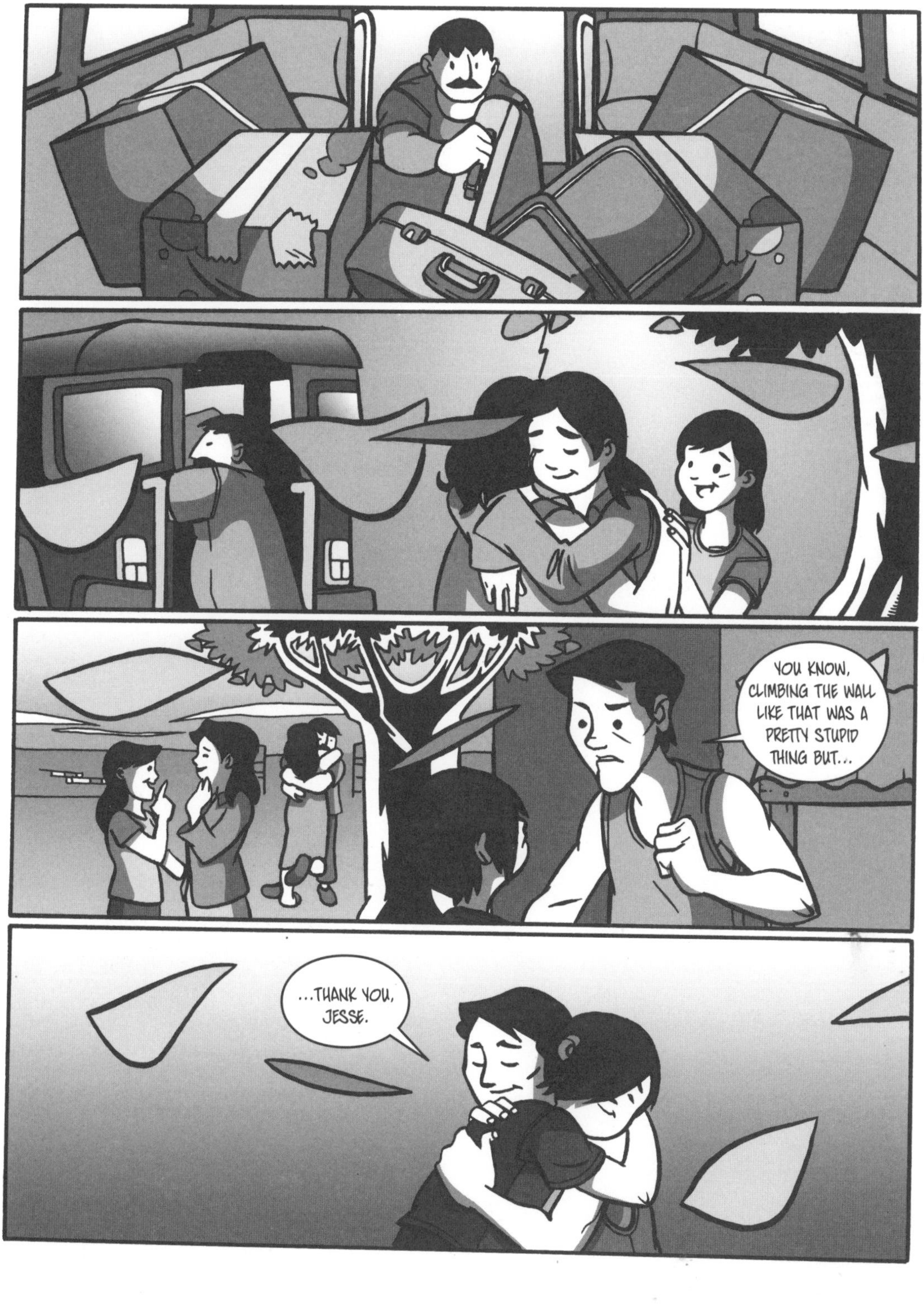
YOU KNOW, CLIMBING THE WALL LIKE THAT WAS A PRETTY STUPID THING BUT...
...THANK YOU, JESSE.

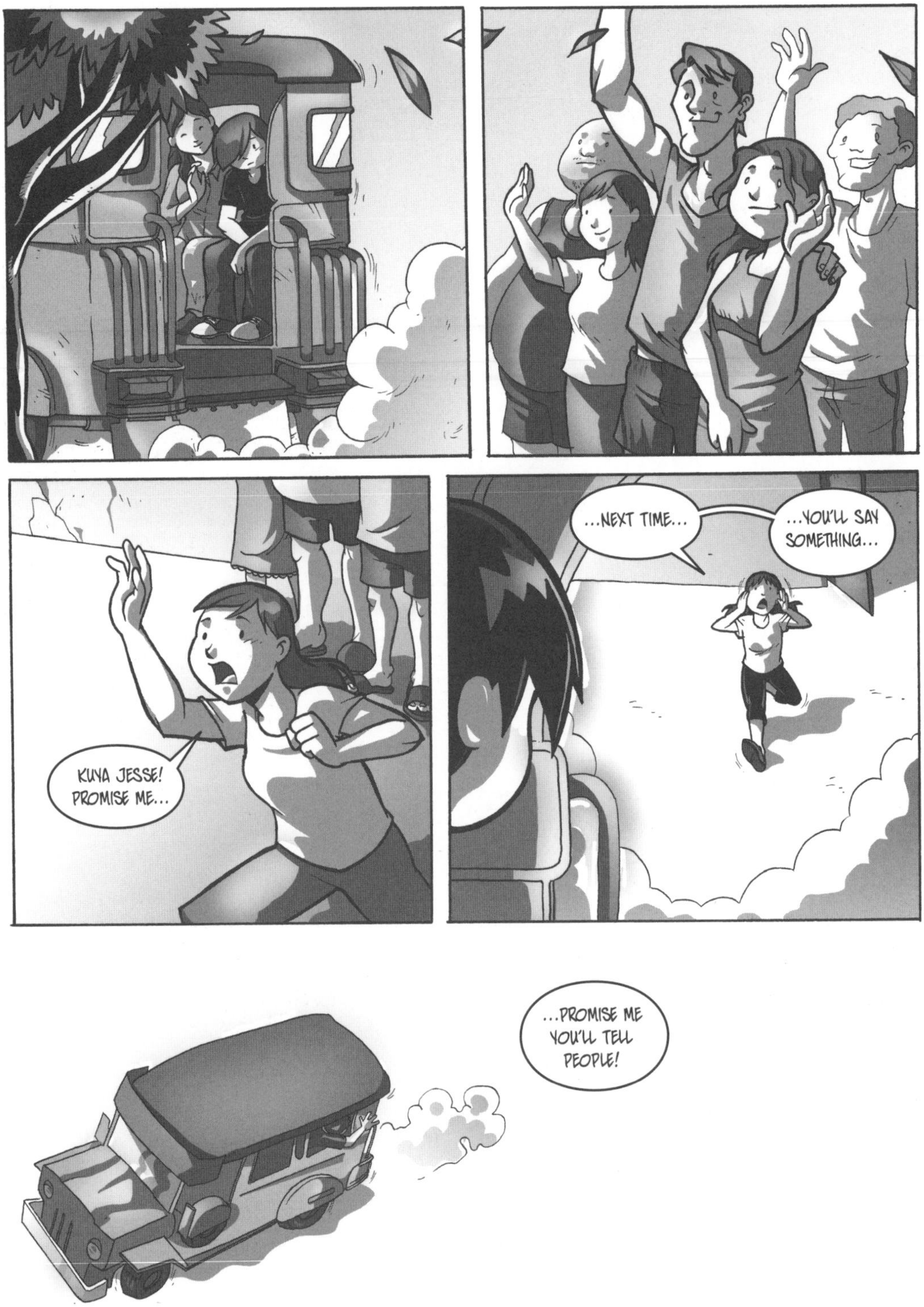
KUYA JESSE! PROMISE ME...
...NEXT TIME...
...YOU'LL SAY SOMETHING...
...PROMISE ME YOU'LL TELL PEOPLE!

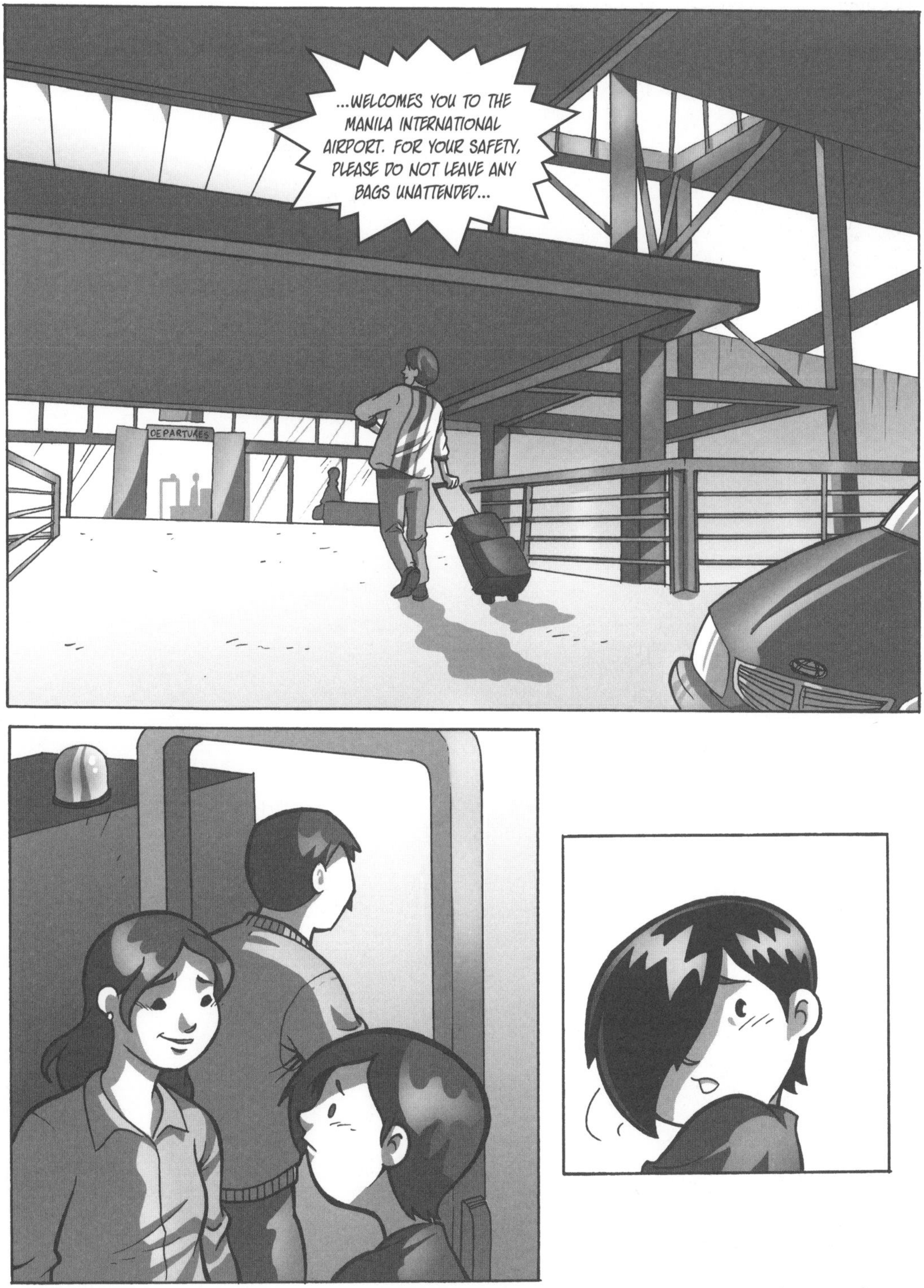
...WELCOMES YOU TO THE MANILA INTERNATIONAL AIRPORT. FOR YOUR SAFETY, PLEASE DO NOT LEAVE ANY BAGS UNATTENDED...
DEPARTURES

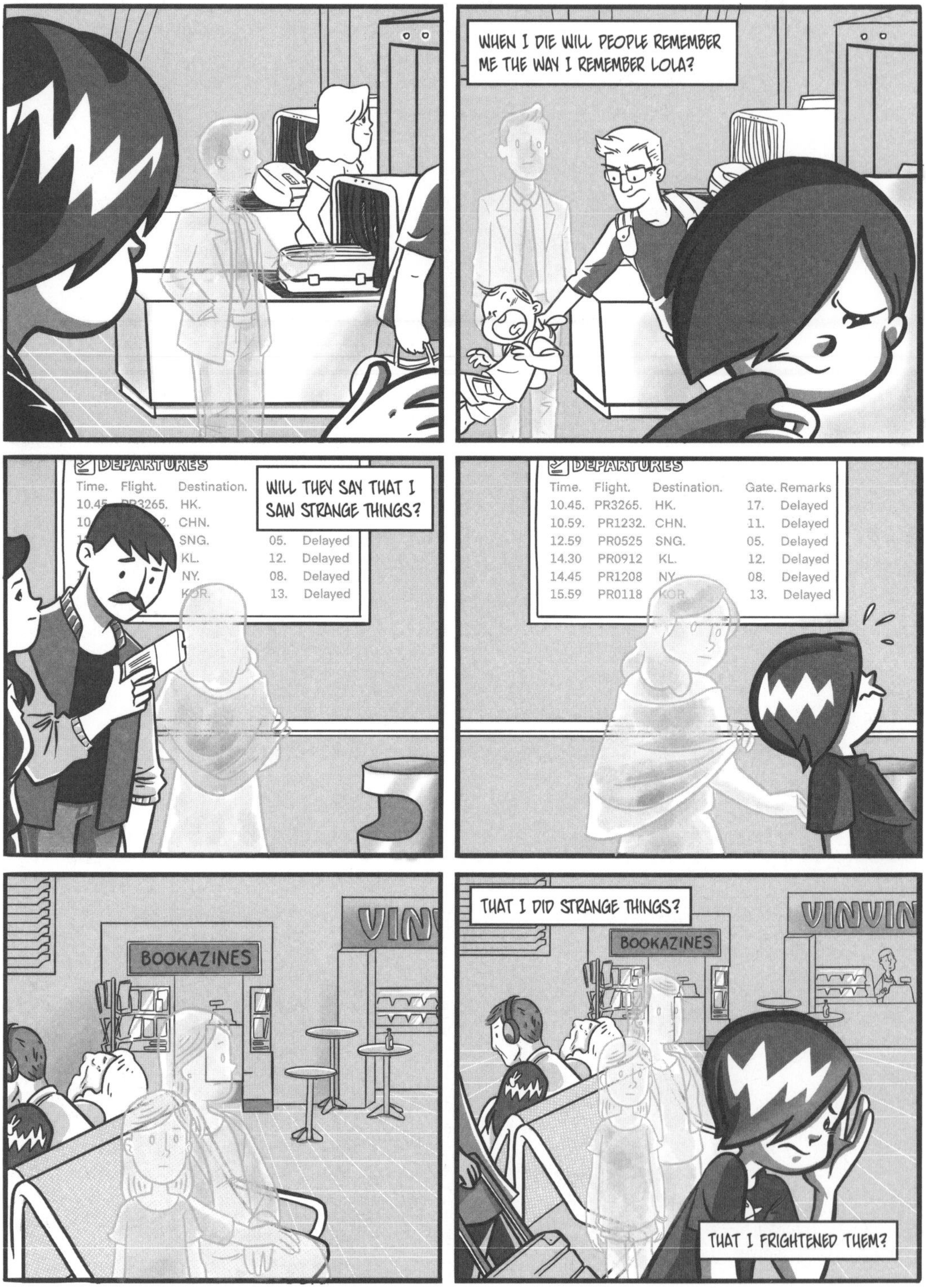
WHEN I DIE WILL PEOPLE REMEMBER ME THE WAY I REMEMBER LOLA?
DEPARTURES
WILL THEY SAY THAT I SAW STRANGE THINGS?
DEPARTURES
Time. Flight. Destination. Gate. Remarks
10.45. PR3265. HK. 17. Delayed
10.59. PR1232. CHN. 11. Delayed
12.59 PR0525 SNG. 05. Delayed
14.30 PR0912 KL. 12. Delayed
14.45 PR1208 NY. 08. Delayed
15.59 PR0118 KOR. 13. Delayed
BOOKAZINES
VINV
THAT I DID STRANGE THINGS?
BOOKAZINES
VINVIN
THAT I FRIGHTENED THEM?

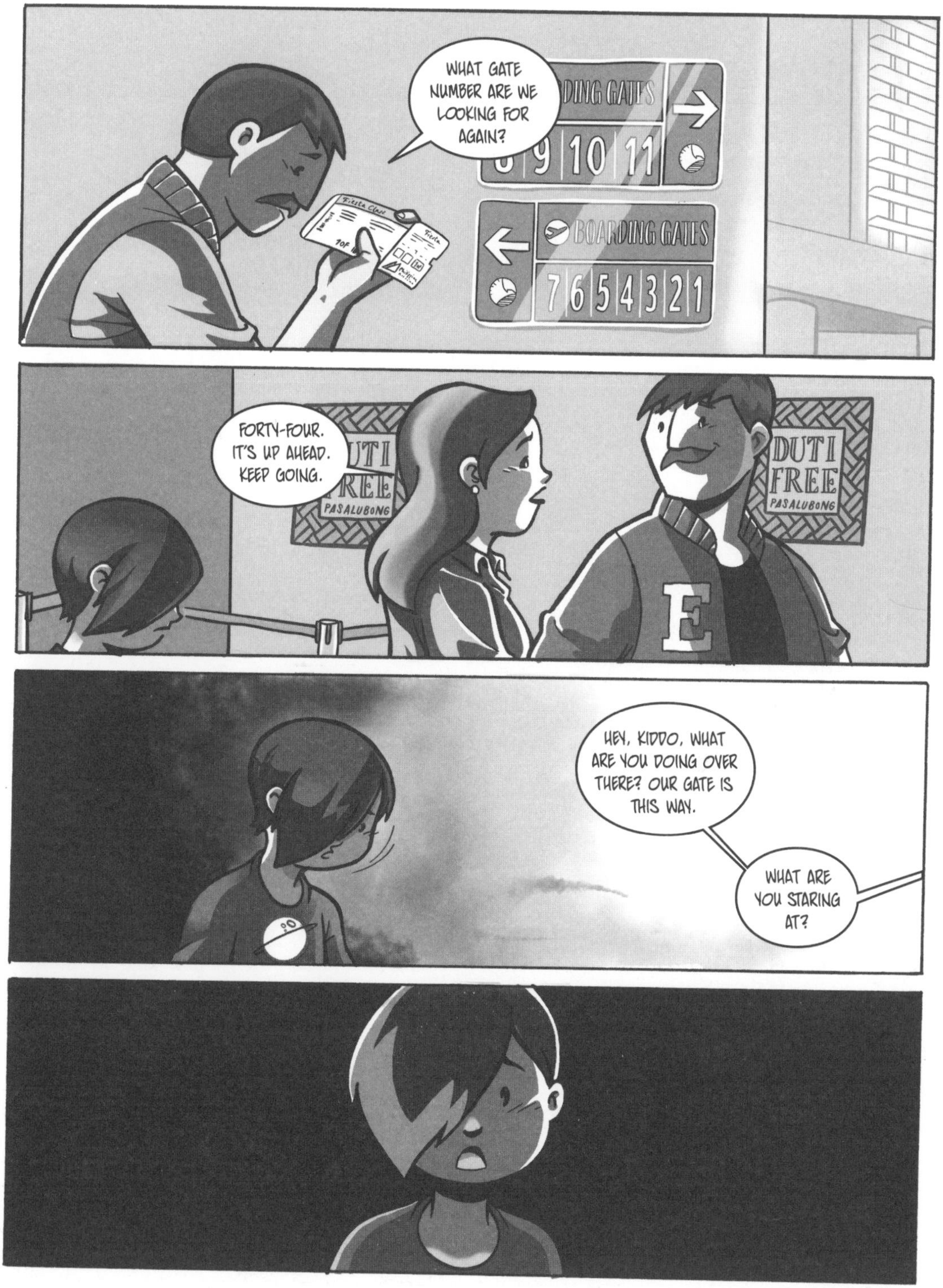
WHAT GATE NUMBER ARE WE LOOKING FOR AGAIN?
DING GATES
9 10 11
BOARDING GATES
7 6 5 4 3 2 1
FORTY-FOUR. IT'S UP AHEAD. KEEP GOING.
PASALUBONG
DUTI FREE
PASALUBONG
E
HEY, KIDDO, WHAT ARE YOU DOING OVER THERE? OUR GATE IS THIS WAY.
WHAT ARE YOU STARING AT?

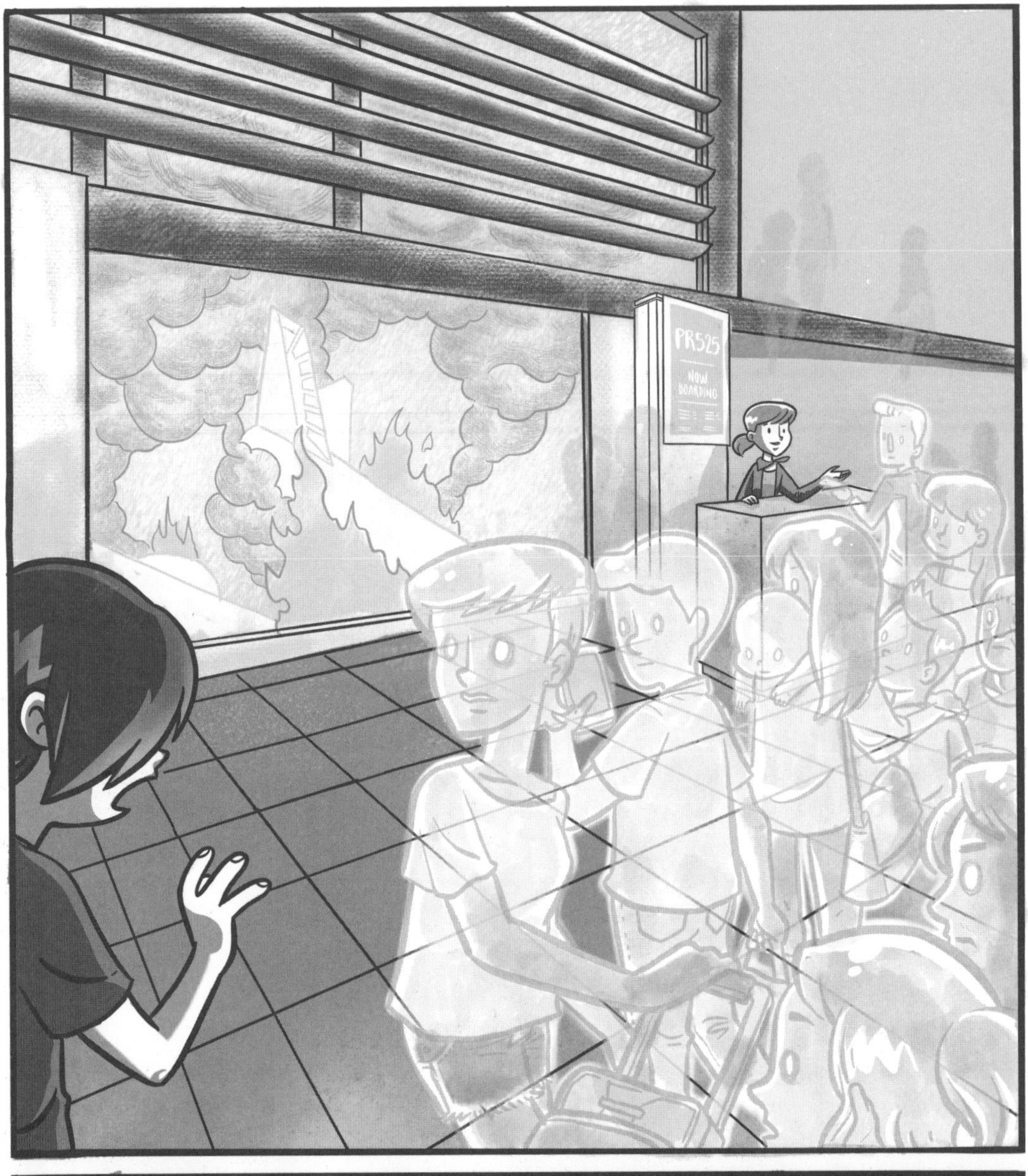
PR525
NOW BOARDING

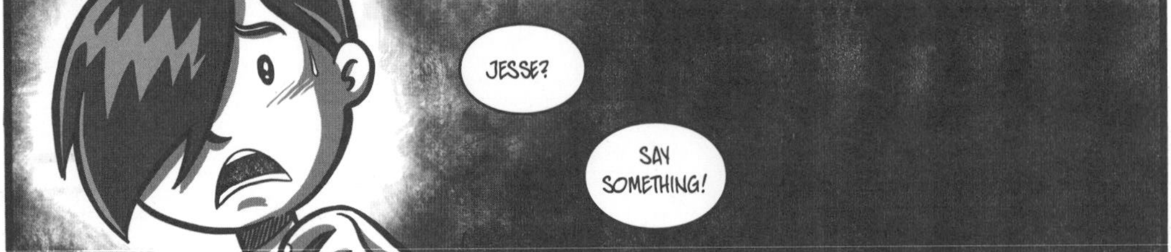
JESSE?
SAY SOMETHING!

THE END

A GLOSSARY OF FILIPINO MONSTERS & LEGENDARY CREATURES

Aswang
A generic term for evil, often shape-changing monsters found in Filipino folklore that include vampire, werewolf, and witch-like creatures.

Bakunawa
Meaning "bent snake," a gigantic sea serpent believed to be the cause of earthquakes, mudslides, rain, wind, etc. in times past.

Bangungot
Meaning "nightmare," a creature often resembling a very large person that sits on a sleeping person's face to suffocate them; in times past, this was used to explain why people seem to inexplicably die in their sleep.

DIWATA
Fairy or elf-like creatures in Filipino folklore who can be both troublesome spirit and benevolent deity; they are often depicted as being beautiful with fair or even luminous skin.

DWENDE
A dwarf-like creature who lives in dark places like caves, dead trees, or even abandoned houses, and sometimes within anthills and termite mounds (as in the legend of "Nuno Sa Punso," the "Old Man of the Mound"); they are said to be good or evil depending on how they are treated.

KAPEROSA
"The White Lady" of the Philippines is a ghost in a white flowing gown who appears late at night to people traveling alone on dark roads or passages, sometimes causing accidents or warning of potential trouble ahead.

KAPRE
Large, often giant, goblin-like nocturnal creatures who dwell in trees or are found sitting beneath them waiting to play tricks on (and sometimes befriend) humans; in times past, fireflies were believed to be embers from the kapre's cigars or tobacco pipe.

GLOSSARY CONTINUED...

Manananggal
Meaning "the separator," an evil flesh-eating, blood-sucking monster or witch that can separate at the waist and fly off in search of its favourite prey: sleeping pregnant women; in times past, these creatures were an explanation for miscarriage.

Sarimanok
A legendary rooster-like creature with colourful ornate wings and a big feathered tail said to bring good fortune to whomever can catch it; the creature is used throughout the Philippines as a symbol, icon, and design motif in popular culture.

Tikbalang
A creature from Filipino folklore that resembles a cross between a horse and a human with really long limbs; it is a forest and mountain-dwelling trickster figure that likes to scare travellers or otherwise lead them astray.

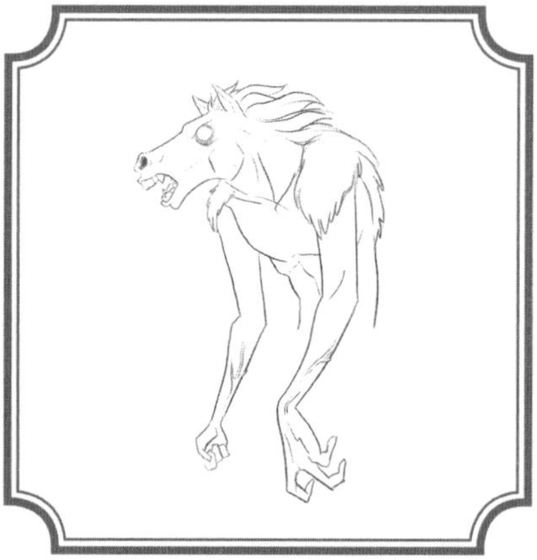

TIYANAK

An evil shape-changing, vampire-like creature that lives in forests and lures its victims by taking the form of a crying baby and then changes back to its true (sometimes dwarf-like, often demonic-looking) form when picked up.

WAK WAK

A scary bird with bat-like wings and sharp talons that hunts at night, often accompanying a vampire or witch; its name comes from the sound its wings make as it flies.

ABOUT THE AUTHORS

∞

J. TORRES IS AN AWARD-WINNING FILIPINO CANADIAN WRITER PERHAPS BEST KNOWN FOR HIS RUN ON DC'S *TEEN TITANS GO*. HIS OTHER CREDITS INCLUDE *BROBOTS*, *LOVE AS A FOREIGN LANGUAGE*, AND *THE MIGHTY ZODIAC* FOR ONI PRESS. AMONG HIS FAVORITE GHOST STORIES ARE *A CHRISTMAS CAROL*, *BELOVED*, AND THE FIRST *GHOSTBUSTERS* MOVIE.

VISIT HIS WEBSITE AT
JTORRESONLINE.BLOGSPOT.COM

∞

ELBERT OR IS BASED IN MANILA, PHILIPPINES, WHERE HE LIVES WITH WIFE AND TWO KIDS. HIS COMICS INCLUDE *THE AMAZING TRUE-ISH STORY OF ANDRES CELESTIAL, AMORSOLO ESPERANZA, FAITH HEALER OF TALINHAGA,* AND *HOMEYCOMB: A MARRIED LIFE.* HE IS CO-FOUNDER OF COMMUNICATIONS FIRM PUSHPIN VISUAL SOLUTIONS.

FOLLOW HIM ON INSTAGRAM
@ELBERTOR